RELIGION
IN THE
WORKPLACE

A COMPREHENSIVE GUIDE TO LEGAL RIGHTS AND RESPONSIBILITIES

MICHAEL WOLF • BRUCE FRIEDMAN • DANIEL SUTHERLAND

TORT AND INSURANCE PRACTICE

AMERICAN BAR ASSOCIATION

The views expressed in this book by Messrs. Friedman and Sutherland are a result of their independent research and do not represent the views of the U.S. Department of Justice.

Cover design by Kathy Karrys.

The materials contained herein represent the opinions of the authors and editors and should not be construed to be the action of either the American Bar Association or the Tort and Insurance Practice Section unless adopted pursuant to the bylaws of the Association.

Nothing contained in this book is to be considered as the rendering of legal advice for specific cases, and readers are responsible for obtaining such advice from their own legal counsel. This book and any forms and agreements herein are intended for educational and informational purposes only.

02 01 00 99 98   5 4 3 2 1

Wolf, Michael, 1948–
    Religion in the workplace : a comprehensive guide to legal rights
and responsibilities / Michael Wolf, Bruce Friedman,
Daniel Sutherland.
        p.   cm.
    Includes index.
    ISBN 1-57073-597-2
    1. Religion in the workplace—Law and legislation—United States.
I. Friedman, Bruce, 1960–   .   II. Sutherland, Daniel, 1961–   .
III. Title.
KF3466.5.W65   1998
658.3'0088'2—dc21   98-29829
                                                       CIP

Discounts are available for books ordered in bulk. Special consideration is given to state bars, CLE programs, and other bar-related organizations. Inquire at Book Publishing, ABA Publishing, American Bar Association, 750 North Lake Shore Drive, Chicago, Illinois 60611.

www.abanet.org/abapubs

Contents

Foreword

The tremendous growth in employment statutes and common law over the last 25 years has presented employers, employees, unions, and their lawyers with enormous questions over compliance and their respective rights. A review of the daily media demonstrates that, while most people have a general understanding of our discrimination laws, few understand the law of religious discrimination. Each day brings new stories of disputes between employers and employees over religious practices.

That is not surprising when one considers the unique aspects of the prohibitions on religious discrimination. For one, those prohibitions go beyond membership in a protected class, and deal with religious beliefs and practices. Employee choices of dress, hairstyle, and days of work can all raise questions of religious discrimination. Moreover, the law not only prohibits discrimination, but imposes a duty on employers to "accommodate" their employees' religious practices. It is a wonder that the growth in religious discrimination cases is not more dramatic than it already has been.

Many fine volumes have been written on discrimination law including the ABA's own Lindemann and Grossman, *Employment Discrimination Law* (3d ed., BNA, 1996). Few, however, concentrate on the questions peculiar to religious discrimination, the complexities of which demonstrate the need for this volume. Of particular interest is the discussion of the interplay between Title VII of the Civil Rights Act of 1964, other federal employment laws such as the National Labor Relations Act, and the First Amendment.

Messrs. Wolf, Friedman, and Sutherland's guide to this "minefield" is most welcome. It will be equally valuable to employers, human resource professionals, unions, and lawyers. Unlike many guides to the law it does not bury the reader in arcane case citations and footnotes. Rather, it gives readily understandable, practical advice. Thus, it is a volume that most will want to keep close at hand for ready reference.

Stephen A. Bokat
Senior Vice President & General Counsel
U.S. Chamber of Commerce
Washington, D.C.

Acknowledgments

The authors would like to express appreciation to our families for their support and patience during the writing of this book. The authors are also grateful to the many colleagues who read all or part of the manuscript and whose suggestions were invaluable in helping us to shape this book.

Introduction

As the population diversifies, conflicts between work and religion inevitably arise. Not surprisingly, the Equal Employment Opportunity Commission (EEOC) has reported a significant increase in the number of religious discrimination charges it has received over the last ten years. In this environment, employers and employees must understand each other's rights and responsibilities. The goal of this book is to describe these rights and responsibilities in a way that is useful to both the layperson and lawyer. More precisely, our objective is to provide a *practical* guide for lawyers, as well as human-resource personnel, union officials, and employees, in dealing with the myriad legal and practical issues arising out of the conflict between work and religion.

Religious conflicts at work arise in a wide variety of contexts. A common example is an employer's denial of an employee's request for leave to observe a religious holiday, forcing the employee to choose between career and conviction. Other situations are more complex. For example, one employee may actively espouse religious views in the workplace, while co-workers find the proselytizing offensive. Whose side should the employer take when an employee demands freedom of speech, while others demand a cessation of what they see as harassment?

In many such conflicts, the dispute between employer and employee can be resolved through simple mediation efforts. The real cause of most conflicts is simple ignorance on the part of both management and employees as to the requirements of the law.

One reason that religion in the workplace has caused more problems than one might expect is that the law does much more than prohibit discrimination based on religion. Religion, in the eyes of the federal law, is more than a status (such as one's race or sex). The law protects religious *practices,* as well as beliefs. What employees *do* in the practice of their religion is entitled to protection.

At the same time, federal law obligates employers to take certain affirmative actions to satisfy employees' religious needs. If religious practices conflict with workplace rules, the employer may be required to "accommodate" those practices. Of course, to say that accommodation "may" be required is to beg a variety of questions: When? How? At whose initiative? At whose expense? A lack of understanding of these basic yet complex questions frequently causes a breakdown in the relationship between employer and employee. This book addresses these questions and provides to both employers and employees basic guidelines for resolving workplace disputes involving religion.

To satisfy our objective of making this a practical resource, we endeavor to be as concise as possible. We resist the temptation toward esoteric ruminations. For example, we do not discuss legislative histories, except to the very limited extent that they are necessary to understand the current state of the law. At the same time, this book addresses all of the major issues and judicial decisions that lawyers will need to advise their clients. Where appropriate, we summarize cases that involve recurring fact patterns in the expectation that such examples will prove helpful to practitioners. To the extent that there are conflicts between courts on particular subjects (or between the courts and the EEOC), these conflicts are noted. The leading Supreme Court, circuit court, and district court decisions are all discussed.[1] We also believe that the employment-law practitioner will find this book to be the most comprehensive resource available for all of the federal laws and decisions that regulate religion in the workplace.

---

1. This book addresses only the governing federal laws and federal judicial decisions. We have not summarized state laws or state court decisions. In our experience, most of the governing principles have been developed by the courts under the federal statutes. Any lawyer confronting an issue of religious discrimination would do well, however, to consult the relevant state law and decisions before providing advice.

About the Authors

Michael Wolf is an attorney and labor/employment arbitrator with offices in Washington, D.C., and New York. He serves as a permanent member of arbitration panels in both the public and private sectors and is on the roster of arbitrators for the American Arbitration Association, the Federal Mediation and Conciliation Service, and the National Association of Securities Dealers. Prior to becoming an arbitrator, Mr. Wolf was in private practice, specializing in labor, employment, and ERISA litigation, and spent four years supervising the prosecution of Nazi war criminals for the U.S. Department of Justice. He clerked for Judge Joseph C. Waddy of the U.S. District Court for the District of Columbia. Mr. Wolf is a graduate of Cornell University (A.B.) and New York University School of Law (J.D.).

Bruce Friedman is a senior trial attorney with the Civil Rights Division of the U.S. Department of Justice. Prior to entering government service, Mr. Friedman was in private practice with the law firm of Wilmer, Cutler and Pickering, in Washington, D.C., and clerked for Judge Oscar H. Davis of the U.S. Court of Appeals for the Federal Circuit. Mr. Friedman is a graduate of the University of Rochester (B.A.) and the National Law Center, George Washington University (J.D.).

Daniel W. Sutherland is also a senior trial attorney with the Civil Rights Division of the U.S. Department of Justice. Prior to entering government service, Mr. Sutherland practiced law with the firm of Brown, Todd and Heyburn in Louisville, Kentucky. Mr. Sutherland is a graduate of the University of Louisville (B.S.) and the University of Virginia School of Law (J.D.).

▦ CHAPTER 1

Overview of Federal Laws Governing Religion in the Workplace

The protection of employees' religious rights in the workplace is not derived from a single source. Instead, there are several different federal laws and regulations, as well as the U.S. Constitution, that regulate religion in the workplace:

- Title VII of the Civil Rights Act of 1964, as amended, and implementing guidelines promulgated by the Equal Employment Opportunity Commission.
- Executive Order 11246 and guidelines issued by the U.S. Labor Department's Office of Federal Contract Compliance Programs (governing federal contractors).
- National Labor Relations Act.
- Federal personnel laws and regulations.
- First Amendment to the U.S. Constitution.
- Religious Freedom Restoration Act.[1]
- White House Guidelines on Religious Exercise and Religious Expression in the Federal Workplace.

---

1. The Religious Freedom Restoration Act was declared unconstitutional in City of Boerne v. Flores, 117 S.Ct. 2157 (1997), but remains applicable to the executive branch of the federal government by virtue of Guidelines on Religious Exercise and Religious Expression in the Federal Workplace, issued by the White House after the *Boerne* decision.

Subsequent chapters analyze these mandates in detail and the relevant case law. This chapter provides a brief overview.

Title VII, Civil Rights Act of 1964[2]

In addition to prohibiting employment decisions based on an employee's race, color, sex, or national origin, Title VII of the 1964 Civil Rights Act (as amended) also bars discrimination in the workplace on the basis of religion.[3] Hiring, promotion, and discharge decisions must be untainted by a religious motivation or animus. The law applies to all public sector employers and to most private sector employers.[4]

In 1972, the definition of religion in Title VII was amended to require employers to "reasonably accommodate" an individual's religious observances or religious practices.[5] The employer can avoid making an accommodation only if doing so would constitute an "undue hardship" on the employer's business.[6] As a result of this amendment, an employer's obligation to refrain from discriminatory employment decisions is coupled with an affirmative obligation to accommodate employees who notify the employer of a conflict between their religious beliefs or practices and a work rule.

The Equal Employment Opportunity Commission (EEOC) has issued "Guidelines on Discrimination Because of Religion,"[7] which adopt a very broad definition of a religious practice: actions taken as a result of "moral and ethical beliefs as to what is right and wrong which are sincerely held with the strength of traditional religious views."[8] The EEOC emphasizes that the moral or ethical belief does not need to be one that is

---

2. 42 U.S.C. §§ 2000e, *et seq.* The relevant provisions of Title VII are reprinted at Appendix A.

3. *Id.* at § 2000e-2.

4. *Id.* at § 2000e-16 (federal government), § 2000e(a) (state and local governmental agencies), and § 2000e(b) (private sector companies with fifteen or more employees "for each working day in each of twenty or more calendar weeks in the current or preceding calendar year").

5. *Id.* at § 2000e(j).

6. *Id.*

7. 29 C.F.R. § 1605, reprinted at Appendix B.

8. *Id.* at § 1605.1.

associated with a recognized religious group or church; if only one individual sincerely holds to the belief, it is a protected religious practice.

The EEOC has additionally promulgated a "Policy Statement on Religious Accommodation under Title VII,"[9] a "Policy Statement on Religious Accommodation under Title VII Based on Objections to Unionism,"[10] and a "Policy Guide on Pay Discrimination by Religious Organizations."[11] Each of these provides guidance on the implementation of Title VII, but does not carry the force of regulation.

Executive Order 11246—Federal Contractors[12]

In 1965, President Johnson signed Executive Order 11246, which requires all companies that contract with the federal government to refrain from discriminating on the basis of race, color, religion, sex, or national origin. The Executive Order requires that this nondiscrimination language be inserted into every federal contract.[13] The contractor is required to post a notice describing its commitment to equal opportunity and it must submit reports to the U.S. Department of Labor documenting its nondiscrimination efforts.[14] Contractors must also agree to take "affirmative action" to ensure that there is no unlawful conduct at the workplace.[15] If a contractor violates the nondiscrimination language of the contract, the contract may be terminated or suspended.[16] The contractor is also required to include the nondiscrimination clauses in any subcontracts it signs.[17]

The Department of Labor's Office of Federal Contract Compliance Programs (OFCCP) has issued a series of guidelines implementing the Executive Order, including guidelines addressing discrimination based on

---

9. Reprinted at Appendix B.

10. Reprinted at Appendix B.

11. Reprinted at Appendix B.

12. Exec. Order No.11246, 42 U.S.C. § 2000e, note. The Executive Order and implementing regulations by the Department of Labor are reprinted at Appendixes C and D.

13. Exec. Order No.11246 at § 202.

14. *Id.* at § 202(5).

15. *Id.* at § 202(B)(i).

16. *Id.* at § 202(6).

17. *Id.* at § 202(7).

religion or national origin.[18] The guidelines start with the assumption that "various religious and ethnic groups" experience considerable discrimination.[19] The guidelines state that many religious and ethnic minorities are not promoted to or hired for upper-management jobs solely because of their religious beliefs or country of origin. The guidelines repeat the Executive Order's requirement that companies must not discriminate on the basis of religion and must undertake "affirmative action" to ensure that religious minorities are provided equal opportunity. The guidelines also require contractors to undertake the following actions as part of their affirmative-action programs:

- communicate regularly to employees that the contractor is committed to equal opportunity for people of all religious faiths;
- foster understanding of religious and ethnic minorities among the contractor's supervisors and management;
- look for opportunities to promote or transfer religious and ethnic minorities to favorable jobs; and
- recruit new employees from schools with substantial enrollments of students from various religious and ethnic groups.[20]

Finally, the OFCCP guidelines repeat the law developed under Title VII: Employers must accommodate an individual's religious observances, unless doing so will cause an undue hardship.[21]

National Labor Relations Act[22]

In 1980, Congress added a "conscientious objector" provision to the National Labor Relations Act (NLRA), which provides limited relief to employees whose religious convictions prevent them from paying union dues or other fees.[23] This provision exempts only employees whose reli-

---

18. 41 C.F.R. § 60-50, reprinted at Appendix E.

19. *Id.* at § 60-50(b).

20. *Id.* at § 60-50.2(b).

21. *Id.* at § 60-50.3.

22. Section 19 of the NLRA (29 U.S.C. § 169) is reprinted at Appendix E. Appendix B also reprints the EEOC's "Policy Statement on Religious Accommodation Under Title VII Based on Objections to Unionism," issued on May 29, 1988.

23. 29 U.S.C. § 169.

gious objections to joining a labor organization are part of "established and traditional tenets or teachings" of their religious organization; the exemption applies only to religious organizations that have "historically held" an objection to participating in a labor organization.[24]

If an employee has a legitimate religious reason for objecting to the payment of union dues, the employee does not pocket the money: The employer and union can require the employee to pay the equivalent amount to a nonprofit charity.[25]

In 1990, the Sixth Circuit Court of Appeals declared this provision of the NLRA unconstitutional because it singled out only certain religions for protection, thereby breaching the Establishment clause of the First Amendment; the Supreme Court declined to review the decision.[26] Since then, there has been no reported decision interpreting this provision.[27]

The First Amendment

Because the Constitution restrains governmental actors, the First Amendment is most pertinent to religious disputes that occur within public-sector workplaces.[28] In this respect, several provisions of the First Amendment are relevant to such disputes.

The Free Exercise and Establishment clauses of the First Amendment are succinct: The government may not pass any law "respecting the establishment of religion, or prohibiting the free exercise thereof. . . ."

---

24. *Id.*

25. *Id.*

26. Wilson v. National Labor Relations Board, 920 F.2d 1282 (6th Cir. 1990), *cert. denied,* 505 U.S. 1218 (1992).

27. As discussed in Chapter 10, the courts have independently interpreted Title VII's accommodation provision to permit employees to opt out of the payment of union dues/fees on religious grounds *and* to permit employers and unions to require an equivalent amount of money to be paid to nonreligious charities as a "reasonable accommodation." These decisions have not limited the definition of religious beliefs entitled to this accommodation and therefore do not appear to have the constitutional infirmity that the Sixth Circuit found with the NLRA. Therefore, whether or not the conscientious objector provision of the NLRA is unconstitutional seems to be moot, since the courts have imposed comparable requirements under Title VII.

28. *See* Brown v. Polk County, Iowa, 61 F.3d 650, 654 (8th Cir. 1995)(en banc), *cert. denied,* 516 U.S. 1158 (1996).

The Free Exercise clause, on its face, bars the government from infringing the exercise of religion by its employees. Indeed, it has been invoked repeatedly by the courts to protect the religious practices of public employees—with two notable exceptions. First, an employer may ban or limit religious activities that hinder the performance of the employer's mission.[29] Second, government agencies are not required to permit employees' religious practices that reasonably convey to the public the impression that the government is supporting or endorsing religion or particular religious practices. In other words, the government employer need not tolerate employee practices that are likely to breach the religious neutrality that lies at the heart of the Establishment clause.[30] As a result, the Free Exercise and Establishment clauses coexist in the public workplace in a perpetual state of tension.

In addition to the religion clauses of the First Amendment, the Free Speech clause also protects government employees who engage in certain religious activities at work. While the courts recognize that the government has much stronger interests in regulating the speech of its employees than it does in regulating the speech of private citizens,[31] the restrictions it may place on the religious speech of employees are still limited by traditional First Amendment principles. Most importantly, government employers may not discriminatorily ban or suppress speech solely because of its religious content.[32] For example, a government employer that permits employees to post general notices on a bulletin board may be precluded from banning the posting of religious notices.[33] On the other hand, employers can and indeed must suppress religious speech that could reasonably be interpreted as having governmental endorsement.[34]

---

29. *See, e.g.,* Ryan v. U.S. Department of Justice, 950 F.2d 458 (7th Cir. 1991), *cert. denied,* 504 U.S. 958 (1992).

30. *See, e.g.,* Bishop v. Aronov, 926 F.2d 1066 (11th Cir.), *cert. denied,* 502 U.S. 905 (1991).

31. Lumpkin v. Brown, 109 F.3d 1498, 1500 (9th Cir.), *cert. denied,* 118 S.Ct. 558 (1997).

32. *See, e.g.,* Brown v. Polk County, 61 F.3d at 658.

33. *See, e.g.,* Tucker v. State of California Dept. of Educ., 97 F.3d 1204, 1215 (9th Cir. 1996) ("We conclude that it is not reasonable to allow employees to post materials around the office on all sorts of subjects, and forbid only the posting of religious information and materials.").

34. Peloza v. Capistrano Unified School District, 37 F.3d 517 (9th Cir. 1994), *cert. denied,* 115 S.Ct. 2640 (1995); Bishop v. Aronov, 926 F.2d 1066.

Occasionally, the constitutional principles underlying the First Amendment may conflict with Title VII jurisprudence. Under the First Amendment, a government employer cannot intentionally restrict an employee's religious activities without a compelling state interest, one of the most exacting standards in constitutional law. By contrast, Title VII of the Civil Rights Act of 1964 allows an employer to restrict an individual's religious practices if it can prove that accommodating those practices would impose an "undue hardship" on the employer—a far lower burden of proof than the "compelling interest" test.[35] The greatest practical consequence of these differing standards of proof is that public sector employers must be aware that Title VII does not define the limits of their responsibilities. They must also satisfy the much more stringent requirements of the First Amendment.

Federal Personnel Laws[36]

In addition to the protections of the First Amendment and Title VII, employees of the federal government are guaranteed limited accommodation rights under Section 5550a of Title 5 of the United States Code. Congress enacted this law to ensure that federal employees are given compensatory time off for religious observances. The law requires federal agencies to give employees the opportunity to work overtime in exchange for time that they must miss for religious observances. Pursuant to implementing regulations, the "compensatory overtime" can be worked either before or after the religious observance, but is paid at the employee's straight-time rate.[37]

Religious Freedom Restoration Act[38]

The Religious Freedom Restoration Act (RFRA) was enacted in 1993 in an effort to reverse the effects of the Supreme Court's decision in *Employ-*

---

35. *See* United States v. Board of Education, 911 F.2d 882, 890 (3d Cir. 1990).

36. Section 5550a of Title 5 and implementing regulations are reprinted at Appendix F.

37. 5 C.F.R. §§ 550.1001, 550.1002. Employees are not entitled to time-and-a-half for any overtime worked to make up for the religious leave; this overtime is exempt from the Fair Labor Standards Act (29 U.S.C. § 201, *et seq.*). *Id.*

38. 42 U.S.C. § 2000bb(b). RFRA is reprinted at Appendix G.

ment Division, Department Of Human Resources of Oregon v. Smith.[39] RFRA required that laws that substantially burden the exercise of religion (even if facially neutral) must be justified by a compelling interest. In *City of Boerne v. Flores,* the Supreme Court declared RFRA unconstitutional, as applied to the states.[40] However, the statute retains some vitality in the workplace in light of the White House's application of the RFRA standards to employment in the executive branch of the federal government, pursuant to the Guidelines discussed below.

White House Guidelines on Religious Exercise and Religious Expression in the Federal Workplace

In August 1997, the Clinton Administration issued an extensive directive on how executive-branch agencies should treat religious practices in the workplace.[41] These Guidelines address religious discrimination, accommodation, harassment, and proselytizing in federal offices. For those in the federal workforce (both managers and employees), the Guidelines are particularly important for three reasons. First, they exhort agencies to maximize efforts to accommodate the religious activities of their workers. The Guidelines instruct federal agencies to "permit personal religious expression by Federal employees to the greatest extent possible[.]"[42] Second, they provide specific and practical guidance through hypothetical examples. In addition to stating general principles of law, the Guidelines contain over two dozen examples of conduct that must be permitted or that can be restricted. Third, the Guidelines require federal agencies to adhere to the compelling interest test of RFRA whenever neutral work rules substantially burden employees' religious practices.

The Guidelines are somewhat peculiar because they are not an Executive Order or a regulation; they are simply a policy statement issued by the White House. Moreover, the Guidelines state that they are not intended to create a right of legal action. For these reasons, their legal significance is likely to remain murky, unless and until they are made the subject of litigation.

---

39. 494 U.S. 872 (1990).

40. 117 S.Ct. 2157 (1997).

41. Guidelines on Religious Exercise and Religious Expression in the Federal Workplace (White House, August 14, 1997), reprinted at Appendix H.

42. *Id.*

▓ CHAPTER 2

Which Employers Are Covered under Federal Law?

Private Sector

Title VII defines an employer as:

> a person engaged in an industry affecting commerce who has *fifteen or more employees* for each working day in each of twenty or more calendar weeks in the current or preceding calendar year, and any agent of such a person. . . . [1]

A "person," in turn, is defined broadly to include:

> . . . individuals, governments, governmental agencies, political subdivisions, labor unions, partnerships, associations, corporations, legal representatives, mutual companies, joint-stock companies, trusts, unincorporated organizations, trustees, trustees in cases under Title 11 [bankruptcy], or receivers.[2]

The definition of "employer" specifically excludes the federal government, agencies of the federal government, corporations wholly owned by the federal government, Indian tribes, and the District of Columbia.[3]

---

1. 42 U.S.C. § 2000e(b) (emphasis added). .
2. 42 U.S.C. § 2000e(a).
3. *Id.* at § 2000e(b).

Labor unions are covered by the law by virtue of their inclusion in the definition of a "person." A "labor organization" is separately defined to be engaged in an industry affecting commerce and therefore subject to liability under Title VII if it operates a hiring hall (or similar operation) or if it has fifteen or more members and meets one of several additional criteria (for example, it is certified as a bargaining representative under the National Labor Relations Act).[4]

Finally, all "employment agenc[ies]" are subject to Title VII's jurisdiction if they "procure employees for an employer or . . . procure for employees opportunities to work for an employer. . . ."[5]

In sum, only the smallest employers and unions in the private sector are exempt from the reach of Title VII. All employment agencies that seek employees for such employers are similarly within the scope of Title VII.

The statute also provides broad coverage to "employees." Any individual employed by a covered employer, as defined above, is protected by Title VII.[6]

Public Sector

The definition of an employer under Title VII includes state and local governments and their agencies. Several categories of public *employees* are excepted, however: elected public office-holders, personal staff to such office-holders, appointees to policy-making positions, and advisors to office-holders who exercise "constitutional or legal powers."[7] These exceptions are explicitly *not* extended to public employees who are subject to the civil service laws governing their states or localities.

---

4. *Id.* at § 2000e(d) and (e).

5. *Id.* at § 2000e(c).

6. *Id.* at § 2000e(f). Independent contractors are not protected by Title VII. *See, e.g.,* Spirides v. Reinhardt, 613 F.2d 826 (D.C. Cir. 1979). In determining whether someone is an employee or independent contractor, most courts use the "economic realities" or "common law control" tests. *See* Mares v. Marsh, 777 F.2d 1066 (5th Cir. 1985) and cases cited therein.

In certain limited circumstances, a claim may be brought under Title VII against an entity that does not directly employ the plaintiff if the entity has sufficient control over the plaintiff's working conditions. *See, e.g.,* Sibley Memorial Hospital v. Wilson, 488 F.2d 1338 (D.C. Cir. 1973); Moland v. Bil-Mar Foods, 76 FEP 180 (N.D. Iowa 1998).

7. 42 U.S.C. § 2000e(f).

Originally, the federal government had exempted itself from Title VII. Instead, a 1965 Executive Order signed by President Johnson required nondiscrimination in federal employment.[8] In 1972, however, Congress extended the statute's coverage to executive-branch employees of the federal government, civilian employees of the military departments, the U.S. Postal Service, the Postal Rate Commission, the District of Columbia, the Library of Congress, and employees of the legislative and judicial branches who are in the competitive service.[9]

Separate provisions of the federal personnel laws mandate nondiscrimination in the hiring and employment of employees for the federal executive branch[10] and for the General Accounting Office.[11] Most recently, Congress agreed to make its own employees subject to the same nondiscrimination principles previously applicable to other public employees.[12]

Federal Government Contractors and Subcontractors

Pursuant to Executive Order 11246, *all* contracts entered into by federal agencies must include a clause barring the contractor from discriminating in employment based on religion.[13] *All* subcontracts must contain the same promise of nondiscrimination by the subcontractor.[14] Therefore, apart from the limitations in Title VII, all employers working under a federal government contract or subcontract (and all unions representing employees of such employers) must comply with the nondiscrimination and accommodation requirements of the Executive Order and the implementing Department of Labor regulations. Noncompliance with these contractual requirements can result in suspension or termination of the contract or a declaration of ineligibility for future contracts.[15]

---

8. Exec. Order No.11246 (Sep. 24, 1965).

9. 42 U.S.C. § 2000e-16.

10. 5 U.S.C. § 2302. *See also* 5 U.S.C. § 7201(b).

11. 31 U.S.C. § 732.

12. 2 U.S.C. § 1301 *et seq.*

13. Section 202, Exec. Order No.11246 (Sep. 24, 1965), reprinted at Appendix C. *See also* 41 C.F.R. § 60-50.1(a).

14. Exec. Order No. 11246 at § 202.

15. *Id.* at §§ 205, 209.

Exemptions for Religious Organizations

Employees of religious organizations who assert employment-related claims against their employers face two obstacles: the First Amendment and two exclusionary clauses in Title VII. One provision of Title VII permits religious institutions to discriminate on the basis of religion, but not on other bases (for example, race, sex, age).[16] Another provision of the statute also permits an employer to discriminate based on religion "where religion . . . is a bona fide occupational qualification reasonably necessary to the normal operation of that business or enterprise."[17] The First Amendment exempts from legal action only certain religious institutions and only those employees functioning as clergy, but the exempt institutions are free to undertake *all* forms of discrimination with respect to their clergy. Although there is overlap between the statutory and constitutional exemptions, each exemption must be analyzed separately.

First Amendment Exemption

Long before the enactment of Title VII, the Supreme Court held that neither a statute nor a court could constitutionally intrude upon the internal governance of a church.[18] Under this rule, the civil courts are obligated to accept the decisions made by the ruling authorities of a church on "matters of discipline, faith, internal organization, or ecclesiastical rule, custom, or law."[19] Essential to the internal governance of a church is the selection of its clergy. For this reason, the First Amendment requires the courts to refrain from exercising jurisdiction in matters relating to a church's selection of employees having ministerial or pastoral duties; even if the selection is challenged on the grounds that it deviates from the church's own internal rules or violates civil-rights laws, the courts must defer to a church's authority in the selection of its clergy.[20] When a minister raises any type of employment claim against a church, including

---

16. 42 U.S.C. § 2000e-1(a).

17. *Id.* at § 2000e-2(e).

18. Kreshik v. Saint Nicholas Cathedral, 363 U.S. 190 (1960); Kedroff v. Saint Nicholas Cathedral, 344 U.S. 94 (1952).

19. Serbian Eastern Orthodox Diocese v. Milivojevich, 426 U.S. 696, 713 (1976).

20. *Id. See also* Gonzalez v. Roman Catholic Archbishop of Manila, 280 U.S. 1 (1929).

claims of discrimination, the civil courts are constitutionally barred from considering those claims.[21] If a court second-guesses a church's ministerial appointments, the government necessarily interferes in the church's free exercise of religion.[22] In addition, the very process of inquiring into and deciding the competing claims on ecclesiastical matters entangles the courts in religious administration to an extent that constitutes an establishment of religion.[23]

For purposes of this exemption, the courts have adopted a liberal interpretation of what constitutes a church and who qualifies as clergy. Although the exemption most clearly applies to churches and the governing bodies of churches (for example, Catholic dioceses, Baptist Convention), the courts have extended the First Amendment's coverage to several related institutions that have pastoral missions.

Similarly, employees who are not ordained ministers may still be barred from bringing suit against their employing churches on the ground that they have some pastoral duties. Several courts have adopted the standard that an employee will fall within the clergy exemption if his or her "primary duties consist of teaching, spreading the faith, church governance, supervision of a religious order, or supervision or participation in religious ritual and worship."[24] As the Fourth Circuit has summed up, the exemption will apply whenever an employee's position is "important to the spiritual and pastoral mission of the church."[25]

---

21. Young v. N. Ill. Conf. of United Methodist Church, 21 F.3d 184 (7th Cir.), *cert. denied*, 513 U.S. 929 (1994); Minker v. Baltimore Annual Conf., 894 F.2d 1354 (D.C. Cir. 1990); Natal v. Christian and Missionary Alliance, 878 F.2d 1575 (1st Cir. 1989); Rayburn v. General Conf. of Seventh-Day Adventists, 772 F.2d 1164 (4th Cir. 1985), *cert. denied*, 478 U.S. 1020 (1986).

22. McClure v. The Salvation Army, 460 F.2d 553 (5th Cir.), *cert. denied*, 409 U.S. 896 (1972).

23. EEOC v. Catholic University of America, 83 F.3d 455 (D.C. Cir. 1996); Maguire v. Marquette University, 627 F. Supp. 1499 (E.D. Wis. 1986), *aff'd in part and vacated in part*, 814 F.2d 1213 (7th Cir. 1987).

24. *See* EEOC v. Catholic University, 83 F.3d 455; Rayburn v. General Conf. of Seventh-Day Adventists, 772 F.2d 1164 (4th Cir. 1985). *See also* Bagni, "Discrimination in the Name of the Lord: A Critical Evaluation of Discrimination by Religious Organizations," 79 COLUMBIA L. REV. 1514, 1545 (1979).

25. Rayburn v. General Conf., 772 F.2d at 1169.

The following decisions exemplify the judiciary's broad interpretation of the First Amendment exemption:

- The Salvation Army is a religious organization and its officers are ordained ministers; a minister is barred from bringing a claim of sex discrimination, even though she had only secretarial duties.[26]
- Teachers at a seminary are akin to ministers and may not bring age-discrimination claims.[27]
- An applicant for a position of "associate in pastoral care" who is not ordained (and cannot be ordained because she is a woman) is still subject to the clergy exemption because the duties of the position are primarily spiritual in nature. Claims of discrimination based on race and sex are therefore barred.[28]
- A theology professor at a Jesuit-run university cannot bring a claim of sex discrimination, since the subject matter of theology courses "is unavoidably intertwined with questions of faith and church doctrine" and a theology professor's duties "go to the very core of what religion is."[29]
- A probationary minister is barred from claiming sex and race discrimination, as well as retaliation, against a conference of churches that denied her promotion to a clergy position.[30]
- A professor of canon law at Catholic University of America cannot bring a claim for sex discrimination.[31]
- A chaplain at a church-affiliated hospital carries out pastoral duties and therefore may not bring sex and age discrimination claims.[32]

---

26. McClure v. The Salvation Army, 460 F.2d 553.

27. Cochran v. St. Louis Preparatory Seminary, 717 F. Supp. 1413 (E.D. Mo. 1989). *Accord* EEOC v. Southwestern Bap. Theological Seminary, 651 F.2d 277 (5th Cir. 1981), *cert. denied,* 456 U.S. 905 (1982) (EEOC is barred from compelling production of employment data relating to seminary teachers).

28. Rayburn v. General Conf., 772 F.2d 1164.

29. Maguire v. Marquette University, 627 F. Supp. at 1506. *Accord* Powell v. Stafford, 859 F. Supp. 1343 (D. Colo. 1994) (suit for age discrimination by theology teacher at Catholic high school would violate First Amendment).

30. Young v. N. Ill. Conf., 21 F.3d 184.

31. EEOC v. Catholic University, 83 F.3d 455.

32. Scharon v. St. Luke's Episcopal Presbyterian Hosp., 929 F.2d 360 (8th Cir. 1991).

Notwithstanding this liberal view of the First Amendment exemption, that liberality is not limitless. In several notable cases, courts concluded that certain religiously affiliated institutions were not entitled to the protection of the First Amendment because they were not "churches" or because the particular employees who brought suit did not function as clergy:

- *Lay* teachers of *non*religious subjects may sue church-operated schools and colleges for race, sex, and age discrimination, even when the education environment is pervasively sectarian.[33]
- Support staff and administrators of a seminary who do not have religious duties are not ministers.[34]
- A publishing business operated as a religious enterprise by the Seventh-Day Adventist church may be sued by a secretary for sex discrimination.[35]
- The administrator of a Jewish temple does not carry out pastoral duties and therefore may assert discrimination claim.[36]
- A chef employed by a monastery may sue for age discrimination.[37]

Although the foregoing decisions may seem to lack a unified theme, there are a few universal standards that can be derived from this body

---

33. EEOC v. Mississippi College, 626 F.2d 477, 485 (5th Cir. 1980), *cert. denied,* 453 U.S. 912 (1981) (Mississippi College is a church-run institution, but not a seminary).

34. EEOC v. Southwestern Bap. Theological Seminary, 651 F.2d 277 (*senior* administrators in education departments of seminary are "ministers," while administrators involved in nonreligious activities—e.g., finance, maintenance—are not "ministers").

35. EEOC v. Pacific Press Pub. Assn., 676 F.2d 1272 (9th Cir. 1982). The court noted that a lawsuit by a secretary would have only a minimal impact on the Church's religious beliefs, since the Church did not espouse views in support of gender discrimination. Similarly, in Geary v. Visitation of the Blessed Virgin Mary, 7 F.3d 324 (3rd Cir. 1993), a claim of age discrimination by a lay teacher against a religious school was not barred, in part because the church did not argue that age discrimination was mandated by religious doctrine. These decisions leave open the question whether churches that espouse theological doctrines supporting gender or age discrimination may avail themselves of the protections of the First Amendment.

36. Weissman v. Congregation Shaare Emeth, 38 F.3d 1038 (8th Cir. 1994) (administrator of Jewish temple has no religious duties and is not treated as a minister).

37. Stouch v. Brothers of Order, 836 F. Supp. 1134 (E.D. Pa. 1993). *Accord* Lukaszewski v. Nazareth Hospital, 764 F. Supp. 57 (E.D. Pa. 1991) (director of plant operations at church-affiliated hospital may sue for age discrimination).

of law. First, disputes involving the employment relationship between churches and ministers are beyond the reach of the courts. For these purposes, a minister will be deemed anyone who has pastoral duties and a church will include any church-affiliated institution (for example, a hospital) that employs persons exercising pastoral duties. Second, lay employees of churches will be permitted to bring employment-discrimination claims against their employers, unless they have significant ecclesiastical duties. Third, the courts will refrain from adjudicating disputes between teachers of religion and the religious schools that employ them; seminaries and similar institutions of religious training will probably be able to exempt *all* teaching employees.

If there is one area in which the courts have not acted uniformly, it is the employment of *lay* teachers by religious schools that are *not* seminaries. The genesis of this problem lies with the Supreme Court's decision in *National Labor Relations Board v. Catholic Bishop of Chicago*.[38] In that case, a union tried to organize the employees of several Catholic high schools. Although the schools taught secular, as well as religious, subjects and although the employees to be organized were limited to lay teachers, the Court concluded that the National Labor Relations Board (NLRB) could not exercise jurisdiction over the schools.

In a convoluted decision, the Court first concluded that the kind of on-going involvement that the NLRB has in investigating and deciding workplace issues risks a conflict of constitutional proportions between the church's religious principles and the interests of employees. If the NLRB were to decide such conflicts, the government would inevitably become entangled in religious matters, thereby violating the ban on the Establishment of religion clause in the First Amendment.[39] To avoid this constitutional conflict, the Court decided that it would review the National Labor

---

38. 440 U.S. 490 (1979).

39. In *Lemon v. Kurtzman*, 403 U.S. 602 (1971), the Court enunciated a three-part test for identifying legislation that survives the Establishment clause of the First Amendment: (1) the statute has a secular legislative purpose, (2) the principal or primary effect of the statute is neither to advance nor to inhibit religion, and (3) the statute does not foster "an excessive government entanglement with religion." In *Catholic Bishop*, the Court concluded that the National Labor Relations Act satisfies the first two criteria, but impermissibly brings about an excessive entanglement of the NLRB in the internal operations of a church.

Relations Act and its legislative history to determine whether Congress intended to apply the law to religious institutions. The Court concluded that Congress did not intend to cover teachers in religious schools. In a 5-to-4 decision, the Court held that the NLRB had no authority to enforce the law against the Catholic schools.

In reaching this conclusion, the Court stated that once the First Amendment provides an exemption, it does far more than result in the dismissal of employee claims—it would require the NLRB to cease its inquiries, since the very process of investigating a church over ecclesiastical matters creates a constitutional conflict. The lower courts have extended this hands-off rule to the EEOC when it investigates discrimination charges brought by *pastoral* employees against churches.[40] However, they have generally limited *Catholic Bishop* to its own particular facts and have permitted the NLRB to exercise jurisdiction over other church-operated institutions that carry out secular functions (for example, child-care facilities and residential treatment facilities for children).[41] More importantly, several circuit courts refuse to extend *Catholic Bishop* to lay employees who bring claims under laws other than the National Labor Relations Act.

The Second, Third, Fourth, and Ninth Circuits have permitted lay teachers in religious schools to sue under the Age Discrimination in Employment Act and the Equal Pay Act.[42] These courts concluded that the EEOC's investigations of allegations of discrimination are much less intrusive than the pervasive and on-going jurisdiction asserted by the NLRB when a workplace becomes unionized; for this reason, the excessive entanglements between church and government that gave rise to constitutional difficulties in *Catholic Bishop* are theoretically not present in statutory discrimination cases. These circuit courts also found that an inquiry

---

40. *See, e.g.,* EEOC v. Catholic University, 83 F.3d 455; EEOC v. Southwestern Bap. Theological Seminary, 651 F.2d 277.

41. *See, e.g.,* Vol. of America-Minnesota-Bar None Boys v. NLRB, 752 F.2d 345 (8th Cir.), *cert. denied,* 472 U.S. 1028 (1985).

42. Geary v. Visitation of the Blessed Virgin Mary, 7 F.3d 324; DeMarco v. Holy Cross High School, 4 F.3d 166 (2d Cir. 1993); Ritter v. Mount St. Mary's College, 814 F.2d 986 (4th Cir.), *cert. denied,* 484 U.S. 913 (1987); EEOC v. Fremont Christian High School, 781 F.2d 1362 (9th Cir. 1986).

into the treatment of lay employees is not likely to require inquiry into church doctrine.[43]

Perhaps the best indication that *Catholic Bishop* will not be extended to EEO claims comes from the Supreme Court itself. In *Ohio Civil Rights Commission v. Dayton Christian Schools*,[44] the court of appeals refused to permit a state human-rights agency to investigate a lay teacher's state-law claim that a religious school had engaged in sex discrimination; the circuit court was persuaded that permitting the state's administrative process to go forward would burden the school's Free Exercise rights and would constitute an unconstitutional entanglement in religion.[45] The Supreme Court reversed, holding that principles of comity prevented the federal courts from enjoining the state administrative process. Without any discussion of *Catholic Bishop*,[46] the Court opined that the state "Commission violates no constitutional rights by merely investigating the circumstances of [the plaintiff's] discharge in this case[.]"[47] It would seem that the circuit courts of appeals have correctly concluded that *Catholic Bishop* should be limited to its precise facts and circumstances and that it may not be a factor in deciding whether EEO claims by lay teachers in religious schools can be investigated and litigated.

This narrowing of the *Catholic Bishop* exception is further reinforced by the EEOC's "Policy Guide on Pay Discrimination by Religious Organizations."[48] The EEOC states that it will respect the ministerial exception under the First Amendment whenever it investigates a Title VII charge of discrimination, but that it will also "carefully examine" the employment relationship to determine whether the exemption applies. As to nonclergy, the Commission will enforce both Title VII and the Equal

---

43. *See also* Dole v. Shenandoah Baptist Church, 899 F.2d 1389 (4th Cir.), *cert. denied,* 498 U.S. 846 (1990) (a church-operated school can be sued for violations of the Fair Labor Standards Act because church doctrine does not require violation of that law).

44. 477 U.S. 619 (1986).

45. 766 F.2d 932 (6th Cir. 1985).

46. The Court accorded *Catholic Bishop* a single "cf." citation, without any commentary.

47. 477 U.S. at 628.

48. Reprinted at Appendix B.

Pay Act[49] even if the religious employer claims that gender discrimination is theologically based.

The EEOC notes that the legislative history of Title VII reflects Congress's belief that religious employers should not be given a blanket exemption from race, sex, color, or national origin discrimination. The Commission also views the elimination of such discrimination as a compelling interest that justifies the burdens of Title VII enforcement on religious institutions. Therefore, in this Policy Guide, the EEOC expresses its willingness to assert jurisdiction over charges of sex discrimination (and presumably other forms of discrimination), even if a religious-organization–employer proclaims that the discrimination is dictated by church doctrine.

Title VII—Religious Organization Exemption

In *Catholic Bishop,* the Supreme Court held that whenever there is a potential conflict between the First Amendment and a civil statute, the courts must first determine whether Congress intended the statute to apply to religious institutions. In the case of Title VII, there is extensive legislative history showing that Congress did intend religious institutions to be treated as employers under the statute—with very limited exceptions. A brief review of the history of this legislation is useful in understanding its limitations.

When first proposed in the House of Representatives, Title VII contained a sweeping exemption for all religious corporations, associations, and societies.[50] As enacted in 1964, the exemption (Section 702(a)) was drastically narrowed; religious organizations were permitted to give preference to employees of a particular religion in jobs relating to the organizations' *"religious* activities"; it did not permit religious organizations to discriminate on other bases (for example, race).[51]

The 1972 revisions to Title VII included changes to Section 702(a). Congress deleted the reference to *religious* activities in that provision, so

---

49. The Equal Pay Act outlaws pay disparity based on gender for work on jobs requiring "equal skill, effort and responsibility." 29 U.S.C. § 206(d).

50. H.R. 7152, H.R. Rep. No. 914, 88 Cong., 1st Sess. 10 (1963).

51. Pub. L. No. 88-352, Title VII, Section 702.

that a religious institution could discriminate *on the basis of religion* with respect to *all* of its activities. Religious schools were also exempted. However, the section continued to outlaw discrimination by religious institutions based on race, sex, and national origin. As currently codified, the religious exemption in Section 702(a) reads as follows:

> This subchapter shall not apply to . . . a religious corporation, association, educational institution, or society with respect to the employment of individuals of a particular religion to perform work connected with the carrying on by such corporation, association, educational institution, or society of its activities.[52]

To emphasize the applicability of this exemption to schools operated by religious institutions, Title VII contains a separate exemption in Section 703(e)(2):

> Notwithstanding any other provision of this subchapter . . . it shall not be an unlawful employment practice for a school, college, university, or other educational institution of learning to hire and employ employees of a particular religion if such school, college, university, or other educational institution or institution of learning is, in whole or in substantial part, owned, supported, controlled, or managed by a particular religion or by a particular religious corporation, association, or society, or if the curriculum of such school, col-

---

52. 42 U.S.C. § 2000e-1(a). The constitutionality of this provision was itself questioned by some lower courts, since it permitted religious organizations to discriminate in a way prohibited to secular institutions. *See, e.g.,* Kings Garden, Inc. v. FCC, 498 F.2d 51 (D.C. Cir.), *cert. denied,* 419 U.S. 996 (1974). The Supreme Court subsequently affirmed the constitutionality of this exemption. Corporation of Presiding Bishop v. Amos, 483 U.S. 327 (1987).

Section 103(c) of the Americans with Disabilities Act, 42 U.S.C. § 12113(c)(1) and (2), contains a similar exemption:

(1) In general. This title shall not prohibit a religious corporation, association, educational institution, or society from giving preference in employment to individuals of a particular religion to perform work connected with the carrying on by such corporation, association, educational institution, or society of its activities.

(2) Religious tenets requirement. Under this title, a religious organization may require that all applicants and employees conform to the religious tenets of such organization.

lege, university, or other educations institution or institution of learning is directed toward the propagation of a particular religion.[53]

The effect of Sections 702(a) and 703(e)(2) is to ensure that all religious institutions, including all church-affiliated schools, may use religious preferences in making employment decisions. This statutory exemption is broader than the First Amendment exemption because it covers a wider range of church-affiliated employers. It also permits religious organizations to restrict their employment of *all* employees (including lay employees) to persons of a particular religion.[54] Religious schools may impose religious requirements upon the hiring of lay teachers and administrators, not just teachers of religion. At the same time, the exemption is considerably narrower than that accorded by the First Amendment, since it does not immunize religious organizations from actions for discrimination on grounds other than religion.[55]

The practical questions arising out of the two statutory exemptions are similar to those confronted under the First Amendment. One question repeatedly addressed by the courts is whether a particular organization is a religious institution within the meaning of the statute. On one hand, the courts have made clear that not every entity affiliated with a religious body will come within the Section 702(a) exemption. On the other hand, because of the constitutional implications, the courts will closely scrutinize the facts of each case to ensure that religious institutions are not deprived of the right to maintain religious cohesiveness in their operations. The following exemplify the divergence of results in these cases:

- *The Christian Science Monitor* is a religious activity of a religious organization and therefore may limit the hiring of journalists to practitioners of the Christian Science faith.[56]

---

53. 42 U.S.C. § 2000e-2(e)(2).

54. Corporation of Presiding Bishop v. Amos, 483 U.S. 327 (section 702 is constitutional notwithstanding its application to lay employees).

55. EEOC v. Pacific Press Pub. Ass'n, 676 F.2d 1272 (9th Cir. 1982); EEOC v. Mississippi College, 626 F.2d 477 (5th Cir. 1980), *cert. denied,* 453 U.S. 912 (1981); Boyd v. Harding Academy of Memphis, Inc., 887 F. Supp. 157 (W.D. Tenn. 1995), *aff'd,* 88 F.3d 410 (6th Cir. 1996).

56. Feldstein v. Christian Science Monitor, 555 F. Supp. 974 (D. Mass. 1983). *See also* EEOC v. Pacific Press, 676 F. Supp. 1272 (publisher affiliated with the Seventh-Day Adventist Church is covered by exemption).

- A university founded by the Alabama Baptist Convention, which teaches both secular and sectarian courses, is a religious educational institution based on: (a) the Baptist Convention is the largest single funding source (7 percent of budget); (b) the school is a member of the Association of Baptist Colleges; (c) the school submits financial reports to Baptist authorities for audit and review; and (d) the school's charter states that its chief purpose is to promote the Christian religion.[57]
- A Methodist home for troubled youth is not a religious organization for purposes of Section 702(a), notwithstanding its oversight by church-appointed trustees; in practice, the home operated primarily as a secular institution with very limited involvement in religious practices and rituals.[58]
- A privately owned for-profit corporation is not a religious corporation merely because the owners are religious and operate the company pursuant to religious principles; mandatory prayer meetings for employees are a violation of Title VII.[59]
- A school created by a private trust dictating that all teachers be of the Protestant faith could not use Section 702 or the First Amendment as a defense to a religious discrimination suit because the school was not operated by a church and provided a largely nonsectarian education.[60]

Another question the courts have grappled with is whether Title VII permits churches to insist upon adherence to religious doctrine by its employees. Clearly, Title VII permits an employer to require that an

---

57. Killinger v. Samford University, 113 F.3d 196 (11th Cir. 1997).

58. Fike v. United Methodist Children's Home of VA., 547 F. Supp. 286 (E.D. Va. 1982), aff'd, 709 F.2d 284 (4th Cir. 1983).

59. EEOC v. Townley Engineering & Mfg. Co., 859 F.2d 610 (9th Cir. 1988), cert. denied, 489 U.S. 1077 (1989).

60. EEOC v. Kamehameha Schools/Bishop Estate, 990 F.2d 458, 463 (9th Cir.), cert. denied, 510 U.S. 963 (1993) ("the religious characteristics of the Schools consist of minimal, largely comparative religious studies, scheduled prayers and services, quotation of Bible verses in a school publication, and the employment of nominally Protestant teachers for secular subjects. References to Bible verses, comparative religious education, and even prayers and services are common at private schools and cannot suffice to exempt such schools from § 2000e-1. . . .").

employee or applicant be a member of the church with which the institution is affiliated. Does it also apply to compliance with the *practices* of that religion? Can a church institution discharge an employee who subscribes to the faith, but who engages in conduct contrary to church doctrine? The answer to both questions is yes, at least to the limited extent that the issue has been litigated.[61] Church organizations may require employees to abide by doctrinal rules, regardless of the church to which the employee actually belongs.[62]

Exemption for Employers for Whom Religion Is a Bona Fide Occupational Qualification

Title VII also permits religious discrimination by employers if the discriminatory condition relates to a bona fide occupational qualification (BFOQ):

> Notwithstanding any other provision of this subchapter, (1) it shall not be an unlawful employment practice for an employer to hire and employ employees, for an employment agency to classify, or refer for employment any individual, for a labor organization, or joint labor-management committee controlling apprenticeship or other training or retraining programs to admit or employ any individual in any such program, on the basis of his religion, sex, or national origin in those certain instances where religion, sex, or national origin is a bona fide occupational qualification reasonably necessary to the normal operation of that particular business or enterprise. . . . [63]

---

61. Little v. Wuerl, 929 F.2d 944 (3d Cir. 1991) (Protestant employee of Catholic school was lawfully fired when she married a Catholic who had previously been married and who had not had the prior marriage annulled, as required by Church doctrine; the fact that the Church hired a Protestant in the first place does not constitute a waiver of its right to insist upon adherence to Church canon); Boyd v. Harding, 887 F. Supp. 157 (a preschool teacher in religious school who was member of the faith was lawfully terminated for engaging in sex outside of marriage, since such conduct violated church doctrine; this motivation was found not to be a pretext for sex discrimination).

62. *Cf.* Vigars v. Valley Christian Center of Dublin, 805 F. Supp. 802 (N.D. Cal. 1992); Dolter v. Wahlert High School, 483 F. Supp. 266 (N.D. Iowa 1980). In both cases, the courts recognized the right of religious schools to impose moral codes on employees based on religious principles, but cautioned that unequal *application* of such codes to men and women would result in forfeiture of the exemptions under Sections 702 and 703.

63. 42 U.S.C. § 2000e-2(e)(1).

This exemption is available to all employers, not merely religious organizations. However, the Supreme Court has cautioned that this exception is to be read narrowly.[64] The Court also held in *International Union, UAW v. Johnson Controls*,[65] that, to be a BFOQ, the qualification must "concern job-related skills" and must relate to the "essence" or "central mission" of the employer.[66] Business necessity, not convenience or preference, must be proved by the employer.[67]

As applied to religious discrimination, the BFOQ exception has rarely been litigated. Most of those cases pre-date the Supreme Court's seminal decision in *Johnson Controls* and are therefore of limited guidance. Nevertheless, these cases do establish that nonsectarian employers may, in limited circumstances, qualify religion as a BFOQ for a particular job or job category. One of the leading cases for this purpose is *Pime v. Loyola University of Chicago*.[68] Loyola was founded by the Jesuit order and had been operated for many years under the control of that order. Starting in 1970, the Jesuits relinquished much of their control over the University's operations. By the mid-1980s, a majority of trustees and 94 percent of the teaching staff were not Jesuits. An applicant for a position as a professor sued the university, charging that he was not selected because of his religious beliefs. The lack of ownership or control by the Jesuit order led the district court to conclude that the university was not entitled to the exemption for religious organizations under Section 703(e)(2) of Title VII.

However, the university was able to establish that religion was a bona fide occupational qualification for the open position. The policy under attack in *Pime* required the Philosophy Department to reserve seven of the 31 faculty positions in that department for Jesuits; Catholics who were not Jesuits were excluded, as were all other non-Jesuits. When three

---

64. Dothard v. Rawlinson, 433 U.S. 321 (1977).

65. 499 U.S. 187 (1991). The employer in *Johnson Controls* excluded all women, except those whose infertility was medically documented, from working in jobs involving exposure to lead. The Court held that the employer's professed concerns about the medical health of its employee's offspring did not go to the essence of its business.

66. *Id.* at 203.

67. *Id.* at 201–203. *See also* Diaz v. Pan American World Airways, 442 F.2d 385, 388 (5th Cir.), *cert. denied*, 404 U.S. 950 (1971); Rasul v. District of Columbia, 680 F. Supp. 436 (D.D.C. 1988).

68. 585 F. Supp. 435 (N.D. Ill. 1984), *aff'd*, 803 F.2d 351 (7th Cir. 1986).

openings arose, the plaintiff was told that he would not be hired for any of them because they had been reserved for Jesuits. Although there was no evidence that the individual courses in question (for example, medical ethics) could be taught only by Jesuits, the university persuaded both the district and circuit courts that "having a Jesuit presence in the Philosophy faculty is 'reasonably necessary to the normal operation' of the enterprise, and that fixing the number at seven out of 31 is a reasonable determination."[69] Although a separate concurring opinion in the circuit court by Judge Posner raises questions about the breadth of this interpretation of the BFOQ exception, *Pime* leaves open an avenue of exclusion for employers that are unable to qualify as exempt organizations under Sections 702(a) or 703(e).[70]

Other decisions addressing religion as a BFOQ present a slim body of precedent, with often contradictory results. For example, can a customer's religious preferences be cited as a basis for an employer's discrimination against certain religions? The EEOC takes the position that client or customer preferences cannot give rise to a BFOQ that justifies a discriminatory employment policy.[71] The following decisions reflect the differing approaches to this question:

- A restaurant rejected a Sikh applicant because his beard conflicted with the company's grooming policy. Based on the perceived (but not proven) preferences of the restaurant's customers, among other things, the court held that the grooming requirements were a BFOQ.[72]
- An employer that hired pilots to fly helicopters to Mecca, Saudi Arabia, restricted its pilots to Muslims, since Saudi Arabia did not permit non-Muslims to enter Mecca.[73]
- Baylor College of Medicine had a contract to supply physicians on rotation at a Saudi Arabian hospital. Believing that Jews could not

---

69. 803 F.2d at 354.

70. *See also* Vigars v. Valley Christian, 805 F. Supp. 808-09 (leading a moral life may be a BFOQ for a librarian at a religious school, but employer must prove at trial that the moral precepts at issue were truly central to plaintiff's job).

71. 29 C.F.R. § 1604.2(a)(1)(iii).

72. EEOC v. Sambo's of Georgia, Inc., 530 F. Supp. 86 (N.D. Ga. 1981).

73. Kern v. Dynalectron Corp., 577 F. Supp. 1196 (N.D. Tex. 1983), *aff'd,* 746 F.2d 810 (5th Cir. 1984).

obtain visas, the College refused to consider any Jews for the assignments. The court held that being non-Jewish was not a BFOQ, since Baylor presented no evidence that Saudi Arabia would actually have refused an entry visa to the Jewish faculty members.[74]

- A school district denied female bus drivers the opportunity to drive certain routes because all of the students on the routes were male Hasidic Jews who, for sincere religious reasons, refused to board a bus driven by a female. The court held that being a male was not a BFOQ, since women and men could drive the routes equally well and since the preference of the riders could not dictate a discriminatory policy.[75]

Whether these decisions would all have been decided the same way after *Johnson Controls* is mere speculation. What is clear is that the determination of a BFOQ is likely to be fact-bound and the courts will be reluctant to grant the BFOQ exception.

Summary

- All public-sector employers and all private-sector employers having fifteen or more employees during each work day in each of twenty calendar weeks are covered by Title VII. In addition, employment agencies and most unions are covered by the statute.
- All employers having contracts or subcontracts with federal agencies are required to include nondiscrimination clauses in their contracts. The Secretary of Labor is responsible for overseeing and enforcing those clauses.
- Churches, church-operated institutions, and educational institutions that are owned, controlled, or managed by religious institutions may discriminate on the basis of *religion* with respect to all of their employees.
- Selected religious institutions may also discriminate on the basis of sex, race, and so on, and may be exempt from other employ-

---

74. Abrams v. Baylor College of Medicine, 805 F.2d 528 (5th Cir. 1986).

75. Bollenbach v. Monroe-Woodbury Cent. Sch. Dist., 659 F. Supp. 1450 (S.D.N.Y. 1987).

ment laws if the employment relationship is between: (a) a church and its clergy; (b) a seminary and its teachers; or (c) a church-affiliated school and its teachers of *religion*. Other lay employees of churches and church-affiliated schools will generally be free to seek enforcement of the antidiscrimination laws against the religious institutions for whom they work, as long as the dispute does not require the court to investigate or decide matters of religious doctrine and faith.

- A BFOQ may permit an employer to discriminate in hiring based on religion, but only if the religious condition is essential to the performance of the job and affects the central duties of the job.

⌘ CHAPTER 3

How Is Religion Defined?

Statutory and Regulatory Definitions

Title VII defines religion broadly:

> "religion" includes all aspects of religious observance and practice, as well as belief. . . . [1]

The Equal Employment Opportunity Commission (EEOC) has published guidelines on religious discrimination that define religious practices to include much more than traditional religious observance. Under these guidelines, religious practices

> include moral or ethical beliefs as to what is right and wrong and which are sincerely held with the strength of traditional religious views. . . .

> The fact that no religious group espouses such beliefs or the fact that the religious group to which the individual professes to belong may not accept such belief will not determine whether the belief is a religious belief of the employee or prospective employee. [2]

Thus, an employee may practice religion in a unique way and still be protected from discrimination; even iconoclasts are safeguarded by Title VII's expansive definition of religion, as interpreted by the EEOC. The courts have mostly followed the EEOC's lead.

---

1. 42 U.S.C. § 2000e(j).
2. 29 C.F.R. § 1605.1.

Can an Employer Challenge an Employee's Religious Beliefs?

Because the statutory definition of religion includes "all aspects" of religious observances, practices, and beliefs, the courts, and especially the EEOC, have shown great deference to employee assertions of adherence to a religious belief system. Both the courts and the EEOC have expressed an unwillingness to second-guess an employee's claim that his or her beliefs are grounded in religion. While an employer may argue that an employee's adherence to a religious practice is fraudulent (discussed below), the courts virtually never reject an employee's assertion that a need for accommodation was derived from a religious belief.

Similarly, efforts to limit the protection of this law to mainstream religions have all failed. In fact, efforts to limit the law to *organized* religion have failed. The courts simply refuse to engage in a theological exploration of religious doctrine. Employers who question an employee's assertion that he or she is acting upon religious faith will face a reluctant judiciary and a hostile EEOC.

The EEOC has derived its definition of religion from two Supreme Court decisions—*Welsh v. United States*[3] and *United States v. Seeger*[4]—that defined religion for purposes of enforcing the conscientious-objector provisions of the then-existing military draft.[5] In view of the EEOC's reliance on these decisions, it is useful to understand their holdings.

First, the Supreme Court emphasized that a person's religious beliefs "need not be confined in either source or content to traditional or parochial concepts of religion."[6] This means that courts defer to an individual's own declaration of "religious" principle:

> The validity of what he believes cannot be questioned. Some theologians, and indeed some [selective service] examiners, might be tempted to question the existence of the registrant's "Supreme

---

3. 398 U.S. 333 (1970).

4. 380 U.S. 163 (1965).

5. Section 6(j) of the Universal Military Training and Service Act exempted from service anyone who was "by reason of religious training and belief . . . conscientiously opposed to participation in war in any form." 62 Stat. 612, reprinted at Welsh v. United States, 398 U.S. at 335.

6. Welsh v. United States, 398 U.S. at 339, summarizing the holding in *Seeger*.

Being" or the truth of his concepts. But *these are inquiries foreclosed to Government.*[7]

Someone who is the sole adherent to a particular religious dogma may still be protected. The fact that beliefs may even be heretical do not rob them of their religious character.

Second, the Supreme Court held that religion, at least for the purposes of the selective-service system, is not dependent on a belief in a "Supreme Being."[8] For purposes of the Universal Military Training and Service Act, a person could hold "religious beliefs" if they "occupy in the life of that individual 'a place parallel to that filled by . . . God'".[9]

These two Supreme Court decisions did not interpret Title VII or any other employment statute. Nor has the Supreme Court directly addressed the propriety of the EEOC's definition of religion under Title VII. However, it has decided two cases involving unemployment-compensation benefits that indicate a fundamental agreement with the EEOC's deference to employees' claims of religious faith.

In the first case, *Thomas v. Review Board of Indiana Employment Security,*[10] a Jehovah's Witness quit his job making tanks, claiming that building war materials violated his religious beliefs. The Supreme Court of Indiana refused the payment of unemployment-compensation benefits to Thomas on the ground that his resignation was for purely personal reasons, as opposed to compliance with the dictates of his religion. The U.S. Supreme Court sided with Thomas. It held that the government may not pass judgment on the validity of an employee's beliefs:

> the resolution of that question [i.e., what is a religious belief] is not to turn upon a judicial perception of the particular belief or practice in question; religious beliefs need not be acceptable, logical, consistent, or comprehensible to others in order to merit First Amendment protection. . . .

> Particularly in this sensitive area, it is not within the judicial function and judicial competence to inquire whether the petitioner or his

---

7. Seeger v. United States, 380 U.S. at 184 (emphasis added).
8. Welsh v. United States, 398 U.S. at 340-43.
9. *Id.* at 340.
10. 450 U.S. 707 (1981).

fellow worker more correctly perceived the commands of their common faith. Courts are not arbiters of scriptural interpretation.[11]

In the second case, *Frazee v. Illinois Department of Employment Security*,[12] Frazee was denied unemployment-compensation benefits because he refused to accept a job that required him to work on Sundays. When the employer argued that Frazee was not a member of a religious sect that barred Sabbath work, the Supreme Court reiterated its holding in *Thomas*:

> Undoubtedly, membership in an organized religious denomination, especially one with a specific tenet forbidding members to work on Sunday, would simplify the problem of identifying sincerely held religious beliefs, but we reject the notion that to claim the protection of the Free Exercise Clause, one must be responding to the commands of a particular religious organization.[13]

Although *Frazee* and *Thomas* did not interpret Title VII, they are repeatedly relied upon by the lower courts to support a hands-off approach in employment-discrimination cases in which an employer contends that an employee's beliefs are motivated by personal preference, rather than religious conviction.[14]

In the abstract, the courts will not accord statutory or constitutional protection to beliefs that are derived from a personal world view. Drawing the line between personal preference and religious belief, however, is exceedingly difficult. As the EEOC stated, "It is a longstanding position of the Commission and the courts that a formal doctrine is not a requirement for a religious belief."[15] In practice, when an employee attaches the appellation "religion" to a set of beliefs, the courts are reluctant to dig beneath the surface.

---

11. 450 U.S. at 714, 716. *Cf.* Hernandez v. C.I.R., 490 U.S. 680 (1989) (under the First Amendment, the government may not challenge the validity of a religious adherent's beliefs, but the burden imposed by government on religious practices may still be permitted if it is *not* "substantial").

12. 489 U.S. 829 (1989).

13. *Id.* at 834. *Cf.* Wisconsin v. Yoder, 406 U.S. 205, 216 (1972) (personal philosophies are not religious beliefs entitled to protection under the First Amendment).

14. *See, e.g.,* Lambert v. Condor Mfg., Inc., 768 F. Supp. 600 (E.D. Mich. 1991).

15. EEOC Decision 81-33, 27 FEP 1834 (1981).

This is not to say that the courts never reject an employee's claim of religious belief. However, those exceptions are exceedingly rare and involve situations so extreme that they reinforce the solidity of the general rule. Thus, the courts have decided that:

- The Ku Klux Klan is not a religion.[16]
- An employee's "personal religious creed" requiring him to eat cat food is not a religious practice, but merely a personal preference.[17]

Absent situations akin to these, employers will find the EEOC and the courts averse to entering into a debate over the definition of a particular religion. Although the courts have not clearly stated whether they agree with the EEOC's willingness to include nontheistic (i.e., "moral or ethical") beliefs within the rubric of "religion," in most other respects the judiciary follows the EEOC's hands-off approach.[18]

Can an Employer Question Whether a Particular Practice Is Mandated by Religious Doctrine?

An employer will commonly accept an employee's professed adherence to a particular religion, but will nevertheless question whether the employee's *practices* are dictated by that religion's theology. As with efforts to have it define religious belief, the EEOC generally refuses to accept this invitation to adjudicate theological issues.

In one such case, *Cardona v. Frank*,[19] a Catholic employee of the U.S. Postal Service requested a full day of leave to observe Good Friday; management denied the request, but permitted the employee to take five hours of annual leave instead. The employer refused to grant the additional leave, contending that Catholic canon law required no more than

---

16. Slater v. King Soopers, Inc., 809 F. Supp. 809 (D. Colo. 1992); Bellamy v. Mason's Stores, Inc., 368 F. Supp. 1025 (E.D. Va. 1973), *aff'd*, 508 F.2d 504 (4th Cir. 1974).

17. Brown v. Pena, 441 F. Supp. 1382 (S.D. Fla. 1977), *aff'd*, 589 F.2d 1113 (5th Cir. 1979).

18. In one case, a court held that Title VII protects an atheist who did not wish to attend her employer's religious sermons at the start of business meetings. Young v. Southwestern Savings and Loan Association, 509 F.2d 140 (5th Cir. 1975).

19. FEOR ¶ 903076 (EEOC 1989), citing Thomas v. Review Bd., 450 U.S. 707 (1981).

two hours of attendance at mass on Good Friday. The EEOC chastised the employer's effort to set up a theological debate:

> Only the individual can determine whether his absence from work is required in order to attend a religious observance. . . . It is not within the agency's [i.e., employer's] function or competence to inquire into whether appellants correctly perceived the commands of their faith, or to dictate the manner in which religious holidays should be observed.[20]

The EEOC later reconsidered its decision in *Cardona,* but came to the same conclusion, pointing out that a religious practice does not have to be theologically mandated:

> There are any number of religious services at which the adherent's presence is not absolutely mandatory. Nevertheless, he may not feel any less compelled to attend. Only the individual can determine whether his absence from work is required in order to attend a religious observance.[21]

In other words, just as the EEOC recognizes that an employee's religion may be unique to that employee, it also permits employees to pursue religious practices that are individualized interpretations of their religion's theology.[22]

Many courts echo the EEOC's reluctance to address the question whether a particular practice is part of a religious belief system. As the Seventh Circuit Court of Appeals has stated, it is improper for the courts to decide "whether a particular practice is or is not required by the tenets of the [employee's] religion."[23]

This same rule has been extended to employees who have declined to perform certain job duties that they consider antithetical to their religious beliefs, even when there was no explicit scriptural basis. For example, an employee whose anti-war beliefs were derived from a Quaker upbringing was practicing her religion when she refused to distribute

---

20. FEOR ¶ 903076 at 90-223.

21. Cardona v. Frank, FEOR ¶ 903088 (EEOC 1989).

22. *See, e.g.,* EEOC v. READS, Inc., 759 F. Supp. 1150 (E.D. Pa. 1991) (a Muslim's insistence on wearing a head covering at work was protected, even though not required by the tenets of her faith).

draft-registration materials in her Postal Service job.[24] Another employee who had religious objections to abortion was practicing his religion when, as an IRS employee, he refused to handle tax-exempt applications from abortion clinics.[25]

As with challenges to religious beliefs, employers have had limited success in attacking employee claims that their *practices* are based on religious principles. The following are the most notable exceptions to the courts' general reluctance to adjudicate the religious basis of an employee's practices:

- A supervisor's directive that a secretary type his Bible-study notes was not a protected practice mandated by his religious beliefs.[26]

- A church-affiliated private school that barred African-American students could not assert that racial segregation was a religious practice, since the court could not find any support in the proffered religious literature that mandated segregation.[27]

- Employees discharged for engaging in extramarital affairs with coworkers could not claim that their sexual conduct was a protected religious practice, since employees were admitted Baptists, whose Church subscribed to the Ten Commandments.[28]

---

23. Redmond v. GAF Corp., 574 F.2d 897, 900 (7th Cir. 1978), citing Fowler v. Rhode Island, 345 U.S. 67, 70 (1953). *See also* Carter v. Bruce Oakley, Inc., 849 F. Supp. 673 (E.D. Ark. 1993) (beard worn by employee who subscribes to "a mix of Christianity and Judaism" is protected); Geller v. Secretary of Defense, 423 F. Supp. 16, 17 (D.D.C. 1976) ("The Court is persuaded . . . that the wearing of beards, although not required, is a well established religious tradition among members of the Jewish faith and that plaintiff wore his beard in furtherance of that religious practice.").

24. McGinnis v. Postal Service, 512 F. Supp. 517 (N.D. Cal. 1980).

25. Haring v. Blumenthal, 471 F. Supp. 1172 (D.D.C. 1979), *cert. denied,* 452 U.S. 939, *reh'g denied,* 453 U.S. 927 (1981).

26. Brown v. Polk County, Iowa, 61 F.3d 650 (8th Cir. 1995), *cert. denied,* 516 U.S. 1158 (1996).

27. Brown v. Dade Christian Schools, Inc., 556 F.2d 310 (5th Cir. 1977) (en banc), *cert. denied,* 434 U.S. 1063 (1978). In an impassioned concurrence, Judge Goldberg castigated the court for belittling the religious origins of the church's practices. In his view, even religions with abhorrent practices are entitled to protection of the First Amendment. He suggested that the court should have recognized the religious basis of the church's practices, but could then strike down its segregationist policies, notwithstanding the First Amendment, because of a compelling state interest in ending discrimination.

28. McCrory v. Rapides Regional Medical Center, 635 F. Supp. 975 (W.D. La.), *aff'd,* 801 F. 2d 396 (5th Cir. 1986).

- An employee who left work early on December 24 to assist children in preparing for a Christmas Eve play was engaged in a family function, rather than a religious practice.[29]

Can an Employer Challenge the Sincerity of an Employee's Religious Practices?

Employees seeking an accommodation of their religious needs have the burden of showing that the practices in which they engage and the beliefs to which they adhere are "sincere." Although the courts are unwilling to define the scope or theological merit of religious beliefs, they are sometimes willing to consider an employer's attack upon the sincerity of an employee's allegations that religious needs conflict with work rules. In reality, there have been very few such cases.

An employee's burden to prove the sincerity of beliefs or practices is minimal.[30] Once that burden is satisfied, the employer must come forward with some evidence that an employee's claim of religiosity is fraudulent. Most often, this takes the form of proof that the employee acted in a manner inconsistent with the professed religious beliefs or was not observant until confronted with an unpalatable work rule.[31] An attack upon an employee's sincerity usually devolves into a credibility contest, so that these issues must be presented to the fact-finder at trial. In the few cases in which "sincerity" has been litigated, the decisions have been fact-intensive. For this reason, there is no universal rule that can guide employers on this issue.

A summary of a few of these cases, all involving similar facts, reveals the difficulty in deriving any guiding principles:

- An employee who claimed that he was a New Testament Christian (without formal affiliation with a church) was terminated because he refused to report to work on a Sunday. The employee claimed that his religious beliefs prevented him from working that Sunday. The evidence showed that he had worked on many Sundays

29. Wessling v. Kroger Co., 554 F. Supp. 548 (E.D. Mich. 1982).

30. Philbrook v. Ansonia Bd. of Educ., 757 F.2d 476 (2d Cir. 1985), *rev'd and remanded on other grounds,* 479 U.S. 60 (1986).

31. *Compare* International Society for Krishna v. Barber, 650 F.2d 430, 441 (2d Cir. 1981) *with* EEOC v. IBP, Inc., 824 F. Supp. 147 (C.D. Ill. 1993).

and had refused to work on other Sundays. As to the Sundays he did work, the employee testified that he "just didn't have the faith" on those days. The court concluded that the employee's religious objection to working on the Sunday in question was not sincere.[32]

- An employee converted to the Seventh-Day Adventist faith approximately nine years after starting work at her employer. For the next two years, she worked numerous Saturdays, but left work sufficiently early to attend church services. When she changed shifts, she informed the employer that she would no longer work on Saturdays. She stated that, in the several years after her baptism, her faith had grown stronger. She resigned, rather than being terminated, when her employer told her she must work Saturdays or take vacation leave for those days. The district court concluded that the employee's asserted conflict between Saturday work and her religious beliefs was not sincere. The court of appeals disagreed and reversed.[33]

- An employee who was available to work Saturdays converted to the Seventh-Day Adventist faith and reported to his employer that he would no longer work Saturdays. After several unexcused absences, the employee was discharged. Approximately one year after his termination, the employee began a new job in which he worked on Saturdays. When asked why he violated the Sabbath in the new job, he stated that he had lost his faith. The court concluded that he was sincere in his faith during the period prior to his termination.[34]

Obviously, the question of sincerity is so dependent upon credibility determinations that very similar facts can give rise to varying results in different courts. The best that can be said is that, in situations in which an employee is not consistently observant, the courts will consider lack of sincerity as a defense. However, employers cannot assume that an employee is insincere merely because he or she is newly observant. Simi-

---

32. Hansard v. Johns-Manville Products Corp., 5 FEP 707 (E.D. Tex. 1973).
33. Cooper v. Oak Rubber Co., 15 F.3d 1375 (6th Cir. 1994).
34. EEOC v. IBP, 824 F. Supp. 147.

larly, imperfect adherence to the dictates of one's religion does not automatically mean that a particular observance is insincere.[35]

Summary

- With few exceptions, the courts will accept an employee's assertion that he or she is acting upon a religious belief, even when those religious beliefs are unique to that employee or are different from the beliefs subscribed to by other adherents of the same religion.

- An employee's personal preferences, political practices, or cultural customs are not entitled to protection under Title VII or the First Amendment and a few courts have so held. However, both the courts and the EEOC are reluctant to doubt an employee's assertion that a particular practice is derived from religious beliefs and will rarely entertain arguments that a practice is not theologically mandated.

- An employee has the initial burden of showing that his or her religious beliefs are sincerely held. If an employer wishes to contest that claim, it must offer its own evidence showing an inconsistency in the employee's practices. Although sincerity of religious conviction is most easily evidenced by consistent observance over time, some courts have been willing to protect employees who undergo either sudden or gradual changes in their religious beliefs; even employees who have been inconstant in their religious practices have withstood employer protests of insincerity and have obtained judgments in their favor.

---

35. *See, e.g.,* EEOC v. Ilona of Hungary, Inc., 108 F.3d 1569 (7th Cir. 1997) (en banc) (a Jew who is not "particularly" observant is still sincere in not wanting to work on Yom Kippur).

▨ CHAPTER 4

When Is an Employer Liable for Intentional Discrimination or Disparate Treatment?

An employer that *intentionally* discriminates against employees or applicants *based on* their religion may be held liable under Title VII for "disparate treatment."[1] In religion cases, this theory of liability has been used by failed job applicants,[2] discharged employees,[3] and employees denied promotions or other benefits.[4]

Absent an accompanying accommodation claim, plaintiffs have tended to fare badly in litigation raising only disparate-treatment claims.[5] The primary cause has much to do with the heavy burden that a plaintiff faces in proving such a claim. Although the courts have permitted plain-

---

1. Chalmers v. Tulon Co. of Richmond, 101 F.3d 1012, 1017 (4th Cir. 1996), *cert. denied*, 118 S.Ct. 58 (1997).

2. *See, e.g.,* EEOC v. Wiltel, Inc., 81 F.3d 1508 (10th Cir. 1996); Wechsler v. R D Management Corp., 73 FEP 195 (E.D.N.Y. 1994).

3. *See, e.g.,* Helland v. South Bend Community School Corp., 93 F.3d 327 (7th Cir. 1996); Liberman v. Brady, 926 F. Supp. 1197 (E.D.N.Y. 1996) (failure to promote and discharge).

4. *See, e.g.,* Stoller v. Marsh, 682 F.2d 971 (D.C. Cir. 1982), *cert. denied*, 460 U.S. 1037 (1983) (denial of promotion).

5. *Compare* Krulik v. Bd. of Ed. of City of New York, 781 F.2d 15 (2d Cir. 1986) (judgment notwithstanding verdict entered against plaintiff on disparate treatment claim) *with* Tincher v. Wal-Mart Stores, Inc., 118 F.3d 1125 (7th Cir. 1997) and Shpargel v. Stage & Co., 71 FEP 1739 (E.D. Mich. 1996) (plaintiffs prevail in combined disparate treatment/failure to accommodate claims).

tiffs to prove a prima facie case through indirect or circumstantial evidence, as well as direct evidence of intent, the plaintiff's ultimate burden of proving that an employment decision was motivated by religious considerations can be difficult.[6] This chapter spells out the essential elements of a disparate-treatment claim and the burdens of proof placed upon both the plaintiff and defendant.

Proof of Disparate Treatment

Direct Evidence of Discriminatory Intent

Direct evidence of disparate treatment may take several forms. One example (albeit rare) is the promulgation of a policy that itself constitutes discrimination.[7] For example, a medical school that had a contract to provide medical services in Saudi Arabia had a policy of excluding Jewish doctors from working in the program; the Fifth Circuit found the employer liable for implementing this discriminatory policy.[8] An exclusionary employment policy that treats members of certain religions differently (either more or less favorably) is presumptively illegal.[9]

Even if an employer does not maintain a policy that is discriminatory on its face, certain actions may constitute direct evidence of discriminatory intent. A blatant example is found in *Blalock v. Metals Trades, Inc.*,[10] in which an employer hired a new salesperson who attended the owner's church. The owner of the business assumed that the new salesperson was devoted to the teachings of the minister who operated the church. However, when the salesperson had a falling out with the church's leader, the employer told him that he was in "doctrinal error in

---

6. *See, e.g.,* Helland v. South Bend, 93 F.3d 327. *Cf.* Rosen v. Thornburgh, 928 F.2d 528, 533 (2d Cir. 1991).

7. EEOC v. Wiltel, 81 F.3d at 1514.

8. Abrams v. Baylor College of Medicine, 805 F.2d 528 (5th Cir. 1986). *Cf.* Kern v. Dynalectron Corp., 577 F. Supp. 1196 (N.D. Tex. 1983), *aff'd,* 746 F.2d 810 (5th Cir. 1984) (an employer with contract to provide helicopter services to Mecca, Saudi Arabia, during religious observances could limit its pilots to Muslims because non-Muslims were not permitted in Mecca).

9. This prohibition would not apply to certain hiring decisions by religious organizations or by employers for whom religion is a "bona fide occupational qualification." See discussion of such exemptions in Chapter 2.

10. 775 F.2d 703 (6th Cir. 1985), *cert. denied,* 490 U.S. 1064 (1989).

parting with the minister." The salesperson was discharged and was given a termination letter that stated:

> Larry was hired with the full knowledge and understanding that Metals Trades is a Christian Company and our rule book is the word of God, or the Bible. He was in full accord and very excited. . . . I hated to lay him off as there are all too few men willing to commit themselves to Jesus—especially salesmen. Larry's problem is that he refuses to submit himself to those in authority over him and the Bible makes it clear that we are to be in submission. Larry was let go for strictly secular reasons but the root of his problem is spiritual, as the scriptures will show. . . .[11]

The Court of Appeals for the Sixth Circuit concluded that, notwithstanding the assertion of "secular reasons," the termination decision was motivated by the employee's religious views:

> [The owner] treated [the salesman] differently at different times depending upon [the salesman's] current religious views. This is the essence of discrimination.[12]

In most other cases where an employee presents direct evidence of discriminatory intent, it comes in the form of derogatory comments, especially if made by a supervisor. However, this type of evidence has caused some problems for the courts. While pervasive expressions of religious animosity may create a "hostile" workplace, the courts find it much more difficult to determine whether a few stray derogatory remarks create the requisite level of hostility.[13] Even when uttered by supervisors, random comments may not be sufficient to prove a plaintiff's case.[14] The courts

---

11. *Id.* at 705–06.

12. *Id.* at 708. The court remanded the case for a determination whether the employer would have discharged the salesman even if his religious views had not changed.

13. An extended discussion of religious harassment and the "hostile" workplace is found in Chapter 5, *infra.*

14. *Cf.* Harris v. Forklift Systems, Inc., 510 U.S. 17, 21 (1993) (mere utterance of sexual epithet does not create a hostile environment); Oncale v. Sundowner Offshore Services, Inc., 118 S.Ct. 998 (1998) ("ordinary socializing," "male-on-male horseplay," and "intersexual flirtation" should not be mistaken for a hostile work environment).

have not developed a uniform rule in this respect, which is not surprising given the fact-bound nature of determining intent.[15]

When derogatory remarks are continuous or at least repeated, a court is more likely to accept it as proof of religious animus.[16] Courts have frequently rejected stray or isolated remarks as insufficient to prove an intent to discriminate. This is especially true when the remarks were not made by the employer's decision-maker. The following are some of the situations in which isolated derogatory remarks have been found *not* to be sufficient proof of discriminatory intent to support a disparate treatment claim:

- A coemployee's religious slurs are not evidence of an employer's discriminatory intent in the absence of evidence of a connection between the comments and the decision to discharge the plaintiff.[17]
- Supervisor's disparaging remarks regarding plaintiff's religious views were not proven to have affected the employer's decision-maker.[18]
- Employer's executive director allegedly referred to plaintiff as that "New York Jew" or "New York kike." The court held that this statement did not prove disparate treatment, absent evidence that the immediate supervisor who made the employment decision harbored anti-Semitic views.[19]
- One of three interviewers recommended against giving applicant a promotion "because she is into all that Jesus s__t and she doesn't fit in." The court held that the statement is not proof of disparate treatment without evidence that the final decision-maker harbored religious animus.[20]

---

15. The courts do seem to be in agreement that the employee must be able to specify the comments and identify the offenders. Generalized complaints about religious hostility are not adequate. *See* Meiri v. Dacon, 759 F.2d 989, 998 (2d Cir.), *cert. denied,* 474 U.S. 829 (1985).

16. Rosen v. Thornburgh, 928 F.2d 528, 534 (2d Cir. 1991). In *Thornburgh,* the Second Circuit reversed the district court's grant of summary judgment to defendants because repeated anti-Semitic remarks created a triable issue of fact.

17. Gillard v. Sears, 32 FEP 1274, 1276 (E.D. Pa. 1983).

18. Sattar v. Motorola, Inc., 72 FEP 10, 14 (N.D. Ill. 1996).

19. Levine v. Navapache Hospital, 25 FEP 1420, 1423-24 (D. Ariz. 1981).

20. EEOC v. Wiltel, 81 F.3d at 1515.

Unlike the plaintiffs in the foregoing cases, employees tend to be more successful in litigation when the person making derogatory remarks (even isolated ones) is their direct supervisor and has decision-making authority. For example, when a supervisor stated that "[a]s long as I'm the warehouse manager, no Jew will run the warehouse for me," the target of the remark prevailed in his disparate treatment claim.[21]

Indirect Evidence of Discriminatory Intent

In most cases, a plaintiff is unable to present direct evidence that an employer has taken action *because of* an employee's or applicant's religion. The far more common scenario involves a plaintiff who circumstantially seeks to prove that an adverse action was based on religion. Fully aware that evidence of a "smoking gun" is rare, the Supreme Court has permitted a plaintiff to proceed to trial even in the absence of direct evidence of religious animus; that is, a plaintiff may still establish a prima facie case of disparate treatment through indirect or circumstantial evidence.[22] To do so, the plaintiff can follow the burden-shifting framework outlined in *McDonnell Douglas Corporation v. Green.*[23] Although *McDonnell Douglas* involved race discrimination, its principles have been adapted to cases of religious discrimination. Under this analysis, the employee must first establish a prima facie case of discrimination by a preponderance of the evidence. Although the Supreme Court has cautioned that "[t]he burden of establishing a prima facie case of disparate treatment is not onerous,"[24] it has also emphasized that the plaintiff cannot prevail in the end if he or she fails to meet the difficult burden of proving that the employer's action was motivated by religious considerations.[25]

---

21. Weiss v. Parker Hannifan Corp., 747 F. Supp. 1118, 1122, 1127-28 (D.N.J. 1990). *See also* Liberman v. Brady, 926 F. Supp. at 1211-13 (a single derogatory comment about applicant's accent was direct proof in claim of religion/national origin discrimination, but that evidence was overcome by employer's proof of nondiscriminatory reasons for discharge).

22. Chalmers v. Tulon, 101 F.3d at 1017-18; EEOC v. Wiltel, 81 F.3d at 1515.

23. 411 U.S. 792 (1973).

24. Texas Dept. of Community Affairs v. Burdine, 450 U.S. 248, 253 (1981).

25. St. Mary's Honor Center v. Hicks, 509 U.S. 502, 515 (1993). The Court made clear that the holding in *McDonnell Douglas* was intended to provide a flexible analytical framework to assist the courts in assessing evidence of discrimination; it does not supplant the plaintiff's ultimate obligation of proving that intentional discrimination occurred.

There are four elements to a plaintiff's prima facie case.[26] First, the plaintiff must establish that he or she was a member of a protected class. In other words, the plaintiff must adhere to a religious belief system or engage in religious practices.[27] Practices that are not derived from a religious belief system are not protected.[28]

Second, the plaintiff must prove that he or she was qualified for the position. If the case involves a job applicant, the plaintiff must prove that he or she applied for the position and met the minimum qualifications for that position. If the case involves an employee who was fired or disciplined, the plaintiff must prove that his or her work was performed satisfactorily.[29]

Third, the plaintiff must prove that he or she suffered an adverse employment action.[30] An applicant for a job must prove that he or she was rejected, despite having the necessary qualifications. An employee must prove some form of disciplinary action (for example, discharge, demotion, or a failure to be promoted), notwithstanding satisfactory performance.

---

26. *See* St. Mary's v. Hicks, 509 U.S. at 506; Texas Dept. of Community Affairs v. Burdine, 450 U.S. 252-54; McDonnell Douglas v. Green, 411 U.S. 802; Chalmers v. Tulon Co., 101 F.3d at 1018-19; Vitug v. Multistate Tax Com'n, 88 F.3d 506, 515 (7th Cir. 1996); Breech v. Alabama Power Co., 962 F. Supp. 1447, 1457 (S.D. Ala. 1997).

27. *See, e.g.,* EEOC v. Wiltel, 81 F.3d at 1515 (evangelical Christians are a protected class). *Cf.* Shapolia v. Los Alamos Nat. Laboratory, 992 F.2d 1033 (10th Cir. 1993), in which a non-Mormon claimed he was discriminated against by Mormons. The Tenth Circuit held that, even though non-Mormons are a majority, the plaintiff could proceed with his claim under a theory of reverse discrimination. Thus, the plaintiff did not need to establish that he belonged to a protected class.

28. *Compare* Wisconsin v. Yoder, 406 U.S. 205 (1972) (personal philosophies are not religious beliefs entitled to protection under the First Amendment) *with* EEOC Guidelines on Discrimination Because of Religion, 29 C.F.R. § 1605.1 (religion includes "moral or ethical beliefs as to what is right and wrong and which are sincerely held with the strength of traditional religious views"). See Chapter 3 for a discussion of the courts' reluctance to define practices as nonreligious.

29. *See, e.g.,* Shapolia v. Los Alamos, 992 F.2d at 1038-39; Lawrence v. Mars, Inc., 955 F.2d 902, 905 (4th Cir.), *cert. denied,* 506 U.S. 823 (1992).

30. *See* Rodriguez v. City of Chicago, 69 FEP 993, 995 (N.D. Ill. 1996) (a threat of adverse action also gives rise to a claim). An employee may also claim that an involuntary resignation because of intolerable working conditions is a "constructive" discharge. Vitug v. Multistate, 88 F.3d at 516-18.

Fourth, the plaintiff must prove that others who do not share his or her religious beliefs or practices received more favorable (or less onerous) treatment. For example, a job applicant might offer evidence that the person hired for the open position practiced a different religion than the plaintiff.[31] An employee could show that other employees with different religious beliefs engaged in the same types of activities, but were not subjected to adverse employment actions.[32] Alternatively, a dismissed employee could argue that the position was filled by a person of a different religion or a person of no religion at all.[33]

Finally, in addition to the four requirements of *McDonnell Douglas,* a plaintiff claiming religious discrimination must meet one other requirement for a prima facie case: The plaintiff must prove that the employer knew of his or her religious beliefs or practices.[34] While an employee's race or sex may be apparent, religion is frequently invisible to an employer. Since intentional discrimination must be knowing, a plaintiff must prove that an employer knew of an employee's or applicant's religion; absent such proof, the courts will dismiss a plaintiff's complaint for failure to prove that discrimination was "because of" religion.[35]

If the employee presents sufficient evidence to satisfy this prima facie case, then the burden shifts to the employer to present evidence demonstrating that it had a legitimate nondiscriminatory reason for its actions toward the employee.[36] When an employee loses a disparate-treatment case, it is usually because the court has found that the

---

31. *See, e.g.,* EEOC v. Wiltel, 81 F.3d at 1515-16.

32. *See, e.g.,* Klein v. Derwinski, 69 FEP 885, 887 (D.D.C. 1994) (summary judgment *against* plaintiff because she was replaced by person of same religion). *See also* St. Mary's v. Hicks, 509 U.S. at 506-8; Breech v. Alabama Power Co., 962 F. Supp. at 1457; EEOC v. Wiltel, 81 F.3d at 1515.

33. Lawrence v. Mars, 955 F.2d 902; Klein v. Derwinski, 69 FEP 885.

34. Rosen v. Thornburgh, 928 F.2d at 532-34; Van Koten v. Family Health Management, Inc., 955 F. Supp. 898 (N.D. Ill. 1997), *aff'd,* 134 F.3d 375 (7th Cir. 1998); Marcus v. Veterans Administration, 32 FEP 464 (N.D. Ill. 1981), *aff'd,* 692 F.2d 759 (7th Cir. 1982).

35. See cases cited *supra* note 34.

36. St. Mary's v. Hicks, 509 U.S. at 506-07; Helland v. South Bend Community School Corp., 93 F.3d at 329.

employer presented performance-based or qualifications-based reasons for its actions. The following are some examples of employers who prevailed on this basis, notwithstanding a plaintiff's evidence supporting a prima facie case of disparate treatment based on religion:

- An employee whose Hebrew accent was criticized by a direct supervisor was properly discharged for making false statements and for pursuing private business while working for the IRS.[37]
- A Catholic applicant who lost a promotion to a person he characterized as a "born-again Christian" was properly rejected for promotion because each member of a three-member interview panel found him to be the least qualified of five applicants.[38]
- A Hindu employee was properly denied promotion and then discharged based on repeated poor performance evaluations and a failure to obtain training on new equipment.[39]
- A non-Mormon employee who claimed he was discriminated against by a Mormon supervisor was properly discharged for posting sexually offensive material in work areas, disobeying orders, and performing work below standards.[40]
- An employee was properly discharged, notwithstanding proof of anti-Semitic slurs by a supervisor, because of complaints from coworkers about her demeanor and difficult attitude.[41]
- An applicant who was criticized for being "into all that Jesus s__t" was properly rejected because she did not have the minimum prior experience listed in the job posting and other persons in same religious group were hired.[42]

Finally, if the employer presents evidence of nondiscriminatory reasons for the employment decision, then the burden shifts back to the

---

37. Liberman v. Brady, 926 F. Supp. at 1212.
38. Vitug v. Multistate, 88 F.3d at 515-16.
39. Gairola v. Virginia Dep't of General Services, 753 F.2d 1281 (4th Cir. 1985).
40. Shapolia v. Los Alamos, 992 F.2d at 1039.
41. Sullivan v. School Board of Pinellas County, 773 F.2d 1182 (11th Cir. 1985).
42. EEOC v. Wiltel, 81 F.3d at 1516-17.

employee to establish that the reasons offered by the employer "were a pretext for discrimination."[43] As the Seventh Circuit has held:

> the pretext inquiry focuses on whether the employer's stated reason was honest, not whether it was accurate. 'Pretext . . . means a lie, specifically a phony reason for some action.'[44]

Proof that the employer's nondiscriminatory reasons are pretextual does not fully satisfy the plaintiff's burden. In order to prevail, the plaintiff must establish *both* that the reason given by the employer was false *and* that religious discrimination was the real reason he or she was treated unfavorably.[45] It is here that the plaintiff faces the greatest hurdle to prevailing. The burden of proving the employer's intent to discriminate "remains at all times with the plaintiff."[46] While the finder of fact may infer a discriminatory motive from proof that an employer's stated reasons were false, the mere proof of pretext, standing alone, does not automatically satisfy a plaintiff's burden of proving that "discrimination was the real reason" for a personnel action.[47] In other words, even though the level of proof necessary for a prima facie case under *McDonnell Douglas* is not onerous, the ultimate burden on a plaintiff to prove religious motivation may well depend upon the employee's ability to offer the same kinds of direct evidence discussed above.

Proof of Discrimination When There Are Dual Motives

It is not uncommon for a plaintiff-employee to provide evidence of a discriminatory motive on the part of a supervisor (for example, derogatory comments), at the same time that the employer offers credible evidence that other officials acted for nondiscriminatory reasons. In other words, an employee is unable to prove that the employer's *sole* motivation was to discriminate. Instead, the evidence points to a mixture of motives, both of

---

43. Texas v. Burdine, 450 U.S. at 253; Chalmers v. Tulon Co., 101 F.3d at 1018.

44. Helland v. South Bend, 93 F.3d at 330, quoting Russell v. Acme-Evans Co., 51 F.3d 64, 68 (7th Cir. 1995).

45. Vitug v. Multistate, 88 F.3d at 515; Liberman v. Brady, 926 F. Supp. at 1201.

46. Texas v. Burdine, 450 U.S. at 253.

47. St. Mary's v. Hicks, 509 U.S. at 515. *See also* Vitug v. Multistate, 88 F.3d at 515-16; DeMarco v. Holy Cross High School, 4 F.3d 166, 170 (2d Cir. 1993); Liberman v. Brady, 926 F. Supp. at 1201-02.

which are credible. This outcome commonly arises in workplaces where there are multiple decision-makers. The reality is that different decision-makers may be motivated by different considerations, some lawful and some unlawful. In these cases, the Supreme Court has directed the courts to move beyond the method of analysis in *McDonnell Douglas*.

In *Price Waterhouse v. Hopkins*,[48] the Supreme Court held that the ultimate proof of an illegal causation for an employment decision must rest with the plaintiff.[49] However, if the fact-finder concludes that an employer acted out of dual motives—one proper and one improper—then the burden shifts to the employer to show by a preponderance of the evidence that it would have taken the same employment action even in the absence of the discriminatory motive.[50] If the employer carries that burden, it will escape liability. As one court of appeals explained in a religious discrimination case:

> the employer has the burden to prove that the adverse employment action would have been taken even in the absence of the impermissible motivation, and that, therefore, the discriminatory animus was not the cause of the adverse employment action.[51]

Other courts have similarly applied this dual motive analysis to religious-discrimination cases.[52]

However, the Price Waterhouse decision provoked considerable criticism and, in 1991, Congress amended Title VII to revise the *Price Waterhouse* standard.[53] The Civil Rights Act of 1991 provides that if a plaintiff proves that unlawful discrimination was "a motivating factor" for an adverse employment decision, he or she has established a violation of Title VII, regardless of the presence of a nondiscriminatory motivation. Congress' alteration of *Price Waterhouse* is nevertheless limited in its scope.

---

48. 490 U.S. 228 (1989).

49. *Id.* at 241–42, 246.

50. *Id.* at 244–45, 253.

51. Blalock v. Metals Trades, Inc., 775 F.2d at 712. *Blalock* predates *Price Waterhouse*, but relies on the same precedent that guided the Supreme Court's opinion. *See* Mt. Healthy City School District Board of Education v. Doyle, 429 U.S. 274 (1977).

52. See EEOC v. Wiltel, 81 F.3d at 1514; Liberman v. Brady, 926 F. Supp. at 1202.

53. 42 U.S.C. § 2000e-2(m).

When the evidence points to dual motives, the employer must be held liable, but the 1991 Act also circumscribes the plaintiff's remedy.[54] If the employer can prove that it "would have taken the same action in the absence of the impermissible motivating factor," then the court may not "award damages or issue an order requiring any admission, reinstatement, hiring, promotion, or payment. . . ."[55] In this circumstance, the plaintiff will only be able to obtain limited injunctive relief and a declaration that the conduct was unlawful, as well as attorneys' fees and costs.[56]

EEOC Regulations on Hiring Discrimination

Title VII explicitly requires that employers accommodate a *"prospective employee's religious observance or practice[.]"*[57] In an effort to provide guidance in the enforcement of this provision, the EEOC has promulgated implementing regulations as part of its "Guidelines on Discrimination Because of Religion."[58] Whether these regulations have any practical utility remains to be seen, since the cases discussed above virtually ignore these EEOC regulations. However, those involved in the hiring process should nevertheless be aware of the EEOC's views.

To the extent that an employer interviews or gives examinations to applicants, the EEOC requires the employer to accommodate applicants whose religious practices or observances conflict with the date of tests or interviews.[59] Consistent with the other provisions of Title VII, an employer's only excuse for not accommodating applicants with religious conflicts is proof that doing so would create an undue hardship.[60]

As to the actual hiring decision, an employer may not permit an applicant's religion to be a factor in the decision.[61] In addition to outlawing an employment decision based on the applicants' religious beliefs, Title VII also prohibits an employer from denying employment to an

---

54. *Id.* at § 2000e-5(g)(2)(B).
55. *Id.*
56. *Id.*
57. 42 U.S.C. § 2000(e)(j) (emphasis added).
58. 29 C.F.R. § 1605.3.
59. *Id.* at § 1605.3(a).
60. *Id.*
61. 42 U.S.C. § 2000e-2(a).

applicant because the person will require an accommodation. As the Ninth Circuit Court of Appeals has held:

> A refusal to hire [an applicant] because she was unable to work on Saturdays would have been a violation of Title VII, in the absence of good faith efforts to accommodate her religious beliefs.[62]

As interpreted by the EEOC, this rule places several restrictions on employers engaging in the hiring process. After conducting hearings, the EEOC determined that pre-hiring inquiries about an applicant's availability had "an exclusionary effect" on employees with certain religious practices.[63] The EEOC therefore decided that it would contest such inquiries as violations of Title VII, unless an employer can show that it:

> (1) Did not have an exclusionary effect on its employees or prospective employees needing an accommodation for the same religious practices; or
>
> (2) Was otherwise justified by business necessity.[64]

Unfortunately, the EEOC does not define "business necessity" in this context.

The EEOC also suggests a mode of interview that is both cumbersome and probably counterproductive. The EEOC advises that, if an employer has scheduling concerns, it should state its normal working hours to applicants and then ask the applicant whether he or she is available to work those hours.[65] When asking this question, however, the employer should preface it with a disclaimer that an applicant is not "required to indicate the need for any absences for religious practices during the scheduled work hours[.]"[66]

The EEOC's proposed hiring scenario continues with a suggestion that the employer make a decision whether to offer a position without asking the employee whether a religious accommodation would be

---

62. Proctor v. Consol. Freightways Corp. of Delaware, 795 F.2d 1472, 1476 (9th Cir. 1986).

63. 29 C.F.R. § 1605.3(b)(2).

64. *Id.*

65. *Id.*

66. *Id.*

needed to permit the applicant to work within the employer's schedule. However:

> . . . after a position is offered, but before the applicant is hired, the employer can inquire into the need for a religious accommodation and determine, according to the principles of these Guidelines, whether an accommodation is possible.[67]

Under this scenario, an employer must decide whether to offer a job to an applicant who states that he or she cannot work the normal schedule without being able to ask whether an accommodation of religion would permit a normal work schedule. Furthermore, the guideline ignores the fact that once an offer is made, acceptance by the employee creates a binding contract of hire, even if the employee has not disclosed any religious conflict.

In practical application, this regulation may well lead to more, rather than fewer, rejections of applicants with special religious needs. Employers naturally want to be as fully informed as possible when making hiring decisions. The EEOC's guidance could produce a situation in which an applicant identifies problems with the employer's work schedule, but declines to identify the source of the conflict or the means of resolving the conflict. The employee may appear not to be forthright, rather than being protective of his or her statutory rights. Applicants anxious to be offered a position will be uncertain as to how to respond to the interviewer's questions, and the employer will not know whether the applicant is being coy or protective of religious rights. That type of uncertainty may well lead employers to reject applicants before ever learning of their religious practices, especially when there is a large pool of applicants with similar qualifications. In that circumstance, rejected applicants may actually be less able to assert a legal claim over the rejection, since the need for religious accommodation will not have been discussed during the interviewing process and prior to the employer's decision not to extend an offer of employment.

A concrete example of this dilemma was presented in the case of *Byrd v. Johnson.*[68] The court there rejected an applicant's claim that he was

---

67. *Id.*
68. 31 FEP 1651 (D.D.C. 1983).

the victim of a discriminatory refusal to hire him based on religion, finding that he presented no evidence that the prospective employer knew his religion. The court stated that the applicant was required to prove that he communicated his religion to the employer as part of his prima facie case.[69] This holding obviously presents a difficulty for any applicant. Should the applicant follow the EEOC guidelines (by not disclosing religion prior to receiving an offer) or the theory in *Byrd* (which requires such disclosure)? There is not a sufficiently developed body of precedent to provide an answer.[70]

The EEOC regulations attempt to ease the applicant's burden of proving a hiring discrimination case by shifting the burden of proof to the employer whenever an applicant needing an accommodation is rejected:

> The Commission will infer that the need for accommodation discriminatorily influenced a decision to reject an applicant when: (i) prior to an offer of employment the employer makes an inquiry into an applicant's availability without having a business necessity justification; and (ii) after the employer has determined the applicant's need for an accommodation, the employer rejects a qualified applicant. The burden is then on the employer to demonstrate that factors other than the need for an accommodation were the reason for rejecting the qualified applicant, or that a reasonable accommodation without undue hardship was not possible.[71]

In effect, the EEOC presumes the existence of a discriminatory motive whenever an employer inquires into an applicant's accommodation needs without having a business justification for doing so and then rejects that applicant in favor of an applicant who does not have any accommodation needs. In that event, the burden is shifted to the employer to prove that nondiscriminatory motives justified the rejection. This system of assigning burdens between the employer and employee is obviously an effort to apply the burden-shifting standards of disparate treatment cases to the accommodation arena. Whether the courts will concur in the EEOC's

---

69. *Id.* at 1668.

70. In the authors' view, the analysis in *Byrd* is likely to prevail. For this reason, an employee desiring to protect his or her rights fully is probably well advised to disclose earlier, rather than later, the need for religious accommodation.

71. 29 C.F.R. § 1605.3(b)(3).

efforts remains to be seen, since this issue has not been the subject of litigation.

Summary

- An employer may not make religion a basis for an employment decision. Whether such a decision was "because of" the applicant's or employee's religion may be proved either by direct evidence of the employer's motivation or by the burden-shifting analysis used in race and sex disparate-treatment cases. In either event, the plaintiff has the ultimate burden of proving that the employer intentionally based its decision on religious beliefs or practices.

- When the evidence points to dual motives on the part of an employer, the employee will prevail if there is proof that discrimination was one of the motivations for the employment decision. However, if the employer proves that it would have reached the same decision even in the absence of the discriminatory motive, then the aggrieved employee's remedy will be limited to costs, attorneys' fees, declaratory relief, and certain forms of injunctive relief; the employee is not entitled to reinstatement or monetary relief.

- If an employer wishes to abide by the EEOC's guidelines for hiring decisions, it needs to proceed as follows:

    1. The employer may not inquire about scheduling and an applicant's need for an accommodation unless the employer has a business necessity for doing so.
    2. Assuming an employer has a business necessity, it must explore an applicant's accommodation needs without asking whether religion forms the basis for the conflict; if the employer asks about religion, the EEOC will apparently infer a discriminatory intent.
    3. Even if an employer has a business justification for inquiring into an applicant's ability to work a particular schedule and even if no inquiry into religion is made, the employer has the burden of showing that it had nondiscriminatory reasons for hiring an applicant who did not need an accommodation or that any accommodation would result in an undue hardship.

CHAPTER 5

When Is an Employer Liable for Religious Harassment or a Hostile Work Environment?

The same general principles that govern sexual harassment in the workplace also apply to religious harassment.[1] Two types of harassment are outlawed: "quid pro quo" harassment and "hostile work environment." Each is a variant of the disparate treatment claim and each is discussed separately below.

Quid Pro Quo Harassment

"Quid pro quo" harassment occurs whenever an employer demands that an employee abandon, alter or adopt a religious practice as a quid pro quo for a job benefit or to avoid adverse action.[2] This form of harassment, at least when it involves religious discrimination, is exceedingly rare.

---

1. Turner v. Barr, 806 F. Supp. 1025 (D.D.C. 1992), *mot. to alter judgment denied*, 811 F. Supp. 1 (D.D.C. 1993). *See generally* Meritor Savings Bank v. Vinson, 477 U.S. 57, 62 (1986) (defining sexual harassment).

When the EEOC proposed new guidelines for religious harassment that were modelled on the sexual harassment guidelines, several religious organizations protested on First Amendment grounds. 58 Fed. Reg. 51266 (Oct. 1, 1993). The proposed regulations were then withdrawn. 59 Fed. Reg. 51396 (Oct. 11, 1994).

2. Weiss v. United States, 595 F. Supp. 1050, 1056 (E.D. Va. 1984). *Cf.* Meritor Savings Bank v. Vinson, 477 U.S. at 62 (recognizing the court of appeals' similar definition of quid pro quo sexual harassment); Nichols v. Frank, 42 F.3d 503, 511 (9th Cir. 1994) (quid pro quo harassment arises when a supervisor "conditions a job, a job benefit, or absence of a job detriment, upon an employee's acceptance of sexual conduct").

The best example of quid pro quo religious harassment is found in a case that actually pre-dates the Supreme Court's approval of this cause of action. In *Young v. Southwestern Savings & Loan Association,*[3] an employee was ordered to attend meetings that were opened by a minister giving religious talks and prayers. The employee objected on religious grounds to attending these meetings; the employer responded that attendance at the entire meeting, including the prayers, was mandatory. The employee resigned, claiming that she was constructively discharged. The Fifth Circuit sided with the employee, using a traditional accommodation analysis. Although the court noted that the events did not rise to the level of an "atmosphere of religious intimidation,"[4] a constructive discharge did take place because the employee was faced with a choice between compliance with a religious mandate or possible discharge; in effect, the employee's attendance at the prayers was a quid pro quo for maintaining her employment.[5]

Because cases of quid pro quo religious harassment are so rare, there is no developed standard of a plaintiff's prima facie case. However, drawing upon precedent in sexual-harassment cases,[6] the essential proof required of a plaintiff should be: (1) evidence that the employee was required to submit to a religious demand or requirement as a condition of a job benefit or to avoid a job detriment, and (2) the employee's response to the demand or requirement was "used as the basis for decisions affecting the compensation, terms, conditions, or privileges" of employment.[7]

In response to the plaintiff's prima facie proof, the employer may either offer evidence that the demands were based on factors other than

---

3. 509 F.2d 140 (5th Cir. 1975).

4. *Id.* at 143.

5. *Id.* at 145 n.8. *See also* Blalock v. Metals Trades, Inc., 775 F.2d 703 (6th Cir. 1985), *cert. denied,* 490 U.S. 1064 (1989) (a "Christian" company could not discharge an employee because he had a falling out with a minister with whom the owner was close, unless it could prove that it would have taken the same action in the absence of the religious motivation).

6. The law of sexual harassment is, in turn, built upon precedent addressing the discriminatory harassment based on race and national origin. *See* Faragher v. City of Boca Raton, _____ S.Ct. _____, 77 FEP 14, 1998 WL 336322 at *8 (June 26, 1998).

7. Karibian v. Columbia University, 14 F.3d 773, 777 (2d Cir.) *cert. denied,* 512 U.S. 1213 (1994). *See also* Sparks v. Pilot Freight Carriers, Inc., 830 F.2d 1554, 1564 (11th Cir. 1987).

religion or that an adverse action against the employee was not based on religious considerations.[8] As in any other type of disparate treatment case, the employee should be given a final opportunity to prove that the employer's proffered nonreligion-based motive for action was merely a pretext.[9]

One issue relating to quid pro quo harassment that had long vexed the circuit courts was whether a plaintiff could make out a claim for this type of action if a supervisor had threatened adverse job action but had not actually carried out the threat. In *Burlington Industries, Inc. v. Ellerth*,[10] the Supreme Court finally ended the debate by holding that an employer may be liable for unfulfilled threats made by supervisors, but that such liability is not automatic. Harassment that does not result in a "tangible employment action" is not considered quid pro quo harassment for purposes of employer liability but, instead, should be analyzed under the guidelines applicable to "hostile work environment" harassment, as discussed below.

Hostile Work Environment

A more common form of religious harassment takes the form of a "hostile work environment." In a nutshell, employees have "the right to work in an environment free from discriminatory intimidation, ridicule, and insult."[11] Looking to the analogous standards for sexual harassment, an employee has the right to be free of harassment that is "sufficiently severe or pervasive" to alter the conditions of employment and to create an abusive work environment.[12] However, the plaintiff must prove that he or she was subjected to the harassing conduct "because of" religion.[13]

---

8. *See, e.g.,* Blalock v. Metals Trades, 775 F.2d at 709–12; Hicks v. Gates Rubber Co., 833 F.2d 1406, 1414 (10th Cir. 1987) ("adverse job consequences [plaintiff] suffered did not arise from her refusal to acquiesce in her supervisors' sexual conduct, but rather, were due solely to her inadequate job performance").

9. See Chapter 4 for a discussion of pretext.

10. ____ S.Ct. ____, 77 FEP 1, 1998 WL 336326 (June 26, 1998).

11. Turner v. Barr, 806 F. Supp. at 1027, *quoting* Kishaba v. Hilton Hotels Corp., 737 F. Supp. 549, 555 (D. Haw. 1990), *aff'd,* 936 F.2d 578 (9th Cir. 1991). The court in *Kishaba* was quoting, in turn, the Supreme Court's decision in *Meritor.*

12. Meritor Savings Bank v. Vinson, 477 U.S. at 67.

13. Oncale v. Sundowner Offshore Services, Inc., 118 S.Ct. 998 (1998).

The EEOC has adopted Guidelines on national origin harassment that can be analogized to a religious harassment claim:

> Ethnic slurs and other verbal or physical conduct relating to an individual's national origin constitute harassment when this conduct: (1) Has the purpose or effect of creating an intimidating, hostile or offensive working environment; (2) has the purpose or effect of unreasonably interfering with an individual's work performance; or (3) otherwise adversely affects an individual's employment opportunities.[14]

Applying this standard and the standards in sexual harassment cases, a plaintiff's prima facie case in a hostile-work-environment claim must satisfy four elements of proof:

1) the employee is a member of a protected religious group;
2) the employee was subjected to unwelcome harassment;
3) the harassment was based on the employee's religion; and
4) the harassment affected a term, condition, or privilege of employment.[15]

An alternative formulation suggested by one court requires a plaintiff asserting a religious harassment claim to prove that:

1) unwelcome comments, jokes, acts, and other verbal or physical conduct of [a] . . . religious nature were made in the workplace;
2) such conduct had the effect of creating an intimidating, hostile, or offensive working environment or unreasonably interfered with an individual's work performance. . . .[16]

Reduced to its practical terms, the employer may not subject an employee to ridicule or insults (including derogatory jokes) that the employee considers unwelcome and that have the effect of altering the conditions of work or creating an abusive work environment.[17] These

---

14. 29 C.F.R. § 1606.8(b). *See* Sarin v. Raytheon Co., 69 FEP 856, 858 (D. Mass. 1995) (applying Section 1606.8(b) to religious harassment).

15. *See, e.g.,* Henson v. City of Dundee, 682 F.2d 897, 903–4 (11th Cir. 1982).

16. Sarin v. Raytheon, 69 FEP at 858. The court additionally held the plaintiff must prove that the employer knew or should have known of the harassment.

17. Weiss v. United States, 595 F. Supp. at 1056.

abusive comments are not necessarily limited to language that is explicitly religious (or anti-religious) in nature. If an employee is subjected to any type of harassment *because* of that employee's religious beliefs, then the employer may become liable.[18]

Altering the conditions of work may come in the form of actually obstructing an employee in the performance of duties. It may be evidenced by a diminution in the quality of the employee's work. An employer may not, for example, discipline or terminate an employee for poor work performance if the employer is on notice that religious harassment impaired the employee's ability to carry out his or her work.[19]

In deciding whether the harassing conduct rises to the level of an abusive work environment, the courts use both a subjective and objective analysis. In other words, the victimized employee must subjectively believe the harassing conduct is abusive *and* the court or jury must objectively conclude that a reasonable person would find the conduct hostile or abusive.[20]

Obviously, there is no all-purpose rule that can guide an employer in such matters, since each case will have its own peculiar set of facts. The factors that an employer must consider in determining whether it has created or fostered a hostile work environment include: the severity of the harassing conduct; the frequency of the conduct; whether the conduct is likely to interfere in job performance; and whether the conduct may be physically intimidating.[21] An employer cannot wait until the victimized employee has suffered economic injury or exhibits signs of emotional or psychological harm, since the courts do not require such evidence before holding an employer liable.[22]

At the same time that the Supreme Court has cautioned that harassment need not produce tangible economic injuries to create liability, it has also warned that Title VII is not a "general civility code"[23] and that

---

18. Turner v. Barr, 811 F. Supp. at 4.

19. Weiss v. United States, 595 F. Supp. at 1057.

20. Kantar v. Baldwin Cooke Co., 69 FEP 851, 854 (N.D. Ill. 1995), citing Harris v. Forklift Systems, Inc., 510 U.S. 17, 21-22 (1993) (sexual harassment). *See also* Oncale v. Sundowner, 118 S.Ct. 998.

21. Harris v. Forklift Systems, 510 U.S. at 23.

22. *Id.* In *Harris,* the Court made clear that harassment claims are not limited to situations in which employees suffer "economic" or "tangible" discrimination.

23. Oncale v. Sundowner, 118 S.Ct. at 1002.

the "'mere utterance of an . . . epithet which engenders offensive feelings in an employee' would not sufficiently alter terms and conditions of employment to violate Title VII."[24]

The following are a few examples of conduct that the courts have found contributed to a work environment hostile to religion:

- Jokes about the Holocaust to Jewish employees.[25]
- Daily transmission of prayers over the employer's public-address system.[26]
- Telling a Jewish employee that he is a "Christ killer."[27]
- A supervisor preaching religion on the job in such a way that employees feel that he is trying to convert them.[28]
- Telling an employee that she is a sinner and that she needs to repent.[29]
- A supervisor prominently displaying a coffee mug with a swastika in a workplace with Jewish employees.[30]

Although the Supreme Court has held that an isolated incident of harassment that is "extremely serious" may give rise to a claim, the courts and the EEOC have mostly concluded that an employer is not liable if an employee has only been subjected to random or isolated comments or conduct.[31] Most reported cases have in fact involved harassing actions that were repeated, if not pervasive.[32] However, the courts have concluded that

---

24. Faragher v. City of Boca Raton, 1998 WL 336322 at *8, quoting Rogers v. EEOC, 454 F.2d 234, 238 (5th Cir. 1971).

25. Turner v. Barr, 811 F. Supp. at 3.

26. Hilsman v. Runyon, FEOR ¶ 951211 (EEOC OFO, 1995) (reversal of agency dismissal of complaint).

27. Weiss v. United States, 595 F. Supp. at 1053. The plaintiff was also subjected to such other epithets as "Jew faggot," "resident Jew," and "nail him to the cross."

28. EEOC Decision No. 72-1114 (1972).

29. Peck v. Sony Music Corp., 68 FEP 1025 (S.D.N.Y. 1995).

30. Yudovich v. Stone, 839 F. Supp. 382 (E.D. Va. 1993).

31. Kantar v. Baldwin Cook, 69 FEP at 854; Weiss v. United States, 595 F. Supp. at 1056; Ledesma v. Frank, FEOR ¶ 921072 (EEOC 1992). Cf. Oncale v. Sundowner, 118 S.Ct. 998 ("ordinary socializing," "horseplay," and "intersexual flirtations" should not be mistaken for unlawful harassment).

32. Weiss v. United States, 595 F. Supp. at 1056; Ledesma v. Frank, FEOR ¶ 921071 at 238.

the harassment need not have been concentrated in a particular time period to create liability and may be varied in character.[33]

How much is too much? When do repeated derogatory comments cross the line? Again, there is no all-purpose answer. The employer must consider both the victimized employee's perception of the conduct, as well as the objective perceptions of a "reasonable person."

Proselytizing versus Harassment

The development of the law of harassment has pointed up the potential for conflict when one employee decides to proselytize during work, notwithstanding objections by coworkers.[34] A graphic example of this problem, in more ways than one, is found in the Eighth Circuit's decision in *Wilson v. U.S. West Communications.*[35] The plaintiff in that case had taken a religious vow to wear a graphic anti-abortion button at all times. The button showed a color photograph of an 18- to 20-week-old fetus. The plaintiff asserted that she believed that the Virgin Mary would have chosen this very same button to wear as a protest against abortion.

The button caused "immediate and emotional reactions" from coworkers and the employer was able to establish a 40 percent decrease in productivity during the times that the button was displayed.[36] Some employees threatened to walk off their jobs because of the button. Even employees who opposed abortion tried to persuade the plaintiff to take off the button during work. When other employees accused the employer of subjecting them to unwanted religious harassment, the plaintiff was ordered to cease wearing the button. When she refused, she was fired.

The Court of Appeals upheld the termination. It found that the employer had offered a reasonable accommodation when it told the plain-

---

33. Turner v. Barr, 806 F. Supp. at 1027. *Cf.* Kantar v. Baldwin Cooke, 69 FEP at 854 (a handful of employee comments over a two-year period was not sufficient to establish a pervasive atmosphere of hostility).

34. This problem is made even more complicated in the public-sector workplace, since the First Amendment rights of both the proselytizer and the target of the proselytizing must be taken into account. Proselytizing in the public sector is discussed separately in Chapter 11.

35. 58 F.3d 1337 (8th Cir. 1995).

36. *Id.* at 1339.

tiff that she could wear the button, as long as she covered it during working hours. The Court of Appeals found this to be reasonable in light of the plaintiff's professed religious vow to wear the button until there was an end to abortion or she could no longer fight it.[37] By rejecting this accommodation, the plaintiff put the employer in an impossible situation vis à vis other employees. As the court ultimately held, "[T]itle VII does not require an employer to allow an employee to impose his religious views on others."[38]

The Fourth Circuit Court of Appeals had a similar case only one year later, in which it approvingly cited *Wilson* and came to the same conclusion. In *Chalmers v. Tulon Company of Richmond*,[39] the plaintiff was a midlevel supervisor who had frequently discussed religion with her supervisor, without any objection on his part. When the plaintiff came to believe that her supervisor had misrepresented facts to potential customers, she felt "led by the Lord" to write her supervisor a letter in which she accused him of unethical conduct:

> The last thing is, you are doing somethings [sic] in your life that God is not please [sic] with and he wants you to stop. All you have to do is go to God and ask for forgiveness[.][40]

On the same day, the plaintiff sent a letter to an unmarried subordinate who had just given birth to a child. She advised this employee:

---

37. *Id.* at 1341–42. The court also found that the employer was not discriminating against employees who had religious objections to abortion, since another employee with a less graphic anti-abortion button was permitted to wear her button. The employer also did not object to other religious symbols that the plaintiff kept at her desk. *Id.* at 1341.

38. *Id.* at 1342. An interesting reversal of this principle is found in Turic v. Holland Hospitality, Inc., 842 F. Supp. 971 (W.D. Mich. 1994), in which an employee discussed with coworkers her plans to have an abortion. Some of those employees, who were opposed to abortion on religious grounds, were deeply offended by the discussion and made their feelings clear to management. The plaintiff was disciplined for her "morally offensive" discussions with "Christian employees," while the latter employees were not disciplined for the "allegedly disruptive 'uproar' over abortion." *Id.* at 979–80. Ultimately, the plaintiff was terminated and filed a Title VII claim of disparate treatment. The employer moved for summary judgment on this claim, but the court denied the motion because of the employer's apparent disparate rule-making and discipline based on the religious beliefs of the employees involved. *Id.* at 980.

39. 101 F.3d 1012 (4th Cir. 1996), *cert. denied,* 118 S.Ct. 58 (1997).

40. *Id.* at 1015.

You probably do not want to hear this at this time, but you need the Lord Jesus in your life right now. . . .

One thing about God, He doesn't like when people commit adultery. You know what you did is wrong, so now you need to go to God and ask for forgiveness.[41]

When these incidents came to the attention of management, the plaintiff was fired for her "serious error in judgment" in criticizing the "personal lives and beliefs" of her coworkers. The plaintiff's Title VII claim was dismissed by the district court and that dismissal was affirmed by the court of appeals. The appellate court noted that the plaintiff had not provided any notice to the employer of the religious need to engage in such conduct and that, even if she had, there was no way that her letter-writing could have been accommodated. One of the reasons for this conclusion was the probability that the letter-writing would subject the employer to lawsuits by other employees for religious harassment.[42] The fact that the plaintiff was a supervisor and had written one of the offending letters to a subordinate only increased the likelihood that a claim of harassment could be lodged against the employer.[43]

The EEOC took exactly the same position when it ruled that an employer had failed to maintain a work environment free of religious harassment when one of its supervisors "preach[ed] religion while on the job," over the objection of employees.[44] One employee claimed that the supervisor was trying to convert him, while another contended that his job security was endangered by his refusal to agree with the supervisor's religious views. These complaints were sufficient to trigger a violation of Title VII.

These cases show that the tendency to merge the secular and religious worlds can have serious consequences in workplaces of increasing diversity. While employers may not discriminate against employees who proselytize in the workplace, proselytizing activities have the potential of interfering in normal business operations and may give rise to harassment claims by employees who object to the proselytizing. Although the divid-

---

41. *Id.* at 1016.
42. *Id.* at 1021.
43. *Id.*
44. EEOC Dec. No. 72-1114, 4 FEP 842 (1972).

ing line between permissible and unacceptable proselytizing may be difficult to locate, the courts have begun to develop basic parameters of conduct and have upheld employers that suppress proselytizing activities that become harassing. The careful employer, however, can avoid a charge that it is biased against a proselytizing employee if it has fully investigated the facts surrounding the proselytizing and has a sound factual basis for concluding that the employee has either disrupted work or has harassed coworkers.

The Employer's Responsibility for Religious Harassment Committed by Its Employees

The fact that an employee has been subjected to harassing conduct by a coworker does not necessarily mean that the employer will be held liable. In *Meritor Savings Bank v. Vinson*, the Supreme Court confronted—and then sidestepped—the important question of when an employer should be liable for the sexually harassing conduct of its employees. The Court held that an employer is not strictly liable for every hostile act of its employees, even supervisory employees; instead, it directed the lower courts to apply traditional agency principles to decide, on a case-by-case basis, when an employer must pay for the consequences of a hostile work environment.[45] Not surprisingly, the Supreme Court's refusal to provide more concrete guidance led to considerable confusion for employers and the courts. The resulting disagreement among the circuit courts was finally addressed by the Supreme Court in *Faragher v. City of Boca Raton*[46] and *Burlington Industries Inc. v. Ellerth.*[47]

Although there is no guarantee that the courts will apply the new rules of liability in sexual harassment cases to religious harassment, the precedent certainly points in that direction. The holdings in *Faragher* and *Burlington* must therefore be consulted in analyzing liability issues in religious discrimination actions.

First, the Court approved the view of those circuit courts holding that an employer will be directly liable for a hostile work environment

45. 477 U.S. at 72–3.
46. 77 FEP 14, 1998 WL 336322 (June 26, 1998).
47. 77 FEP 1, 1998 WL 336326 (June 26, 1998).

created by any of its employees (including nonsupervisors) if it "knew or should have known about the [harassing] conduct and failed to stop it."[48] In effect, this imposes a negligence standard on employers.[49] Once an employer is on notice of the harassing conduct, it is obligated to take remedial action that effectively eradicates the unwelcome conduct and returns the victimized employee to a normal working relationship.[50]

The types of corrective action that need to be taken will vary from situation to situation. Merely enunciating a policy in opposition to religious intolerance will not be sufficient where an employee has already suffered a change in working conditions because of the abusive environment.[51] Similarly, pointing to the existence of a nondiscrimination or nonharassment policy, without effective implementation of that policy, is not likely to absolve an employer of responsibility.[52] Disciplining the offending employee is one possibility, although it is not mandatory if other means are successful in bringing an end to the harassment.[53]

Second, and most importantly, the Court devised a new standard of vicarious liability for the acts of *supervisors* who engage in harassing conduct. Eschewing some of the common law agency principles that had

---

48. Burlington v. Ellerth, 1998 WL 336326 at *11. *See also* EEOC v. Hacienda Hotel, 881 F.2d 1504, 1515-16 (9th Cir. 1989); Turner v. Barr, 811 F. Supp. at 2-3. *Cf.* EEOC National Origin Guidelines:

> With respect to conduct between fellow employees, an employer is responsible for acts of harassment in the workplace on the basis of national origin, where the employer, its agents or supervisory employees, knows or should have known of the conduct, unless the employer can show that it took immediate and appropriate corrective action. [29 C.F.R. § 1606.8(d).]

49. Burlington v. Ellerth, 1998 WL 336326 at *11.

50. Weiss v. United States, 595 F. Supp. at 1057. *See also* Andrade v. Mayfair Management, Inc., 88 F.3d 258, 261 (4th Cir. 1996) (sexual harassment); Bouton v. BMW of North America, Inc., 29 F.3d 103, 107 (3rd Cir. 1994); Kauffman v. Allied Signal, Inc., 970 F.2d 178, 184 (6th Cir. 1992).

51. Weiss v. United States, 595 F. Supp. at 1057. *See* Meritor v. Vinson, 477 U.S. at 72 (existence of a grievance procedure and a policy against discrimination is relevant to, but not dispositive of, an employer's liability).

52. Meritor v. Vinson, 477 U.S. at 72-73. *See also* Gary v. Long, 59 F.3d 1391, 1398 (D.C. Cir.), *cert. denied,* 116 S.Ct. 569 (1995).

53. Sarin v. Raytheon, 69 FEP 859 (employer avoided liability, even absent disciplinary action against harassers, by promptly speaking to harassers, holding a hearing, and forcing the harassers to apologize, resulting in no repetition of the conduct).

caused so much disagreement in the lower courts,[54] the Supreme Court held that employers will be vicariously liable if a supervisor engages in harassing conduct that results in "tangible employment action."[55] The latter action is defined as a "significant change in employment status, such as hiring, firing, failing to promote, reassignment with significantly different responsibilities, or a decision causing a significant change in benefits"—in other words, it causes direct economic harm.[56] If a supervisor takes such action, the employer is not entitled to assert any affirmative defense and the lack of knowledge of the harassment by senior management is irrelevant; the plaintiff will not be required to prove negligence.

In keeping with the holding in *Harris v. Forklift Systems* that tangible or economic harm is not a necessary pre-condition to asserting a hostile work environment claim, the Court also permitted an employer to be held vicariously liable in those circumstances where no direct employment action is taken if the harassing conduct is sufficiently severe or pervasive. For example, in *Ellerth,* a supervisor threatened to take certain job actions against plaintiff, but never carried out the threats. Notwithstanding the absence of a "tangible employment action," the pervasive nature of the harassment could still give rise to vicarious liability for the employer. However, in this circumstance—where no concrete job action is taken—an employer is given the opportunity to put forward an affirmative defense:

> The defense comprises two necessary elements: (a) the employer exercised reasonable care to prevent and correct promptly any sexually harassing behavior, and (b) that the plaintiff employee unreasonably failed to take advantage of any preventive or corrective opportunities provided by the employer or to avoid harm otherwise. While proof that an employer had promulgated an anti-harassment policy with complaint procedure is not necessary in every instance as a mat-

---

54. *See, e.g.,* Burlington Industries, Inc. v. Ellerth, 123 F.3d 490 (7th Cir. 1997) (per curiam), *affd.,* 1998 WL 336326 (June 26, 1998). Sitting *en banc,* the circuit court was unable to agree on a standard for determining liability and produced seven separate concurring and/or dissenting opinions.

55. Burlington v. Ellerth, 1998 WL 336326 at *13-14; Faragher v. City of Boca Raton, 1998 WL 336322 at *19.

56. Burlington v. Ellerth, 1998 WL 336326 at *13.

ter of law, the need for a stated policy suitable to the employment circumstances may appropriately be addressed in any case when litigating the first element of the defense. And while proof that an employee failed to fulfill the corresponding obligation of reasonable care to avoid harm is not limited to showing any unreasonable failure to use any complaint procedure provided by the employer, a demonstration of such failure will normally suffice to satisfy the employer's burden under the second element of the defense.[57]

Obviously, trial courts and juries will have to balance the two prongs of this defense and decide how much weight to attach to an employer's and/or employee's actions in the face of workplace harassment. This uncertainty ensures that this new test of liability will be an evolving one.[58]

Summary

- "Quid pro quo" harassment occurs when an employee is required to submit to a religious demand or requirement as a condition of receiving a job benefit or of avoiding a job detriment.
- A "hostile work environment" occurs when an employee is subjected to unwelcome religious harassment that is sufficiently severe or pervasive to alter the conditions of employment.
- Whether harassment creates an abusive work environment depends upon proof that the conduct was subjectively perceived by the victimized employee as being abusive and proof that a reasonable person would perceive the conduct as being abusive.
- Employers may discipline employees (especially supervisors) who engage in proselytizing activities at work if the proselytizing creates a hostile work environment.
- An employer will be held liable for employee actions creating a hostile work environment if it knew or should have known of the conduct and negligently failed to take steps to correct it.

---

57. Faragher v. City of Boca Raton, 1998 WL 336322 at *19; Burlington v. Ellerth, 1998 WL 336326 at *15.

58. Justices Thomas and Scalia dissented from this standard of vicarious liability. They complained, in part, that the vagueness of the two-part affirmative defense will only lead to more, rather than less, litigation. Burlington v. Ellerth, 1998 WL 336326 at *20.

- Even in the absence of knowledge by management, an employer will be liable for harassment perpetrated by a supervisor if it results in a "tangible employment action" (for example, firing or withholding promotion) against an employee. If there is no tangible employment action, the employer may still be held liable for a supervisor's religious harassment, but the employer may avoid liability through an affirmative defense showing that it exercised reasonable care to prevent and correct the harassment *and* that the employee unreasonably failed to take advantage of corrective or preventive opportunities to avoid or ameliorate the harassment.

☒ CHAPTER 6

When Is an Employer Obligated to Accommodate an Employee's Religious Beliefs or Practices?

Title VII imposes an affirmative duty upon employers to "reasonably accommodate" the religious observances or practices of employees and applicants. This duty of reasonable accommodation appears in Title VII's definition of religion:

> The term "religion" includes all aspects of religious observance and practice, as well as belief, unless an employer demonstrates that he is unable to *reasonably accommodate* to an employee's or prospective employee's religious observance or practice *without undue hardship* on the conduct of the employer's business.[1]

Proof that an Employer Has Failed to Accommodate Religious Beliefs or Practices

Virtually every circuit court has adopted the same three-pronged test for deciding whether an employer has failed to accommodate an employee's religious beliefs or practices.[2]

---

1. 42 U.S.C. § 2000e(j) (emphasis added). The statutory duty to accommodate did not appear in Title VII as originally enacted. Rather, in 1972, Congress amended the statute to include the duty to accommodate already set forth in the EEOC's 1967 Guidelines on Religious Discrimination. *See* 29 C.F.R. Part 1605 (Appendix A to §§ 1605.2 and 1605.3) (1997).

2. *See generally* Chalmers v. Tulon Co. of Richmond, 101 F.3d 1012, 1019 (4th Cir. 1996); Protos v. Volkswagen of America, 797 F.2d 129, 133 (3d Cir.), *cert. denied,* 479

First, the employee must prove that he or she has a sincere religious belief that conflicts with an employment requirement.[3] Second, the employee must prove that the employer was put on notice of the conflict.[4] Third, the employee must prove that he or she was disciplined or would otherwise suffer for the adherence to his or her religious beliefs or for the failure to comply with the conflicting employment requirement.

If the employee presents such proof (that is, establishes a prima facie case), then the burden shifts to the employer. It can avoid liability if it proves that it offered an accommodation that was reasonable, but the employee refused to accept the accommodation.[5] The employer is not required to select the employee's proposed accommodation or the "best" accommodation; the employer satisfies its burden if it establishes that it offered *any* reasonable accommodation that resolved the conflict between the individual's religious practices and the requirements of the job.[6]

Alternatively, the employer can offer proof that it would have been futile to attempt an accommodation because any accommodation, even a reasonable one, would have caused "undue hardship."[7] In *Trans World Airlines, Inc. v. Hardison,* the Supreme Court defined an undue hardship as any cost to an employer that is more than de minimis.[8]

The remainder of this chapter addresses the essential elements of a failure to accommodate claim, including the evidence that an employee

---

U.S. 972 (1986); Turpen v. Missouri-Kansas-Texas R. Co., 736 F.2d 1022, 1026 (5th Cir. 1984); Cooper v. Oak Rubber Co., 15 F.3d 1375, 1378 (6th Cir. 1994); EEOC v. Townley Engineering & Mfg. Co., 859 F.2d 610, 614 n.5 (9th Cir. 1988), *cert. denied,* 489 U.S. 1077 (1989).

3. Chalmers v. Tulon Co., 101 F.3d at 1019. The Eighth Circuit Court of Appeals adopted a slight variation on the first element: "A plaintiff must plead and prove that (1) he has a bona fide belief that compliance with an employment requirement is contrary to his religious faith[.]" Brown v. General Motors Corp., 601 F.2d 956, 959 (8th Cir. 1979).

4. Chalmers v. Tulon Co., 101 F.3d at 1019.

5. EEOC v. United Parcel Service, 94 F.3d 314, 318 (7th Cir. 1996); Cooper v. Oak Rubber Co., 15 F.3d at 1378.

6. Ansonia v. Philbrook, 479 U.S. 60, 68-69 (1986); Wilson v. U.S. West Communications, 58 F.3d 1337, 1342 (8th Cir. 1995). The Supreme Court's holding in *Ansonia* is discussed at greater length in Chapter 7.

7. Chalmers v. Tulon Co., 101 F.3d at 1019.

8. 432 U.S. 63, 84 (1977). *See also* Cooper v. Oak Rubber Co., 15 F.3d at 1378. Compare this standard with the definition of "undue hardship" in the Americans with Disabilities Act (ADA). The implementing regulations to the ADA define an "undue hardship" as a "significant difficulty or expense incurred by a covered entity[.]" 29 C.F.R.

must present for a prima facie case and how the employee must respond in the event that the employer offers an accommodation. Chapters 7, 8, and 9 are devoted to a detailed analysis of an employer's obligations when presented with an employee's request for an accommodation. Finally, Chapter 10 describes the special obligations of unions to accommodate religious objections to the payment of dues.

Adherence to Sincere Religious Beliefs or Practices

The first element of a prima facie accommodation case requires the employee to prove that he or she has a sincere religious conflict. As explained in Chapter 2, the courts are extremely reluctant to question the sincerity or religious basis of an employee's beliefs and practices. Although there have been a few cases rejecting claims of religious-based practices (for example, the Ku Klux Klan is not a religion[9] and eating cat food is not a sincere religious practice[10]), they are so rare that they do not have a serious impact on Title VII jurisprudence.

The Employee's Duty to Notify Management of a Conflict Between Religion and Work

The second element of a prima facie accommodation case is proof that the employer was put on notice of the conflict between the employee's religious beliefs or practices and a requirement of the job. The EEOC's Religious Discrimination Guidelines provide:

> After an employee or prospective employee notifies the employer or labor organization of his or her need for a religious accommodation, the employer or labor organization has an obligation to reasonably accommodate the individual's religious practices.[11]

---

§ 1630.2(p); 28 C.F.R. § 36.104. The preamble to these regulations states that this definition was clearly mandated by Congress in the legislative history of the ADA. 29 C.F.R. § 1630. There is no similar legislative history providing guidance on Title VII's definition of undue hardship vis à vis a religious accommodation. As a result, an employer has a much lower burden to meet in religious accommodation cases than it does in disability accommodation cases.

9. Slater v. King Soopers, Inc., 809 F. Supp. 809, 810 (D. Co. 1992).

10. Brown v. Pena, 441 F. Supp. 1382, 1385 (S.D. Fla 1977), *aff'd,* 589 F.2d 1113 (5th Cir. 1979).

11. 29 C.F.R. § 1605.2(c).

The employee is required to inform the employer that a conflict exists and that it is caused by the employee's religious observance or practice.[12] The court may not presume that the employer has such knowledge. One court described the employee's duty as one to "acquaint the employer 'with his religion and its potential impact upon his ability to perform his job.'"[13]

Whom should the employee tell of the need for an accommodation? Notice must be provided to a supervisor or other member of management.[14] If the employee merely informs a coworker, the employer has not received adequate notice of the conflict.[15]

The requirement that an employee or applicant notify the employer of the conflict is grounded upon common sense; the employer must have notice of the problem so that it can address the problem. Otherwise, an employer would have the burden of continually searching for each potential religious conflict for each employee—clearly, an unworkable solution.[16] Notice also assists the employer in avoiding any harm to its business that religious activities may cause.[17]

---

12. EEOC v. Hacienda Hotel, 881 F.2d 1504, 1512 (9th Cir. 1989); EEOC v. Ilona of Hungary, Inc., 108 F.3d 1569, 1575 (7th Cir. 1997) (en banc); Chalmers v. Tulon Co. of Richmond, 101 F.3d at 1019; Wilson v. U.S. West Communications, 58 F.3d at 1340; Turpen v. Missouri-Kansas-Texas R. Co., 736 F.2d at 1026; Cooper v. Oak Rubber Co., 15 F.3d at 1378; Rourke v. New York State Dept. of Correctional Services, 915 F. Supp. 525, 538 (N.D.N.Y. 1995); Banks v. Service America Corp., 952 F. Supp. 703, 708 (D. Kan. 1996).

13. Brown v. General Motors Corp., 601 F.2d at 959 n.4, quoting Chrysler Corp. v. Mann, 561 F.2d 1282, 1285 (8th Cir. 1977), *cert. denied,* 434 U.S. 1039 (1978).

14. *See* Johnson v. Angelica Uniform Group, Inc., 762 F.2d 671, 673 (8th Cir. 1985) (stating that plaintiff should have notified plant manager or another supervisor of conflict); Boomsma v. Greyhound Food Management, Inc., 639 F. Supp. 1448, 1453 (W.D. Mich. 1986) (employee properly notified an immediate supervisor and the district manager of his beliefs).

15. EEOC v. J.P. Stevens and Co., 740 F. Supp. 1135, 1137 (M.D.N.C. 1990) (notice to fellow employee but not management fatal to claim); Van Koten v. Family Health Management, Inc., 955 F. Supp. 898, 903 (W.D. Ill. 1997), *aff'd,* 134 F.3d 375 (7th Cir. 1998) (vague statement to coworkers not sufficient notice). *See also* Chalmers v. Tulon Co., 101 F.3d at 1020 ("notice to coworkers at the same time as an employee violates employment requirements is insufficient to provide adequate notice to the employer and to shield the employee's conduct").

16. *See, e.g.,* Redmond v. GAF Corp., 574 F.2d 897, 902 (7th Cir. 1978).

17. *See* Chalmers v. Tulon Co., 101 F.3d at 1020.

In providing notice, the employee is not required to impart to the employer encyclopedic knowledge about his or her religion and the conflict. Rather, as one court stated:

A sensible approach would require only enough information about an employee's religious needs to permit the employer to understand the existence of a conflict between the employee's religious practices and the employer's job requirements.[18]

Conversely, a Title VII claim will be rejected when the employee does "little to acquaint [the employer] with his religion and its potential impact upon his ability to perform his job."[19]

In practice, informing the employer should be rather simple. For example, suppose a supervisor asks an employee to work on a Saturday, because the company is experiencing an unexpected demand for its product. If the employee observes the Sabbath on Saturdays and refuses to work on that day, the employee must inform the supervisor of his or her religious practices and the conflict with the Saturday schedule.[20]

If an employee fails to inform the employer of the conflict, or informs the employer of the conflict but does not link it to a religious belief, the employer is not legally required to accommodate the employee. In turn, the employer may take adverse action, including termination, if the employee fails to report for duty. The following are examples of situations in which the courts found an employee's notice to be inadequate.

- A teacher's aide wore a head-covering that violated the school district's dress-code policy. When questioned by the school's principal, the aide referenced her Afro-American heritage and culture. She did not connect her actions to her religious faith. The aide claimed that her actions were based upon her religious beliefs only

---

18. Heller v. EBB Auto Co., 8 F.3d 1433, 1439 (9th Cir. 1993). *Accord* Brown v. Polk County, Iowa, 61 F.3d 650, 654 (8th Cir. 1995) (en banc), *cert. denied,* 516 U.S. 1158 (1996); Redmond v. GAF Corp., 574 F.2d at 902.

19. Chrysler v. Mann, 561 F.2d 1282, 1285 (8th Cir. 1977), *cert. denied,* 434 U.S. 1039 (1978).

20. *See* EEOC v. Hacienda Hotel, 881 F.2d at 1512-13. *See also* Proctor v. Consol. Freightways Corp., 795 F.2d 1472, 1475 (9th Cir. 1986) (employee notified company that working on Saturday was contrary to her religious beliefs).

after the school district decided to terminate her. The court upheld the termination.[21]

■ An employee who was also a Baptist minister refused to take a drug test required by his employer, claiming that "[m]y religious faith as an ordained Baptist minister prohibits me from exhibiting my own personal assent to duress."[22] The employee refused to provide the employer with additional information concerning the conflict. The court ruled that the employee did not provide adequate notice, making it impossible for the employer to understand the nature of the conflict.[23]

■ The employer did not have knowledge that its employee observed the "Wiccian" religion merely because (1) the employee allegedly stated to several coworkers that he considered Halloween to be the holiest day of the year, (2) his supervisor observed that he was a vegetarian, (3) his supervisor called him "brutally agnostic," and (4) his supervisor observed that he prepared astrology charts.[24]

In short, an employee should be clear when explaining why an accommodation is needed. Vague references to culture, heritage, or personal preferences are not the same as clearly stating that one's actions are required by *religious* beliefs. When an employee cannot work on a Sabbath day and informs the employer of the conflict, the employer has adequate knowledge to address the issue and to propose a reasonable accommodation. However, when an employee presents only a vague objection to a work rule, the employer may be relieved of the obligation to propose a reasonable accommodation.

Although this notice requirement usually works well enough in practice, there are potential gray areas as shown by the Fourth Circuit's split decision in *Chalmers v. Tulon Company*.[25] Chalmers was an evangelical Christian who testified she was "led by the Lord" to send personal letters

---

21. McGlothin v. Jackson Mun. Separate School Distr., 829 F. Supp. 853 (S.D. Miss. 1992).

22. Cary v. Carmichael, 908 F. Supp. 1334, 1344 (E.D. Va. 1995), *aff'd*, 116 F.3d 472 (4th Cir. 1997).

23. *Id.* at 1346.

24. Van Koten v. Family Health Management, Inc., 955 F. Supp. at 903-04. The religion in this case is also spelled as "Wiccan."

25. 101 F.3d 1012.

to two coworkers in which she criticized their morality and urged each of them to "go to God and ask for forgiveness."[26] After Chalmers was terminated for writing the letters, she claimed that the employer had failed to accommodate her religious activities (i.e., the letter-writing). The majority upheld the lower court's grant of summary judgment to the employer, in part because Chalmers failed to provide notice of her need for an accommodation.[27] The dissent pointed out, however, that Chalmers may not have understood that her conduct violated company policy or needed her employer's accommodation. The dissenting judge then posited several troublesome hypothetical situations:

> The majority's rule would mean that *as a matter of law* a Jew could not make out a *prima facie* case under Title VII if, on the first day of work, he was fired for wearing a yarmulke that, unknown to him, violated his company's dress code. Similarly, a Muslim would have no case for being fired the first time mandatory company meetings conflicted with his prayer schedule; a Jehovah's Witness would have none upon being fired for her disrespect in refusing to attend a company-wide celebration of the CEO's birthday; a Mormon would have none for being fired the first time he refused to work late on church-wide family nights.[28]

These hypotheticals point up the need for common sense on the part of both the employer and employee. The employee needs to make certain that the employer is on notice that an accommodation is necessary. However, neither the employee nor the employer will necessarily foresee every conflict that might arise. While Chalmer's provocative and disruptive conduct might have been a foreseeable problem, the wearing of a yarmulke or the refusal to sing happy birthday is less clearly a potential conflict in the workplace. For this reason, neither the courts nor employers should be overly rigid in enforcing the notice requirement.

One last problem that frequently arises between employees and employers concerns the *timing* of the employee's notice to the employer of

---

26. *Id.* at 1015–16. Chalmers accused one employee of adultery and the other of lying to the employer's customers.

27. *Id.* at 1019.

28. *Id.* at 1026 (Niemeyer, dissenting, emphasis in original).

a religious conflict. In several cases, employers have argued that a delay in notifying the employer of a religious conflict resulted in the employee's waiver of rights under Title VII.[29] The courts generally reject this defense.

For example, in *Wangsness v. Watertown School Dist.,*[30] a teacher who belonged to the Worldwide Church of God submitted a request in early September 1973 for a religious leave of absence for October 11 through October 19 of that year. Rejecting the employer's argument that the notice did not provide sufficient time to secure a substitute teacher, the court held that one month's notice satisfied the requirements of Title VII.

A similar result was reached in a case where the employees were accused of giving too much notice. In *Willey v. Maben Manufacturing, Inc.,*[31] employees told their immediate supervisor well in advance of the date when they would need to take off work for two religious days. The supervisor had no authority to act on the requests. He therefore passed them along to the plant manager, who asked the supervisor to have the employees notify him when the two days got closer; they did not do so. The court concluded that the employer was still obliged to seek an accommodation because the original notification to the supervisor was sufficient to put the employer on notice of the religious conflict.[32]

---

29. In other cases, the employer argues that the delay in notice shows that the employee's asserted religious belief is insincere. For example, an employee may have worked on his Sabbath for a number of years before informing the employer that he could not, consistent with his religious beliefs, continue working on that day. This type of argument is usually rejected by the courts because a person may have a genuine change or renewal in commitment to his or her religion. *See, e.g.,* Cooper v. Oak Rubber Co., 15 F.3d at 1379 (rejecting argument that plaintiff, who worked Saturdays for approximately seven months after her baptism, did not express a sincere religious belief); Smith v. Pyro Min. Co., 827 F.2d 1081, 1086 (6th Cir. 1987), *cert. denied,* 485 U.S. 989 (1988) (rejecting argument that plaintiff, who worked from 11:00 P.M. to 12:00 A.M. on Sunday, was not sincere in objecting to working on Sunday morning). The sincerity of an employee's belief is discussed in detail in Chapter 2.

30. 541 F. Supp. 332, 336–37 (D.S.D. 1982).

31. 479 F. Supp. 634 (N.D. Miss. 1979). *Cf.* EEOC Decision No. 81-19 (1981) (employee did not satisfy notice requirement when employer was given church calendar for the year showing holy days, but with no indication of which days would require an accommodation).

32. Willey v. Maben Mfg., 479 F. Supp. at 636–37.

In *EEOC v. Townley Engineering & Manufacturing Co.,*[33] an employee was required upon hire to sign a commitment to attend weekly "nondenominational devotional services" on the employer's premises. The employee attended the services for a number of months before protesting and refusing to attend the services on religious grounds. Ultimately, the employee left work, and claimed a constructive discharge. Before the court, the employer argued that the employee waived his rights by not objecting upon hire and by attending the services for a substantial period of time before complaining. The Ninth Circuit rejected the employer's argument: "An employee does not cease to be discriminated against because he temporarily gives up his religious practice and submits to the employment policy."[34]

Similarly, in a case heard by the Equal Employment Opportunity Commission (EEOC), an employee objected on religious grounds to paying union dues.[35] The union questioned the sincerity of the employee's religious objections because he waited four years after being hired to object. The EEOC rejected the notion that a delay in notification proves insincerity; it also noted that the union did not actually seek to enforce the obligation against the employee until four years after hire, so that the actual conflict between the employee and the union did not arise until that time.[36]

The foregoing cases do not mean that belated notification by an employee will never lead to dismissal of a claim.[37] However, most courts view a delay in employee notification as something that may reduce the number of accommodation options, but not as something that vitiates the employer's obligation to attempt to reach an accommodation after it becomes aware of the religious conflict. Courts will decide on a case-by-case basis whether a particular delay prevented an accommodation from being reached. However, the courts are reluctant to permit a delay to work a complete waiver of an employee's rights.

---

33. 859 F.2d 610, 612 (9th Cir. 1988), *cert. denied,* 489 U.S. 1077 (1989).

34. *Id.* at 615 n.5.

35. EEOC Dec. 81-83, 27 FEP 1835 (1981).

36. *Id.*

37. *See* Johnson v. Angelica Uniform Group, 762 F.2d at 673 (employer did not violate Title VII when it disciplined an employee who gave notice of the need for religious leave immediately before her absence).

*Proof that an Employee has Suffered an Adverse Consequence
as a Result of the Religious Conflict*

This last element of a plaintiff's burden of proof has not posed any difficulties for the courts. In most cases, plaintiffs have brought action after
they were discharged or otherwise disciplined for failing to comply with a
work rule.[38] A plaintiff may also seek to prove a cause of action based on
constructive discharge; that is, an employee who resigns rather than violate his or her religious beliefs does not waive the right to bring suit.[39]
Monetary losses (such as loss of pay resulting from absences) are also sufficient to support a Title VII claim.[40]

*The Employee's Duty to Cooperate with the Employer
in Reaching an Accommodation*

Establishing the three elements of a failure to accommodate claim is not
the sole burden placed on employees. The employee also has the obligation to respond appropriately if the employer makes an effort to reach a
reasonable accommodation. The Supreme Court has held that "bilateral
cooperation is appropriate in the search for an acceptable reconciliation of
the needs of the employee's religion and the exigencies of the employer's
business."[41] The Court relied on the legislative history for the 1972
amendments to Title VII, especially the comments of Senator Randolph,
who sponsored the reasonable accommodation amendment; he expressed
the view that accommodation should be made with flexibility and the
desire to achieve an acceptable adjustment in working conditions.[42]

---

38. Proctor v. Consolidated Freightways Corp., 795 F.2d 1472; Smith v. Pyro Min.
Co., 827 F.2d 1081; Brener v. Diagnostic Center Hospital, 671 F.2d 141 (5th Cir. 1982);
EEOC v. Ilona of Hungary, 108 F.3d 1569. *See also* EEOC v. Townley Engineering, 859
F.2d at 614 n.5 (court recognized that the "*threat* of discharge (or of other adverse employ-
ment practices)" is sufficient to satisfy third prong) (emphasis in original).

39. Young v. Southwestern Savings and Loan Ass'n, 509 F.2d 140, 144 (5th Cir.
1975). *Cf.* Vitug v. Multistate Tax Com'n, 88 F.3d 506, 517 (7th Cir. 1996) (disparate-
treatment claim based on constructive discharge was rejected for lack of evidence).

40. Ansonia v. Philbrook, 479 U.S. at 71.

41. *Id.* at 69.

42. *Id.* (citing statement of Senator Randolph, 118 Cong. Rec. 706 (1972)).

It is important to emphasize in this context what the employee is *not* required to do. An employee is under no duty to propose to the employer the specific means by which religious practices or beliefs will be accommodated.[43] The employer is better situated to understand the business and the intricacies of its operation; it therefore is in the better position to propose an accommodation that does not present an undue hardship to itself. An employee is also not required to compromise the religious beliefs giving rise to the conflict; if an employer were to offer an accommodation that required an employee to violate his or her religious principles, it would not be a reasonable accommodation.[44]

On the other hand, nothing prohibits the employee from suggesting appropriate accommodations to the employer. Indeed, the employee has a duty to cooperate with the employer's attempt to reach an accommodation.[45] This duty is triggered once the employer makes its initial effort to accommodate.[46] If the employer proposes a reasonable accommodation, the employee must cooperate with the employer by accepting the accommodation offered. This responsibility on the part of the employee has been described in numerous ways by the courts. The most common explanation is that "the employee has a correlative duty to make a good faith attempt to satisfy his needs through means offered by the employer."[47] This does not mean compromising religious beliefs, but it does preclude employee intransigence in the face of a reasonable accommodation.[48]

---

43. Toledo v. Nobel-Sysco, Inc., 892 F.2d 1481, 1488-89 (10th Cir. 1989), *cert. denied,* 495 U.S. 948 (1990); Brener v. Diagnostic Center Hospital, 671 F.2d at 145; Redmond v. GAF Corp., 574 F.2d at 901; Cary v. Carmichael, 908 F. Supp. at 1347.

44. Wilson v. U.S. West, 58 F.3d at 1342; Brener v. Diagnostic Center Hospital, 671 F.2d at 146 n.3; Cary v. Carmichael, 908 F. Supp. at 1346.

45. Toledo v. Nobel-Sysco, 892 F.2d at 1488-89; Brener v. Diagnostic Center Hospital, 671 F.2d at 146; EEOC v. IBP, Inc., 824 F. Supp. 147, 153 (C.D. Ill. 1993).

46. Toledo v. Nobel-Sysco, 892 F.2d 1488-89.

47. Brener v. Diagnostic Center Hospital, 671 F.2d at 146. *See also* Lee v. ABF Freight System, 22 F.3d 1019, 1022-23 (10th Cir. 1994); Heller v. EBB Auto, 8 F.3d at 1440; Chrysler Corp. v. Mann, 561 F.2d 1282, 1285 (8th Cir. 1977); Breech v. Alabama Power Co., 962 F. Supp. 1447, 1460 (S.D. Ala. 1997); Cary v. Carmichael, 908 F. Supp. at 1347.

48. Yott v. North American Rockwell Corp., 602 F.2d 904 (9th Cir. 1979), *cert. denied,* 445 U.S. 928 (1980).

Once the employer offers any reasonable accommodation, the employee must accept it; the employee cannot insist on his or her own alternative.[49]

Summary

- An employee is entitled to have his or her religious beliefs or practices accommodated if he or she can show:
  1) adherence to a sincere religious belief that conflicts with an employment requirement, and
  2) timely notification to the employer of the conflict.
- An employer may avoid the requirement of providing an accommodation if:
  1) it offered the employee a reasonable accommodation that the employee refused, or
  2) all accommodations, including reasonable ones, would cause undue hardship.
- Employees have no obligation to propose an accommodation or to compromise their religious beliefs, but they must cooperate with the employer in exploring and implementing an accommodation.
- Employees must accept any reasonable accommodation offered by the employer.
- If an employee brings suit claiming a failure to accommodate, the employee must prove that he or she was disciplined or was otherwise adversely affected by adherence to the religious belief or failure to comply with the conflicting employment requirement.

---

49. Ansonia v. Philbrook, 479 U.S. at 69.

✖ CHAPTER 7

What Steps Must an Employer Take in Response to an Employee's Request for an Accommodation?

The Employer's Obligation to Respond to an Employee's Request for Accommodation

The general rule in accommodation cases is simply stated: An employer *must* propose a reasonable accommodation unless it can prove that *all* reasonable accommodations would entail an undue hardship.[1] Although an employee must cooperate with an employer's effort to accommodate, the full burden of exploring all avenues of accommodation falls upon the employer.[2]

Several circuit courts of appeals have held that an employer need not futilely pursue accommodations of work-religion conflicts that are inher-

---

1. *See generally* Heller v. EBB Auto, 8 F.3d 1433, 1440 (9th Cir. 1993). *See also* Ansonia Bd. of Educ. v. Philbrook, 479 U.S. 60, 69 (1986); EEOC v. Ilona of Hungary, Inc., 108 F.3d 1569, 1575 (7th Cir. 1997); Opuku-Boateng v. California, 95 F.3d 1461, 1467 (9th Cir. 1996), *cert. denied,* 117 S.Ct. 1819 (1997); Toledo v. Nobel-Sysco, Inc., 892 F.2d 1481, 1489 (10th Cir. 1989), *cert. denied,* 495 U.S. 948 (1990); Brener v. Diagnostic Center Hospital, 671 F.2d 141, 145-46 (5th Cir. 1982).

2. Heller v. EBB Auto, 8 F.3d at 1440; EEOC v. Sterling Merchandise Co., 46 FEP 1448 (N.D. Ohio 1987), *aff'd,* 845 F.2d 325 (6th Cir. 1988) (employer failed to prove undue hardship when it did not explore all possible accommodations with employee).

ently irreconcilable.[3] Under this theory, an employer may offer a defense of undue hardship even in the absence of accommodation efforts. However, as the Sixth Circuit observed, a court should be "somewhat skeptical of hypothetical hardships that an employer thinks might be caused by an accommodation that never has been put into practice."[4] In fact, most courts have held that, once an employee has made an accommodation request, the employer cannot ignore the request. It must initiate a good faith discussion with the employee to determine whether it can reasonably accommodate the employee's religious beliefs.[5] This burden to initiate discussions rests solely upon the employer.[6] It may not put the onus of devising or suggesting accommodations on the employee:

> Title VII complainants are under no burden to propose to their employers specific means of accommodating their religious practices.[7]

Numerous courts have held that employers violate Title VII when they fail to discuss any accommodations with the employee; the defense of undue hardship in such cases was rejected because of the factual vacuum in which they were raised. In effect, the undue-hardship defense was deemed too hypothetical.[8]

---

3. Toledo v. Nobel-Sysco, 892 F.2d at 1489; EEOC v. Townley Engineering & Mfg. Co., 859 F.2d 610, 615 (9th Cir. 1988), *cert. denied,* 489 U.S. 1077 (1989).

4. Draper v. United States Pipe & Foundry Co., 527 F.2d 515, 520 (6th Cir. 1975).

5. Heller v. EBB Auto Co., 8 F.3d 1433, 1440 (9th Cir. 1993); Opuku-Boateng v. California, 95 F.3d at 1467; Redmond v. GAF Corp, 574 F.2d 897, 903-04 (7th Cir. 1978); EEOC v. Ithaca Ind., 849 F.2d 116, 118 (4th Cir.), *cert. denied,* 488 U.S. 924 (1988). *But see* Ryan v. United States Department of Justice, 950 F.2d 458, 461 (7th Cir. 1991), *cert. denied,* 504 U.S. 958 (1992). In *Ryan,* the court rejected the plaintiff's argument that Title VII required the employer to negotiate with him about an accommodation. According to the *Ryan* court, "Title VII requires employers to act not talk (it is not a collective bargaining law)." 950 F.2d at 461.

6. Proctor v. Consol. Freightways Corp., 795 F.2d 1472, 1475 (9th Cir. 1986).

7. Gordon v. MCI Telecommunications Corp., 59 FEP 1363, 1365-66 (S.D.N.Y. 1992), quoting Brener v. Diagnostic Ctr. Hosp., 671 F.2d 141, 145 (5th Cir. 1982). *See also* Toledo v. Nobel-Sysco, 892 F.2d at 1488 (employer bears the burden to accommodate; employee's duty to cooperate is irrelevant until employer satisfies its initial obligation).

8. *See, e.g.,* EEOC v. Hacienda Hotel, 881 F.2d 1504; Boomsma v. Greyhound Food Management, 639 F. Supp. 1448 (W.D. Mich. 1986), *app. dismissed,* 815 F.2d 76 (6th Cir. 1987).

The most extreme example of an employer's intransigence is found in a case before the Seventh Circuit, in which an employee's Saturday morning Bible-study class conflicted with infrequently scheduled overtime.[9] When the employee learned that he was scheduled for overtime on a Saturday, he notified his employer of the conflict. Rather than attempt to accommodate the employee, the employer simply told him that he would have to work on Saturday "or else."[10] The company refused to discuss any alternative arrangements with the employee. The court held that the company failed to make any effort to accommodate the employee.[11]

Such blatant intransigence, however, is not the sole basis for employer liability. On occasion, an employer may attempt to accommodate the schedules of each of its employees before assigning overtime or weekend work. For example, an employer may seek volunteers before assigning any employee overtime work on a Saturday. The employer may do this because it understands that weekend work may conflict with the family or personal schedules of its employees. This type of flexibility, unrelated to religion, does not rescue an employer from Title VII's obligations. An employer's generally flexible personnel policies that are extended to all employees may not always provide an accommodation of a particular employee's religious needs. Even when the employer is particularly sensitive to the needs and schedules of its employees, it is still obligated to propose a reasonable accommodation to an employee who raises a religious conflict.[12]

In a case before the Fourth Circuit, an employee informed his company upon hire that he could not work on Sunday because it would violate his religious beliefs.[13] As a matter of practice, the supervisor attempted to accommodate all employees when Sunday work was assigned by asking for volunteers from the same shift before ordering employees to work. The supervisor asked for volunteers, regardless of whether an individual objected to working for religious reasons. He did not, however, ask for volunteers from other shifts. After the company failed to find enough vol-

---

9. Redmond v. GAF Corp., 574 F.2d 897.

10. *Id.* at 903.

11. *Id.* at 904. *See also* Toledo v. Nobel-Sysco, 892 F.2d at 1488-89 (employer made no attempt to accommodate applicant and relied upon speculative hardships).

12. EEOC v. Ithaca Ind., 849 F.2d at 119.

13. *Id.* at 117.

unteers to work on a particular Sunday, the plaintiff was told that he had to work. The company refused to discuss the matter with him; it believed that it could rely on its efforts to accommodate all of its employees who preferred not to work on Sunday. The court of appeals rejected the company's position:

> It is true that . . . [the employer] did demonstrate an effort to accommodate all their employees when Sunday work was assigned. These accommodations, however, were clearly not for reasons of religion, nor were they specifically aimed at addressing [the plaintiff's] beliefs.[14]

The court noted that, if the employer had made the extra effort, it would have learned that some employees were willing to volunteer to substitute for the plaintiff.[15]

The employer's duty to propose a reasonable accommodation continues even in a number of situations that the employer may believe is counter-intuitive. For example, the Ninth Circuit has held that an employer was obligated to discuss possible accommodations of an employee's Sabbath despite the fact that she applied for a position that she knew was likely to conflict with her religious objection to working on the Sabbath.[16] An employer is similarly required to participate in discussions with an employee, even though the employee proposes an accommodation that is unreasonable.[17]

The employer's duty to discuss a reasonable accommodation with an employee also applies to a situation in which a current employee is being accommodated by the employer, but then applies for a new position

---

14. *Id.* at 119.

15. *Id.* at 118. *Contra* Beam v. General Motors Corp., 21 FEP 85 (N.D. Ohio 1979) (employer need not make special effort to accommodate plaintiff when collective-bargaining agreement provided means to avoid religious conflict).

16. *Cf.* Proctor v. Consol. Freightways, 795 F.2d at 1476 (employee knew of conflict when she applied for promotion); EEOC Decision 81-83, 27 FEP 1834 (union must accommodate employee's religious objection to union dues, even though employee knew of the religious conflict at the outset of employment). An employer violates Title VII if it refuses to hire an applicant simply because of the need to devise a reasonable religious accommodation. See Chapter 4.

17. Toledo v. Nobel-Sysco, 892 F.2d at 1849; EEOC v. IBP, Inc., 824 F. Supp. 147, 153 (C.D. Ill. 1993).

within the company. Even though the employer has provided a reasonable accommodation to the employee in the old position, it must again accommodate the employee after the move to a new position.[18] In other words, each separate conflict requires a particularized effort at accommodation.

An Employer that Offers a Reasonable Accommodation Is not Required to Accept the Accommodation Requested by an Employee

The Supreme Court has made clear that an employer that offers a means of reasonably accommodating an employee's religious needs is not required to accept another solution recommended by the employee, even if the employee's solution does not result in an undue hardship to the employer.

In *Ansonia Board of Education v. Philbrook,*[19] a high school teacher was a member of the Worldwide Church of God. His religious beliefs prohibited him from working on designated holy days, including six scheduled school days. The collective-bargaining agreement between the board of education and the Ansonia Federation of Teachers provided that teachers could take only three days of leave each year for "mandated religious observance" without losing annual or sick leave. Although the agreement also provided that employees could take an extra three days of sick leave for necessary personal business, religious leave was explicitly excluded from this category.[20] Nonetheless, Philbrook sought to use six days of leave each year for religious observances (i.e., three days more than permitted). He offered to reimburse the school district for the cost of a substitute teacher, which was less than the cost incurred if Philbrook took leave without pay. When the school board refused to permit the use of personal leave for the three religious days and insisted that Philbrook take leave without pay for those three days, he brought suit under Title VII.[21]

The Court held that the school board's policy of requiring an employee to take leave without pay for religious absences in excess of three days each year was reasonable.[22] The Court also held that the school board did not have to accept Philbrook's recommended solutions to the

---

18. Proctor v. Consol. Freightways, 795 F.2d at 1477.
19. 479 U.S. 60 (1986).
20. *Id.* at 63–64.
21. *Id.* at 64–65.
22. *Id.* at 70–71.

conflict because Title VII only required an employer to offer an employee *any* reasonable accommodation. Once the board offered a reasonable accommodation, it was neither required to offer the best accommodation nor accept an alternative proposed by Philbrook.[23]

The Court, however, remanded the case to the district court for further factual inquiry because the record did not clearly show whether the school board offered paid leave for all purposes *except* religious ones. If so, the Court noted that "[s]uch an arrangement would display a discrimination against religious practices that is the antithesis of reasonableness."[24] On remand, the district court found that the school board had not deviated for any reason from its written personal-leave policy; accordingly, that policy, as applied to Philbrook, was not discriminatory and was deemed reasonable.[25]

In addition to relieving an employer of the obligation to accede to an employee's proposed accommodation, the *Ansonia* holding provided employers with one additional benefit. It confirmed that an accommodation that imposes a financial cost on employees is not, for that reason alone, unreasonable. Even when less costly accommodations to the employee are available, an employer is not required to choose one of those accommodations.[26]

Another example of an employer offering its own proposed accommodation, rather than accepting an employee's alternative "reasonable" accommodation, is found in *Wright v. Runyon.*[27] Wright, a postal worker, was a member of the Seventh-Day Adventist Church; his religious beliefs forbade work on Saturdays. After Wright's position was abolished, the Postal Service permitted him to bid for a number of positions, some of which did not require work on the Sabbath. Wright bid only for positions that required Sabbath work, but he was unsuccessful in those bids. As a

23. *Id.* at 68-69. In the Supreme Court's view, such a rule was necessary to avoid encouraging employees to hold out for the most advantageous accommodation, even though the employer has already offered a reasonable resolution of the conflict.

24. *Id.* at 71.

25. Philbrook v. Ansonia Bd. of Educ., 925 F.2d 47, 54 (2d Cir.), *cert. denied,* 501 U.S. 1218 (1991).

26. *See* Ansonia v. Philbrook, 479 U.S. at 74 (Marshall, J., dissenting).

27. 2 F.3d 214 (7th Cir. 1993), *cert. denied,* 510 U.S. 1121 (1994).

result, Wright was assigned involuntarily to a position that required work on Friday evenings. Wright protested that the new assignment would require his resignation. The Postal Service refused to change the assignment or schedule, and Wright resigned.[28]

The Seventh Circuit held that the Postal Service offered a reasonable accommodation when it allowed Wright to bid for positions that did not require work on the Sabbath, two of which he would have received had he bid for them.[29] The court noted that Title VII "requires only 'reasonable accommodation,' not satisfaction of an employee's every desire."[30] The court continued:

> The USPS admittedly did not investigate every possible way in which Wright could avoid a conflict between his work requirements and his religious practices. But, by providing at least one reasonable accommodation, the USPS discharged its obligations.[31]

In *Ansonia,* the Supreme Court suggested that both the employer and employee should engage in "bilateral cooperation" in reaching an accommodation.[32] The decision in *Wright* points out the limits of that bilateral cooperation. In the Seventh Circuit's view, the dialogue recommended by the Supreme Court is not mandatory. Once a single reasonable accommodation presents itself, an employer need not discuss other possible accommodations with the employee. Put differently, an employer's decision does not have to be informed by an exploration of all of the possible accommodations. Once an employer finds a reasonable accommodation (even one imposing a cost on the employee) it is not required to pursue any other possibilities.

On the other hand, if—after discussion between the employer and employee—the employer *fails* to propose a reasonable accommodation that eliminates the religious conflict, the employer *must* accept the proposal proffered by the employee if it is reasonable (or, it must demon-

---

28. *Id.* at 215-15.

29. *Id.* at 217. Wright could have selected a position, similar in skill to the one that was abolished, that did not require work on the Sabbath.

30. *Id.*

31. *Id.*

32. 479 U.S. at 69.

strate that the employee's proposed accommodation would cause an undue hardship).[33]

An Employer Must Eliminate All Religious Conflicts, Unless Doing So Would Cause an Undue Hardship

Employers must eliminate *every* conflict presented by the employee, unless doing so will cause an undue hardship.[34] A partial accommodation is not sufficient to terminate an employer's duty to explore resolution of the conflict. As the Sixth Circuit has held:

> An employer does not fulfill its obligation to reasonably accommodate a religious belief when it is confronted with two religious objections and offers an accommodation which completely ignores one.[35]

Although this situation may arise in a number of different contexts, the following is one that has been repeatedly confronted by the courts: An employee seeks an accommodation for a shift schedule requiring work on his or her Sabbath; the employer agrees to allow the employee to swap

---

33. EEOC v. Townley Engineering, 859 F.2d at 615 (employer violated Title VII when it offered no accommodation, and turned down an employee's proposed reasonable accommodation); Opuku-Boateng v. California, 95 F.3d at 1467 ("Where the negotiations do not produce a proposal by the employer that would eliminate the religious conflict, the employer must either accept the employee's proposal or demonstrate that it would cause undue hardship were it to do so."). *But see* Ryan v. U.S. Dept. of Justice, 950 F.2d at 461, in which an FBI agent (Ryan) refused to investigate a pacifist group based upon his religious beliefs. Although another agent volunteered to swap assignments, Ryan refused. In a confusing decision, the court was apparently upset that Ryan simply refused an assignment based upon religious grounds and proposed only one accommodation—that he be excused from working on any assignment that clashed with his religious beliefs. In turn, the court held that any accommodation would have posed an undue burden on the FBI, even though Ryan's colleagues had successfully swapped assignments with him during earlier conflicts.

34. Cooper v. Oak Rubber Co., 15 F.3d 1375, 1379 (6th Cir. 1994), citing EEOC v. University of Detroit, 904 F.2d 331, 335 (6th Cir. 1990). *See also* EEOC v. Universal Mfg. Co., 914 F.2d 71, 73 (5th Cir. 1990); Wright v. Runyon, 2 F.3d at 217; EEOC v. IBP, 824 F. Supp. at 152. *But see* Lee v. ABF Freight System, Inc., 22 F.3d 1019, 1023 n.4 (10th Cir. 1994) (refusing to decide "whether a reasonable accommodation is one which must completely eliminate the employee's conflict").

35. Cooper v. Oak Rubber, 15 F.3d at 1379.

shifts with another worker; *but* the employee believes it is a sin to solicit someone else to work on the Sabbath. Three courts, including the Sixth Circuit, have held that permitting the employee to arrange his or her own shift swaps in this circumstance is not a reasonable accommodation, since it does not obviate all religious conflicts. The employer must also take it upon itself to ask its other employees if they are willing to swap shifts, as long as doing so does not impose an undue hardship on the employer. Absent this additional effort, the employer fails to fully accommodate the employee.[36]

Other situations in which an employer accommodated only one of several religious conflicts presented by an employee and consequently failed to provide a reasonable accommodation include:

- An employee requested seven days of unpaid leave to allow her to attend seven days of religious observances by the Worldwide Church of God. Based upon her religious beliefs, the employee both had to attend the festival *and* refrain from working at any time during its celebration. The employer offered a choice of two accommodations: (1) five working days off, or (2) seven working days off, but only if the employee worked one shift within the seven-day period. Thus, the employer offered only to accommodate the employee's request to attend the festival during her normal working hours, but did not permit the employee to miss work all week. The employee refused both options, attended the celebration, and was terminated. The Fifth Circuit found in favor of

---

36. *See* Smith v. Pyro Min. Co., 827 F.2d 1081, 1088 (6th Cir. 1987), *cert. denied,* 485 U.S. 989 (1988); EEOC v. IBP, 824 F. Supp. at 152; EEOC v. J.P. Stevens and Co., 740 F. Supp. 1135, 1138-39 (M.D.N.C. 1990). This situation is different than a case in which an employee refuses to work on his or her Sabbath, is permitted by the employer to ask other employees to swap shifts, does *not* have a religious objection to arranging shift swaps with other employees, but believes that the employer should actively assist him or her in finding a replacement. In this circumstance, one court of appeals held that the employer was not obligated to do more than permit the plaintiff to request shift swaps with other employees. Beadle v. Hillsborough County Sheriff's Dept., 29 F.3d 589 (11th Cir. 1994), *cert. denied,* 514 U.S. 1128 (1995).

the employee because the employer should have, but did not, seek to accommodate both of her religious needs.[37]

- A professor at a University objected to paying union dues and associating in any way with a union because it supported pro-abortion activities. To accommodate the professor's objection to paying union dues, the union offered to reduce the dues by the percentage that supported pro-abortion activities. The union, however, did not offer to accommodate the professor's association claim. The professor refused the partial accommodation offered by the union, and was terminated. The Sixth Circuit held that the lower court's decision incorrectly excused the union from making any effort to accommodate the professor's association claim.[38]

Summary

- The employer need offer only one reasonable accommodation.
- The accommodation offered by the employer must accommodate *every* religious conflict raised by the employee, unless doing so causes an undue hardship.
- The employer need not accept an employee's recommended accommodation, even if it is reasonable and even if it is less costly to the employee.
- If the employer *fails* to propose a reasonable accommodation that eliminates the religious conflict, the employer *must* accept the proposal proffered by the employee if it is reasonable and does not cause an undue hardship.

---

37. EEOC v. Universal Mfg., 914 F.2d at 73. The court remanded to permit the district court to determine whether providing each accommodation sought by the employee would have resulted in an undue burden. It noted that "[t]he Supreme Court has never held that the question of 'reasonable' accommodation focuses upon the number of conflicts or even upon the proportion of a single conflict eliminated by the employer's offer of accommodation." *Id.*

38. EEOC v. Univ. of Detroit, 904 F.2d 331 (6th Cir. 1990). The court noted that "the employer was confronted with two religious objections, one of which was completely ignored." *Id.* at 335. The case was remanded to the district court to determine whether it was feasible to accommodate each of the professor's objections. *See also* Cooper v. Oak Rubber Co., 15 F.3d at 1379. For a complete discussion of religious objections to the payment of union dues, see Chapter 10.

CHAPTER 8

What Accommodations Are Considered Reasonable?

Over the years, the courts and the Equal Employment Opportunity Commission (EEOC) have recognized that there are several common workplace mechanisms through which an employer may (or must) provide a reasonable accommodation of religious practices. This chapter describes common accommodations that the courts have deemed reasonable.

EEOC Guidelines on Religious Discrimination

The EEOC's Guidelines on Discrimination Because of Religion suggest three common methods for accommodating conflicts between an employer's work schedule and an employee's religious needs:[1]

1) Voluntary substitution and "swaps" of work assignments between employees.
2) Flexible scheduling of work hours, breaks, and holiday leave.
3) Lateral transfers of employees with religious conflicts to different assignments or locations.

While the courts have embraced these accommodations in various contexts, they have not always done so in the precise way suggested by the EEOC. The courts have also devised other accommodations appropriate to

1. 29 C.F.R. § 1605.2(d) (reprinted at Appendix B). These accommodation provisions of the Guidelines have been cited approvingly by the courts. *See, e.g.*, EEOC v. Ithaca Indus., 849 F.2d 116, 119 (4th Cir. 1988), *cert. denied*, 488 U.S. 929 (1988).

the circumstances of different workplaces. The reasonableness of an accommodation will obviously vary from situation to situation, and the case law reflects this fact.

Permitting Use of Leave Without Pay or Accrued Paid Leave

When an employee cannot work on particular days because of religious conflicts, the courts frequently approve accommodations that provide the employee with leave without pay or use of accrued paid leave—unless the employee's absence would impose an undue hardship upon the employer.[2]

In *Ansonia Board of Education v. Philbrook*,[3] the Supreme Court concluded that the provision of unpaid leave is a reasonable accommodation:

> The provision of unpaid leave eliminates the conflict between employment requirements and religious practices by allowing the individual to observe fully religious holy days and requires him only to give up compensation for a day that he did not in fact work.[4]

The Supreme Court's approval of unpaid leave leads to an interesting disparity in the treatment of employers and employees. Unpaid leave is routinely approved as an accommodation, even though it can impose a significant financial impact upon the employee; at the same time, anything greater than a de minimis expenditure by an employer is considered an undue hardship under *Trans World Airlines, Inc. v. Hardison*.[5] In effect, the Court has interpreted Title VII to give primary importance to an employer's economic interests; a cost that is an undue hardship when

---

2. *See, e.g.,* Smith v. United Refining Co., 21 FEP 1481, 1484-87 (W.D. Pa. 1980) (where plaintiff was only employee with necessary skills, his absence from work to attend religious event created undue hardship).

3. 479 U.S. 60 (1986).

4. *Id.* at 70 (1986). The Court continued, "Generally speaking, 'the direct effect of unpaid leave is merely a loss of income for the period the employee is not at work; such an exclusion has no direct effect upon either employment opportunities or job status.'" *Id.* at 70-71 (*quoting* Nashville Gas Co. v. Satty, 434 U.S. 136, 145 (1977)). However, the Court cautioned employers that refusing to provide paid leave as an accommodation would be discriminatory "when paid leave is provided for all purposes except religious ones." 479 U.S. at 71. This, the Court stated, "would display a discrimination against religious practices that is the antithesis of reasonableness." *Id.*

5. 432 U.S. 63, 84 (1977).

borne by the employer may nevertheless be reasonable when paid by the employee.[6]

As originally promulgated, the EEOC Guidelines suggested that such a disparity in the apportionment of economic costs was not appropriate. The Guidelines provided that, when there is more than one accommodation that does not cause undue hardship, the Commission will evaluate whether the accommodation offered by the employer is reasonable by examining:

> (i) The alternatives for accommodation considered by the employer . . . and

> (ii) The alternatives for accommodation, if any, actually offered to the individual requiring accommodation. Some alternatives for accommodating religious practices might disadvantage the individual with respect to his or her employment opportunities, such as compensation, terms, conditions, or privileges of employment. Therefore, when there is more than one means of accommodation which would not cause undue hardship, the employer or labor organization *must offer* the *alternative* which *least disadvantages* the individual with respect to his or her employment opportunities.[7]

To the extent that the Guidelines require an employer to accept the accommodation that "least disadvantages" the employee, they have been overruled by the Supreme Court's holding in *Ansonia* that an employer is not required to offer more than one reasonable accommodation and is not obligated to offer the employee's preferred resolution.[8] However, in a policy statement issued after the *Ansonia* decision, the Commission asserted that the Guidelines are consistent with *Ansonia* because they do not require the employer to provide any alternative favored by the employee:

> The Guidelines should be consulted when determining the reasonableness of an accommodation offered by an employer. Whether a particular religious accommodation is reasonable must be determined on a case by case basis. Where leave of absence for secular pur-

---

6. *Compare* Ansonia v. Philbrook, 479 U.S. at 70-71, *with* TWA v. Hardison, 432 U.S. at 84.

7. 29 C.F.R. § 1605.2(c)(2) (emphasis added).

8. Ansonia v. Philbrook, 479 U.S. at 69 n.6.

poses is granted more liberally than for religious purposes the accommodation is not reasonable. Where the burden on an employee's employment status is more than de minimis or inconsequential an accommodation is unreasonable.[9]

Whether the EEOC is accurate in its assessment of *Ansonia* and the survival of its Guidelines is questionable—especially with respect to its warning that an accommodation imposing more than a de minimis cost on the *employee* is unreasonable. In *Ansonia,* the Supreme Court held that a loss of three days' pay to an employee was an acceptable cost to be borne by the employee, without endangering the reasonableness of the accommodation. That is certainly more than a de minimis cost to a teacher. In other words, an accommodation is not made unreasonable merely because it involves a significant loss of pay for the employee. In the Supreme Court's view, requiring an employee to take unpaid leave for a day he or she did not work is generally reasonable.[10] The loss of pay does not compromise an employee's "employment opportunities or job status."[11]

The case law subsequent to the EEOC's 1988 Policy Statement suggests that the EEOC has not vigorously litigated the accommodation principles enunciated in the Statement. The courts seem to have paid it no heed whatsoever. Employers and employees are probably safe in applying the principles of *Ansonia* without the qualifications implied by the EEOC Policy Statement.

Consistent with the Supreme Court's approval of leave without pay as a reasonable accommodation, the lower courts have also approved employer policies that permit employees to apply accrued annual leave (or other paid leave) to religious absences.[12] Again, the fact that these policies

---

9. EEOC Policy Statement on Religious Accommodation Under Title VII (May 9, 1988) (reprinted at Appendix B).

10. Ansonia v. Philbrook, 479 U.S. at 70.

11. *Id.* at 70–71. *Cf.* Cooper v. Oak Rubber Co., 15 F.3d 1375, 1379 (6th Cir. 1994) (accommodation that requires employee to use up all vacation leave for religious purposes is not reasonable, but employer still prevails because all alternatives impose more than de minimis costs on employer).

12. *Ansonia* stands for the proposition that an employer cannot be compelled to permit employees to use paid leave for religious observances if it has an established nondiscriminatory policy that limits the type of paid leave that is permitted. It must be emphasized again, however, that a leave policy that singles out religious observances for harsher treatment is discriminatory. 479 U.S. at 71.

have a negative impact on the employee (i.e., reduction in the number of paid leave days available for nonreligious purposes) does not render them unreasonable.

Situations in which the use of accrued leave or unpaid leave have been deemed a reasonable accommodation include:

- A teacher's one-week absence from school without pay to attend the week-long Feast of Tabernacles was reasonable and would not cause the employer to suffer an undue hardship.[13]
- A company should have considered whether staff assistant, who needed to leave work early on Fridays for Sabbath observance, would have accepted a reduction in salary to cover the lost hours.[14]
- An Orthodox Jewish woman who was required to refrain from work on thirteen days during the year, only some of which fell on workdays, was provided reasonable accommodation through use of personal and annual leave.[15]

However, one circuit court has indicated that there may be limits to the economic costs that can be shifted to the employee when leave without pay or accrued annual leave is offered as an accommodation for religious absences. In *Cooper v. Oak Rubber Company*,[16] the Sixth Circuit held

---

13. Wangsness v. Watertown School District, 541 F. Supp. 332 (D.S.D. 1982). *See also* Heller v. EBB Auto Co., 8 F.3d 1433 (9th Cir. 1993) (used car dealership failed to provide a reasonable accommodation when it rescinded its earlier decision to approve leave for a Jewish employee to attend his wife's conversion ceremony; dealership was unable to show that accommodating the employee would have caused undue hardship); Man-of-Jerusalem v. Hill, 769 F. Supp. 97 (E.D.N.Y. 1991) (leave without pay for religious observance was reasonable); Edwards v. School Board of the City of Norton, 483 F. Supp. 620 (W.D. Va. 1980) (school board failed to provide a reasonable accommodation when it refused to approve the absence of a teacher's aide during the Feast of Tabernacles); *judgment vacated in part on other grounds,* 658 F.2d 951 (4th Cir. 1981).

14. Gordon v. MCI Telecommunications Corp., 791 F. Supp. 431 (S.D.N.Y. 1992). *See also* Pinsker v. Joint Dist. No. 28J, 735 F.2d 388, 390–91 (10th Cir. 1984) (school district offered a reasonable accommodation to Jewish teacher through two days of paid leave and one day of unpaid leave for observance of Jewish holidays).

15. Getz v. Pennsylvania, 802 F.2d 72 (3d Cir. 1986) (even after taking leave, plaintiff still had nearly three weeks of paid leave remaining after observing religious holidays). *See also* United States v. Albuquerque, 545 F.2d 110, 114 (10th Cir. 1976), *cert. denied,* 433 U.S. 909 (1977) (permitting an employee to take annual leave or leave without pay is a reasonable accommodation).

16. 15 F.3d 1375.

that it is not a reasonable accommodation to require an employee to use all paid leave to avoid working on the Sabbath: "Such an employee stands to lose a benefit, vacation time, enjoyed by all other employees who do not share the same religious conflict, and is thus discriminated against with respect to a privilege of employment."[17] The court nevertheless held for the employer because all possible reasonable accommodations would have resulted in an undue hardship.

Temporary Scheduling Changes or Shift Swaps

Scheduling changes and shift swaps between employees are two ways employers can accommodate employees who seek leave for religious reasons. The EEOC's Guidelines on Religious Discrimination expressly provide for voluntary substitutes and shift swaps, as long as the substitute has "substantially similar qualifications" as the person for whom he or she is substituting.[18] In *TWA v. Hardison*,[19] the Supreme Court noted with approval that TWA had asked the union to search for another employee who would be willing to swap shifts with Hardison.

The Guidelines also state that, rather than leave the procuring of a substitute solely to the individual seeking an accommodation, the employer must facilitate the securing of a substitute. The Guidelines provide that employers should (1) publicize policies regarding accommodation and substitution, (2) promote an atmosphere in which substitutions are favorably regarded, and (3) provide a means for matching voluntary

---

17. *Id.* at 1379. The court did not explain whether an employee's use of an equal number of days of leave without pay (as in *Ansonia*) would be different from using accrued vacation leave. In an interesting case that went beyond the use of leave, a district court concluded that an employer failed to provide a reasonable accommodation to a pilot who refused to fly on his Sabbath because it failed to consider the only feasible accommodation: an extended leave of absence that would have provided the employee with additional seniority. Kendall v. United Air Lines, 494 F. Supp. 1380, 1391 (N.D. Ill. 1980). However, in a later proceeding to determine the appropriate remedy, the court determined that the pilot would require leave for a number of years to achieve sufficient seniority, thereby violating the collective-bargaining agreement and requiring a costly training program upon his return to service. Kendall v. United Air Lines, 28 FEP 948 (N.D. Ill. 1981). Consequently, the pilot was not awarded any compensation or other remedy.

18. 29 C.F.R. § 1605.2(d)(1)(i).

19. 432 U.S. 63.

substitutes with positions for which substitutes are required (for example, bulletin boards, central files, and so forth).[20]

The EEOC Guidelines also state that flexible work schedules, including the following, may provide a reasonable accommodation of employees' religious practices:[21]

- flexible arrival and departure times,
- floating or optional holidays,
- flexible work breaks,
- use of lunch time in exchange for early departure,
- staggered work hours, and
- allowing employees to make up time lost due to religious observance.

For the most part, the lower courts have held that employers must explore scheduling changes and shift swaps as a reasonable accommodation, limited only by proof that doing so creates an undue hardship. For example, in *Opuku-Boateng v. State of California*,[22] the plaintiff applied for a position as a Plant Quarantine Inspector. All such inspectors were required to work an equal number of undesirable shifts, including weekends, holidays, and nights. Although the plaintiff notified the State that he was unable to work on Saturdays, his Sabbath, he received no accommodation and ultimately was terminated.

The trial court ruled in favor of the State's decision to dismiss the employee, but the Ninth Circuit reversed. The court of appeals determined that a schedule could have been arranged for the plaintiff that did not include Saturday work.[23] This arrangement would not discriminate against other employees or provide the plaintiff with preferential treatment because the plaintiff (by working more shifts on nights, Sundays,

---

20. 29 C.F.R. § 1605.2(d)(1)(i). This does not mean that the employer itself is always required to actually contact employees to determine if they are willing to substitute. *See* Beadle v. Hillsborough County Sheriff's Dept., 29 F.3d 589, 593 (11th Cir. 1994), *cert. denied,* 514 U.S. 1128 (1995) (employer need only give employee access to means of locating a substitute; employer is not obligated to take any further affirmative steps).

21. 29 C.F.R. § 1605.2(d)(1)(ii).

22. 95 F.3d 1461 (9th Cir. 1996), *cert. denied,* 117 S.Ct. 1819 (1997).

23. *Id.* at 1470–71.

and holidays) would still work an equal number of undesirable shifts as the other employees (who would simply trade one undesirable shift for another).[24]

The circuit court also ruled that the State could have easily created a voluntary shift-trade system.[25] Such a system would be set up by creating a calendar, arriving at the number of Saturday shifts the plaintiff would be assigned, and then asking other employees whether they would trade a Sunday, holiday, or evening for one of the plaintiff's Saturday shifts.[26]

Other examples where shift trades or schedule changes were recognized as reasonable accommodations include:

- Two Jewish beauty-salon employees requested, but were denied, leave for Yom Kippur (which fell on a Saturday, arguably the salon's busiest day of the week). The employees failed to appear for work and were terminated. The Seventh Circuit upheld a district court's decision finding that the salon could have accommodated the employees by allowing them to reschedule their appointments and not work on Yom Kippur.[27]
- An employee refused to work overtime on Sundays, his Sabbath, and was fired. The court of appeals held against the employer because it failed to (1) look to other shifts to fill the position, (2) inform the employee to find a qualified substitute, or (3) permit use of the company bulletin board for substitute requests.[28]

---

24. *Id.* at 1471–73.

25. *Id.* at 1469, 1471.

26. *Id.* at 1472.

27. EEOC v. Ilona of Hungary, Inc., 108 F.3d 1569, 1576–77 (7th Cir. 1997). The court specifically found that the salon would not suffer financially if it rescheduled the appointments.

28. EEOC v. Ithaca Industries, 849 F.2d 116, 119 (4th Cir. 1988). *See also* Smith v. Pyro Mining Co., 827 F.2d 1081, 1088 (6th Cir. 1986), *cert. denied,* 485 U.S. 989 (1988) (recognizing that one manner of reasonable accommodation includes trading work shifts if both employees are qualified); Protos v. Volkswagen of America, 797 F.2d 129, 134–35 (3d Cir.), *cert. denied,* 479 U.S. 972 (1986) (cost to employer of providing substitute on Saturday for mandatory overtime was de minimis when efficiency, production, quality, and morale were not affected, and higher wages not required).

- An employer that has no procedure whereby plaintiff could arrange on his own for a substitute or shift swap is required to make arrangements for a substitute, especially since the employer had used substitutes for nonreligious employee absences.[29]

This last decision reflects the view of most courts (and the EEOC) that an employer must take an active role in arranging a shift swap or substitute for an employee with a religious conflict. How active that role must be, however, is not entirely clear. In *Beadle v. Hillsborough County Sheriff's Department*,[30] the Eleventh Circuit held that the employer offered a reasonable accommodation to an employee who could not work on Saturdays when it provided him with a roster of the other employees' work schedules and permitted him to advertise the need for a voluntary shift swap at daily roll calls and on the employer's bulletin board. However, the court held that the employer was *not* required to provide more active assistance in locating a substitute for the employee.[31]

Finally, the foregoing examples all involve *voluntary* shift swaps and scheduling changes. The courts virtually never *impose* such swaps or changes upon unwilling employees, finding that one employee should not have to suffer changes in working conditions in order to accommodate another employee's religious needs.[32]

---

29. Redmond v. GAF Corp., 574 F.2d 897, 903 (7th Cir. 1978). *See also* EEOC v. Universal Mfg. Co., 914 F.2d 71, 74 (5th Cir. 1990) (allowing an employee to swap shifts may have been a reasonable accommodation for an employee who requested not to work for one week); Brener v. Diagnostic Center Hosp., 671 F.2d 141 (5th Cir. 1982) (employer reasonably accommodated employee by allowing voluntary shift swaps); Hudson v. Western Airlines, 851 F.2d 261 (9th Cir. 1988) (same); United States v. City of Albuquerque, 545 F.2d 110 (10th Cir. 1976), *cert. denied,* 433 U.S. 909 (1977) (same); Boomsma v. Greyhound Food Management, 639 F. Supp. 1448, 1454 (W.D. Mich. 1986) (employer failed to reasonably accommodate employee when it refused his suggestion that he be permitted to find a qualified substitute); Miller v. Drennon, 56 FEP 274, 279 (D.S.C. 1991), *aff'd,* 966 F.2d 1443 (4th Cir. 1992) (employer satisfied its duty to reasonably accommodate a medical technician when, among other things, it provided him with a list of other employees with whom he could swap shifts).

30. 29 F.3d 589 (11th Cir. 1994), *cert. denied,* 514 U.S. 1128 (1995).

31. *Id.* at 593.

32. This issue is discussed further as a component of "undue hardship" in Chapter 9.

Job Swaps Between Employees or Transfer to New Positions

Schedule changes and shift substitutes are often only temporary solutions to ad hoc problems. In an effort to provide more permanent accommodations, employers may offer employees the opportunity either to swap jobs with a colleague or to transfer to a new position.[33] The EEOC's Guidelines on Discrimination Because of Religion provide:

> Lateral Transfer and Change of Job Assignments.
>
> When an employee cannot be accommodated either as to his or her entire job or an assignment within the job, employers and labor organizations should consider whether or not it is possible to change the job assignment or give the employee a lateral transfer.[34]

The most important aspect of this form of accommodation is that at least two circuit courts have held that the failure to consider the possibility of permanently transferring an employee to a new job or geographic location will be used as evidence of a failure to accommodate.[35] An employer that takes an adverse action against an employee without considering this accommodation option runs the risk of an adverse judicial ruling.

Another important consideration is that, notwithstanding the EEOC's preferences for a "lateral" transfer, many courts have permitted employers to reassign individuals to positions that involve lower pay and lesser responsibilities.[36] The Eighth Circuit has also held that an employer

---

33. *See* TWA v. Hardison, 432 U.S. at 77 (the Court noted approvingly that TWA attempted to find Hardison a new position); Breech v. Alabama Power Co., 962 F. Supp. 1447 (S.D. Ala. 1997) (offering an employee the opportunity to swap jobs and shifts satisfied the employer's burden to provide a reasonable accommodation).

34. 29 C.F.R. § 1605.2(d)(1)(iii).

35. *See* Redmond v. GAF Corp., 574 F.2d at 903 (the company's failure to discuss the possibility of transferring the plaintiff to another warehouse or to another job to eliminate the religious conflict contributed to the court's finding that it made no effort to accommodate the plaintiff); Opuku-Boateng v. California, 95 F.3d at 1474-75 (the failure to provide the plaintiff with a temporary accommodation during which time both employer and employee could have explored reassignment contributed to a finding that the State failed to offer a reasonable accommodation).

36. Breech v. Alabama Power Co., 962 F. Supp. 1447, 1460 (S.D. Ala. 1997) (employer offered a reasonable accommodation when it offered the plaintiff the opportunity to move to another position with lesser responsibilities and lower pay); Mathewson v.

could properly offer an employee a transfer to a different job site where there was less likelihood of a conflict between the work schedule and the employee's Sabbath, even though the transfer may have reduced the employee's chances for a promotion.[37] Conversely, the Sixth Circuit affirmed a district court's decision that an employer failed to accommodate an employee when it refused to demote him to a position that did not conflict with his Sabbath.[38] These decisions confirm that a "reasonable" accommodation may still exact a heavy economic toll on employees.[39]

Apart from the use of job transfers to accommodate conflicts with an employee's religious observances, a variant of this accommodation may also be appropriate when an employee has religious objections to a particular job assignment. However, in the several cases presenting this issue, the courts have split in their approach. In *Haring v. Blumenthal*,[40] an Internal Revenue Service reviewer of applications from organizations seeking tax-exempt status objected to reviewing applications from organizations that favored the right to an abortion. This work constituted less than 2 percent of the employee's workload, leading the court to rule that he could have been accommodated by reassigning those tasks to other supervisors who did not have religious objections.[41]

The Seventh Circuit came to a different conclusion on similar facts in *Ryan v. United States Department of Justice*.[42] There, an FBI agent refused

---

Florida Game & Fresh Water Fish Comm'n, 693 F. Supp. 1044, 1050 (M.D. Fla. 1988), *aff'd mem.*, 871 F.2d 123 (11th Cir. 1989) (employer offered a reasonable accommodation when it offered an employee reassignment to a lower position, but without reduced pay).

37. Mann v. Milgram Food Stores, 730 F.2d 1186 (8th Cir. 1984).

38. EEOC v. Sterling Merchandising Co., 46 FEP 1448, 1454 (N.D. Ohio 1987), *aff'd,* 845 F.2d 325 (6th Cir. 1988).

39. *But see* Cook v. Lindsay Olive Growers, 911 F.2d 233, 241 (9th Cir. 1990), wherein the court held that the transfer of an employee to a lesser position was reasonable in light of the fact that the employer had previously exhausted consideration of other accommodations that did not entail adverse consequences to the employee. This decision is one of the few that are consistent with the statement in the EEOC Guidelines that employers should first explore the least onerous accommodations before settling upon a final accommodation.

40. 471 F. Supp. 1172 (D.D.C. 1979), *cert. denied,* 452 U.S. 939, *reh'g denied,* 453 U.S. 927 (1981).

41. *Id.* at 1180.

42. 950 F.2d 458 (7th Cir. 1991), *cert. denied,* 504 U.S. 958 (1992).

to investigate certain pacifist groups on religious grounds. Although the plaintiff had previously traded assignments with other agents, the court refused to compel the Bureau to reassign the plaintiff's investigations to other agents; it came to this conclusion without any consideration of the percentage of plaintiff's workload that was devoted to the objectionable investigations. The circuit court was apparently influenced by the need for discipline in law-enforcement agencies and the negative impact on discipline if individual agents could veto particular work assignments.[43]

Interestingly, subsequent to *Ryan,* a district court in Chicago held that the City's police department could accommodate an officer's objection to abortion-clinic details with shift changes, changes in starting times, use of paid and unpaid leave or permitting him to apply for a different position in the department.[44] However, the court held that the department was not obligated to grant the officer an exemption from such assignments, even though the other accommodations would functionally produce the same result.[45]

Relaxation of Clothing and Personal Grooming Codes

Grooming conflicts have not been the subject of much litigation.[46] They typically involve a clash between an employee who wears a beard or special clothing for religious reasons and a company policy that demands conformity in appearance or apparel. As discussed in Chapter 9, if the employer can present legitimate evidence that safety or health will be compromised, the courts have concluded that the employer need not accommodate the employee. On the other hand, if the grooming or apparel rule is justified by nothing more than a desire for a uniform or

---

43. *Id.* at 461–62. See discussion in Chapter 9 relating to the courts' general reluctance to interfere in the operations of law enforcement agencies.

44. Rodriguez v. City of Chicago, 975 F. Supp. 1055 (N.D. Ill. 1997).

45. *Id.* at 1059, citing Ansonia v. Philbrook, 479 U.S. at 68 (any reasonable accommodation is sufficient).

46. Interestingly, many of these cases have arisen in the public sector, where both the First Amendment and Title VII apply. These cases are discussed separately in Chapter 9.

"professional" appearance, employers are often found liable for failing to offer the employee a reasonable accommodation. When this occurs, the most common accommodation is simply to permit the employee to continue the grooming or apparel without limitation.[47]

In one unusual case, at least with respect to remedy, the court acted upon an application for a preliminary injunction and ordered Electronic Data Systems (EDS) to rehire the plaintiff prior to trial.[48] The plaintiff, a Jewish computer programmer, asserted that his religion compelled him to wear a beard. The employer prohibited any employee from wearing a beard. When the plaintiff refused to shave his beard, he was terminated. According to the district court, EDS was unable to present any evidence that accommodating the plaintiff would impose an undue hardship upon the company. Moreover, EDS had permitted employees of other religious backgrounds (for example, Sikhs) to wear beards. The court ruled that the plaintiff was likely to succeed on the merits. Since the plaintiff was a computer programmer and worked in a field of constant change, the court also found that he would be irreparably harmed through a loss of job skills if he was unemployed until a full trial on the merits.[49]

---

47. *See* Carter v. Bruce Oakley, Inc., 849 F. Supp. 673, 676 (E.D. Ark. 1993) (the employer failed to demonstrate that it would suffer an undue burden by permitting the plaintiff to wear his beard; contrary to the employer's assertions, the beard did not pose a safety risk and looked "professional"); Karriem v. Oliver T. Carr Co., 38 FEP 882 (D.D.C. 1985) (Title VII prohibits employer from terminating a security guard merely because he insisted on wearing a religious pin that was between a quarter and a half dollar in diameter and that was not obtrusive); EEOC Dec. *81-20,* 27 FEP 1809 (1981) (employer required to permit employee to wear skirt instead of pants). *See also* EEOC v. United Parcel Service, 94 F.3d 314 (7th Cir. 1996) (appeals court reversed summary judgment against plaintiff who wore a beard in violation of the employer's policy because facts were disputed regarding whether employer could offer a reasonable accommodation without undue hardship).

The one significant exception to this rule is found in EEOC v. Sambo's of Georgia, Inc., 530 F. Supp. 86 (N.D. Ga. 1981), in which the court held that a Sikh employee's refusal to shave could not be accommodated; the employee managed a restaurant and the court believed his beard adversely affected the restaurant's public image. Given the cases discussed above, the decision in *Sambo's* is difficult, if not impossible, to defend and should probably be viewed as an aberration.

48. EEOC v. Electronic Data Systems, 31 FEP 588 (W.D. Wash. 1983).

49. *Id.* at 590.

Accommodating Employee Speech or Proselytizing

Employers occasionally confront employees who assert their right to discuss or pronounce their religious beliefs at work. Absent concrete proof that such speech disrupts the business or creates a hostile workplace, the courts have permitted the speech to proceed:[50]

- A supervisor who infrequently and spontaneously allowed prayers in his office during meetings, affirmed his Christianity, and referred to Bible passages related to slothfulness and work ethics, could not be disciplined when such statements had no provable impact upon other employees or the work of the office.[51]
- Food-service workers at a General Motors plant could greet customers with phrases such as "God bless you" and "Praise the Lord" without retribution because the employer failed to demonstrate that it lost any business, the complaint rate was less than .02 percent of customers, and any other loss was speculative.[52]

An interesting variation on this issue is found in *EEOC v. Townley Engineering & Manufacturing Company*.[53] In this case the *employer* (not the employee) proselytized, holding mandatory devotional services in the workplace. The court held that the employer could excuse the plaintiff from attending the services without affecting the efficiency of the business or other employees. The court found that there would be no undue hardship in excusing the employee from participating in these prayers, thereby separating the business functions from the religious services. The court rejected the proposal by the plaintiff's supervisor that he sleep or read during the service, although this proposal did show that failure to attend the religious exercises would not lead to undue hardship.[54]

---

50. Examples of situations where proselytizing has been found to create an undue hardship are discussed in Chapter 9 (private sector) and Chapter 11 (public sector).

51. Brown v. Polk County, Iowa, 61 F.3d 650, 656-57 (8th Cir. 1995), *cert. denied,* 516 U.S. 1158 (1996).

52. Banks v. Service America Corp., 952 F. Supp. 703 (D. Kan. 1996).

53. 859 F.2d 610 (9th Cir. 1988), *cert. denied,* 489 U.S. 1077 (1989).

54. *Id.* at 615-16. *See also* Young v. Southwestern Savings and Loan Ass'n, 509 F.2d 140 (5th Cir. 1975) (employer could accommodate employee's religious objection to opening prayers at staff meetings; employee could absent herself during that portion of meeting).

Summary

- Where appropriate, employers must consider the following accommodations to resolve conflicts between work requirements and religious beliefs or practices:
  a) Permitting employees to voluntarily swap shifts and/or assignments.
  b) Flexible scheduling of hours of work and leave.
  c) Transfers of employees to different duties or locations.
  d) Permitting employees to use unpaid leave or accrued paid leave for absences due to religious needs.
  e) Relaxation of grooming and clothing requirements.
- If an employer offers one or more of the foregoing accommodations and doing so obviates the conflict between work and religion, then the courts will deem such accommodation(s) reasonable.
- An employer may accommodate an employee's religious proselytizing activities by permitting the activities to continue so long as they do not interfere in the operations of the business, do not impair customer relations, and do not create an harassing or hostile work environment.

✱ CHAPTER 9

What Is an Undue Hardship?

TWA v. Hardison

Title VII provides that an employer must reasonably accommodate an employee's religious beliefs unless doing so causes an "undue hardship." This requirement is set forth in the definition section of Title VII:

> The term "religion" includes all aspects of religious observance and practice, as well as belief, unless an employer demonstrates that he is unable to reasonably accommodate to an employee's or prospective employee's religious observance or practice without undue hardship on the conduct of the employer's business.[1]

Although the definition of undue hardship is critical to determining whether an employee is entitled to an accommodation, the statute does not define the term. Moreover, its legislative history offers no assistance.

Ultimately, in *Trans World Airlines, Inc. v. Hardison*,[2] the Supreme Court was presented with a case that required it to define undue hardship. Hardison worked as a clerk in a supply department at TWA's maintenance and overhaul facility in Kansas City, Missouri. The department was open 24 hours per day, each day of the year, and its work was deemed critical to the operation of the entire Kansas City facility. Whenever an employee in the supply department was absent, another employee or supervisor was moved from his or her own department to the supply department. Employees at the facility were covered by a seniority system contained in a collective bargaining agreement.

---

1. 42 U.S.C. § 2000e(j).
2. 432 U.S. 63 (1977).

During his employment, Hardison became a member of the Worldwide Church of God and refused to work Saturdays, his Sabbath. Initially, Hardison was accommodated through a shift transfer that enabled him to observe his Sabbath. Hardison then bid for and received a transfer to a new position. In this new position, however, he did not have sufficient seniority to avoid assignments on his Sabbath.

When Hardison was asked to work on a Saturday to replace a fellow employee who was on vacation, he objected. Although TWA agreed to allow the union to seek a change in work assignments, the union refused to do so because Hardison did not have sufficient seniority to bid for another shift under the seniority provisions of the collective bargaining agreement. TWA also attempted to place Hardison in another job, but without success.

After Hardison refused to work on Saturdays, he was terminated. He then sued TWA and the union, alleging religious discrimination in violation of Title VII. TWA argued that Hardison's job was essential and that supply functions critical to airline operations would be compromised if he was absent on Saturdays. TWA also contended that replacing Hardison with a worker from another department would understaff other operations and that employing someone not scheduled for Saturday work would require the payment of premium wages.

After defendants prevailed at the district court, the court of appeals reversed. It held that TWA could have reasonably accommodated Hardison by permitting him to work four days a week and by using a substitute employee for the fifth day, even though the replacement employee's original job duties would suffer. The court also concluded that TWA could have filled Hardison's Saturday shift with another employee by paying premium wages. Finally, TWA could have arranged a shift swap.

The Supreme Court disagreed with the court of appeals on all grounds. In its view, each of the suggested accommodations imposed an undue hardship upon TWA. The Court's initial task was to define "undue hardship," which it interpreted to mean anything "more than a de minimis cost."[3]

Much of the Court's decision addresses the conflicts between Hardison's proposed accommodations and the collective bargaining agreement. The Court stated that the seniority system "represented a significant

---

3. *Id.* at 84.

accommodation to the needs, both religious and secular, of all of TWA's employees. . . . [It] represents a neutral way of minimizing the number of occasions when an employee must work on a day that he would prefer to have off."[4] The Court then held that the duty to accommodate does not override a company's obligation to comply with the seniority provisions of a valid collective bargaining agreement.[5] Conversely, an employer may not violate the terms of such an agreement in order to accommodate an employee. The Court was unwilling to infer that a collectively bargained seniority system was subordinate to the religious needs of an employee. In reaching this conclusion, the Court emphasized the need to preserve the contractual rights (for example, shift and job preferences) of other employees who would be affected by Hardison's proposed accommodations. The Court believed that any other result would run counter to national labor policy.[6]

The Court's deference to a bona fide seniority system finds its source in Title VII:

> Notwithstanding any other provision of this subchapter, it shall not be an unlawful employment practice for an employer to apply different standards of compensation, or different terms, conditions, or privileges of employment pursuant to a bona fide seniority or merit system . . . provided that such differences are not the result of an intention to discriminate because of race, color, religion, sex, or national origin. . . .[7]

The holding in *Hardison* applies this same exemption to accommodation claims.[8]

---

4. *Id.* at 78.

5. *Id.* at 79–83.

6. *Id.*

7. 42 U.S.C. § 2000e-2(h).

8. The Supreme Court recognized that TWA offered to accommodate Hardison by agreeing to a change of shifts or jobs if the union would agree. The union refused to do so because it would have violated the seniority provision of the collective bargaining agreement. The Court concluded that Title VII did not compel either TWA or the union to abrogate rights that had been collectively bargained, as long as the bargaining agreement was not adopted with a discriminatory purpose. 432 U.S. at 67–68, 82–83.

Although the Supreme Court was primarily concerned with the inviolability of the collective bargaining agreement, it also addressed the other accommodations suggested by the court of appeals. It held that the lower court erred by not recognizing the varied costs to TWA of accommodating Hardison: lost efficiency in jobs (by switching workers from their regular jobs to Hardison's job on Saturdays),[9] higher wages (by paying approximately $150 in premium wages for a Saturday replacement),[10] and discrimination against other employees (who would be required to work on Saturdays so that Hardison could observe his Sabbath).[11] The Court held that all of these actions would entail greater than de minimis cost. The Court also stated that reasonable accommodation does not require an employer to permit one employee to observe his Sabbath at the expense of the shift and job preferences of other employees or to deprive those employees of their rights under a collective bargaining agreement.[12]

The *Hardison* standard of de minimis cost clearly encompasses quantifiable monetary costs (for example, overtime payments), as well as less clearly quantifiable hardships, such as interference in the efficiency of a business' operations, adverse impacts on other employees, and violations of a collective bargaining agreement. The determination of nonmonetary "costs" often involves subjective judgments. Monetary hardships, on the other hand, would seem to have been reduced to little more than a trifle in light of *Hardison*'s holding that a $150 payment by TWA was an *undue* hardship. If an employer the size of TWA is not required to spend $150 in overtime, then there would seem to be little in the way of accommodation costs that would fail to exceed the Supreme Court's de minimis standard.

Given the outcome in *Hardison,* one might assume that there have been virtually no prevailing plaintiffs since that decision. In fact, such is not the case. For this reason, employers need to pay close attention to the lower-court decisions issued subsequent to *Hardison.*

---

9. *Id.* at 84.

10. The dissent observed that TWA would have suffered overtime costs of approximately $150 until Hardison obtained enough seniority to be eligible to transfer to a position that would have accommodated his Sabbath observance. *Id.* at 92 n.6.

11. *Id.* at 84–85.

12. *Id.* at 81, 83.

Undue Hardship May Not Be Speculative

Before addressing the different kinds of hardships that the courts have recognized or rejected, employers should be aware of considerable case law demanding that proof of a hardship be concrete, rather than speculative. For this reason, an employer runs a significant risk if it comes to court having made no offer of accommodation. As the Sixth Circuit has held, it will be "skeptical" of an employer who hypothesizes an undue hardship in the absence of proof that some effort at accommodation was made.[13]

The following are among the examples of court decisions holding that an employer's proof of hardship was too speculative:

- An employer that did not explore voluntary shift trades between plaintiff and other employees could not rely on "hypothetical morale problems" as an excuse not to accommodate.[14] The Ninth Circuit suggested it would be appropriate for employers to experiment with accommodation during a probationary period before declaring an undue hardship.[15]
- An employer did not prove undue hardship in accommodating an employee requesting leave on Friday afternoons for the Sabbath. The employer claimed it needed the employee to input payroll data, but failed to present proof that such work needed to be performed on Friday afternoons.[16]
- A school board's defense that students' education would suffer if a teacher was permitted religious observance was "speculative" and the "product of hindsight created in preparation for this trial."[17]

---

13. Draper v. United States Pipe & Foundry Co., 527 F.2d 515, 520 (6th Cir. 1975). *See also* Smith v. Pyro Mining Co., 827 F.2d 1081, 1085-86 (6th Cir. 1987), *cert. denied*, 485 U.S. 989 (1988).

14. Opuku-Boateng v. State of Cal., 95 F.3d 1461, 1473–74 (9th Cir. 1996), *cert. denied*, 117 S.Ct. 1819 (1997).

15. *Id.* at 1474–75.

16. Gordon v. MCI Telecommunications Corp., 59 FEP 1363, 1367 (S.D.N.Y. 1992).

17. Edwards v. City of Norton, Virginia, 483 F. Supp. 620, 627 (W.D. Va. 1980), *judgment vacated in part on other grounds*, 658 F.2d 951 (4th Cir. 1981).

■ A food-service company fired cafeteria workers who refused to cease saying "God bless you" or "Praise the Lord" to customers in the cafeteria line, claiming that these employees' conduct endangered relations with the customers. The court rejected the employer's defense because its fear that customers would "boycott" the cafeteria and that the company would suffer financially was more "hypothetical than real."[18]

In addition to the foregoing cases, a commonly heard refrain from employers is that they cannot accommodate employees because doing so will set a precedent that will snowball among other employees. The courts are generally unsympathetic to such claims, again because they are too speculative. The EEOC's Guidelines on Discrimination Because of Religion expressly provide that "a mere assumption that many more people, with the same religious practices as the person being accommodated, may also need accommodation is not evidence of undue hardship."[19]

In one district court case, the employer—a school district—was chastised by the court for its refusal to negotiate with a school teacher who believed in the tenets of the Worldwide Church of God.[20] The teacher sought a one-week leave of absence to attend the "Feast of Tabernacles." The court reviewed the school district's efforts to accommodate the teacher, and concluded that the school board "made it quite clear to [the plaintiff] that it did not intend to accommodate his religious beliefs."[21] One day after receiving notice of the teacher's request for an accommodation, the board wrote the teacher a letter stating that the request would be denied because, among other reasons, it would encourage other types of leave requests that could seriously affect the mission of the school. The court rejected the board's defense.[22]

Other courts, including several circuit courts, have similarly held that the argument against opening a floodgate of accommodation claims

---

18. Banks v. Service America Corp., 952 F. Supp. 703, 710 (D. Kan. 1996).
19. 29 C.F.R. § 1605.2(c).
20. Wangsness v. Watertown School Distr., 541 F. Supp. 332 (D.S.D. 1982).
21. *Id.* at 336.
22. *Id.* at 337.

cannot be sustained without concrete evidence; conjecture is not a substitute for proof.[23]

Frequently, employers will also oppose an accommodation because it will cause "grumbling" among coworkers who are not accorded similar flexibility in their schedules. Again, the courts are unsympathetic to such claims. As the Ninth Circuit has held:

> undue hardship requires more than proof of some fellow-worker's grumbling. . . . An employer . . . would have to show . . . actual imposition on coworkers or disruption of the work routine.[24]

While *Hardison* protects coworkers from an infringement of their seniority rights, it does not permit them to veto a religious accommodation merely because of generalized disgruntlement.

Nonmonetary Hardships

As previously explained, the Supreme Court recognized in *Hardison* that an accommodation can impose nonmonetary costs that nevertheless create "undue" hardships for an employer or other employees. Some of these hardships recur in the case law and are discussed below.

Breaches of Collective Bargaining Agreements

In *Hardison,* the Supreme Court gave special attention to the harm that the employer would suffer if it was forced to violate a collective bargaining

---

23. Nottelson v. Smith Steel Workers, 643 F.2d 445, 452 (7th Cir.), *cert. denied,* 454 U.S. 1046 (1981) ("fear of a 'steamroller effect' was purely conjectural"); Brown v. General Motors Corp., 601 F.2d 956, 961 (8th Cir. 1979); Burns v. Southern Pacific Transp. Co., 589 F.2d 403, 407 (9th Cir. 1978), *cert. denied,* 439 U.S. 1072 (1979); EEOC v. Townley Engineering & Mfg. Co., 859 F.2d 610, 615 (9th Cir. 1988), *cert. denied,* 489 U.S. 1077 (1989); Haring v. Blumenthal, 471 F. Supp. 1172, 1182 (D.D.C. 1979), *cert. denied,* 452 U.S. 939, *pet. for reh'g denied,* 453 U.S. 927 (1981).

24. Burns v. Southern Pac. Transp. Co., 589 F.2d at 407. *See also* Opuku-Boateng v. State of California, 95 F.3d at 1473 ("Even proof that employees would grumble about a particular accommodation is not enough to establish undue hardship"), citing Anderson v. General Dynamics Convair Aerospace Div., 589 F.2d 397, 402 (9th Cir. 1978), *cert. denied,* 442 U.S. 921 (1979).

agreement. The EEOC has similarly made seniority rights under a collective bargaining agreement inviolable in accommodation cases:

> Undue hardship would also be shown where a variance from a bona fide seniority system is necessary in order to accommodate an employee's religious practices when doing do so would deny another employee his or her job or shift preference guaranteed by that system.[25]

The *Hardison* legacy is also reflected in the following comment by the Second Circuit: ". . . it has not been established that an employer acting under the terms of a collective bargaining agreement must do more to accommodate religious preferences than is required by the agreement."[26] Indeed, many courts have held that neither the employer nor union need look beyond the collective bargaining agreement for accommodations.[27]

The courts are unwilling to compel an employer, for the sake of an accommodation, to require employees to waive their rights under a collective bargaining agreement or to compel a union to consent to such a waiver.[28] Applying this principle, courts have refused to require accommodations that (1) would permit a plaintiff to transfer to another shift out of seniority;[29] (2) grant a plaintiff regular absences contrary to contractual procedures;[30] (3) permit a plaintiff's name to be skipped on Saturdays on the employer's hiring board, thereby cutting short the next employee's

---

25. EEOC Guidelines on Discrimination Because of Religion, 29 C.F.R. § 1605.2(e)(2).

26. Genas v. New York Dept. of Correctional Services, 75 F.3d 825, 831 (2d Cir. 1996).

27. *See, e.g.,* Wren v. T.I.M.E.-D.C., Inc., 595 F.2d 441, 445 (8th Cir. 1979); Blair v. Graham Correctional Center, 782 F. Supp. 411 (C.D. Ill. 1992), *aff'd,* 4 F.3d 996 (7th Cir. 1993), *cert. denied,* 510 U.S. 1093 (1994); Cook v. Chrysler Corp., 779 F. Supp. 1016, 1025 (E.D. Mo. 1991), *aff'd,* 981 F.2d 336 (8th Cir. 1992), *cert. denied,* 508 U.S. 973 (1993). *But see* Moore v. A.E. Staley Mfg. Co., 727 F. Supp. 1156, 1160-61 (N.D. Ill. 1989) (reasonable accommodation when union and employer solicited and supported voluntary swaps).

28. See, e.g., EEOC v. Caribe Hilton Int'l, 597 F. Supp. 1007, 1013 (D.P.R. 1984), *aff'd,* 821 F.2d 74 (1st Cir. 1987) (neither employer nor union is required to change terms of collective bargaining agreements).

29. Cook v. Chrysler Corp., 779 F. Supp. at 1023.

30. *Id.*

time off;[31] (4) transfer a plaintiff to a different bargaining unit, in violation of the collective bargaining agreement;[32] and (5) relieve a plaintiff of mandatory overtime when doing so would require another employee to work overtime, in violation of that employee's contractual rights.[33]

Notwithstanding the above precedent, the defense of a collective bargaining agreement is not necessarily iron-clad. A few courts have held that an employer must at least make the effort to obtain the union's cooperation in seeking either a contractual waiver or an accommodation within the boundaries of the collective bargaining agreement.

In *EEOC v. Hacienda Hotel*,[34] the Ninth Circuit affirmed that an employer may not use a collective bargaining agreement as a shield to ward off all discussion of potential accommodation.[35] Two women employed as maids at the Hacienda Hotel requested a change of schedule so that they would have a day off on their Sabbath. Rather than discuss the situation with the plaintiffs, the employer simply relied upon the seniority provisions of the collective bargaining agreement that governed their employment. The court held that the hotel failed to make *any* effort to accommodate the religious beliefs of the two plaintiffs.[36] The court noted that the seniority provision governing the employment of the plaintiffs was written in permissive terms: "whenever possible and feasible, seniority shall govern . . . work schedules."[37] Moreover, the hotel accommodated the nonreligious needs of another employee, even though she did not have sufficient seniority, proving that the collective bargaining agreement permitted a degree of flexibility.[38]

In addition, the hotel failed to ask other employees if they could work during the Sabbath day.[39] The court found that at least one employee was

---

31. Lee v. ABF Freight System, Inc., 22 F.3d 1019, 1023 (10th Cir. 1994). *See also* Dickson v. International Longshoremen and Warehouseman's Union, 38 FEP 1253, 1256 (D. Or. 1984) (cannot alter dispatch rules for casual employees).

32. Lee v. ABF Freight System, 22 F.3d at 1023.

33. Mann v. Frank, 7 F.3d 1365, 1369 (8th Cir. 1993).

34. 881 F.2d 1504 (9th Cir. 1989).

35. *Id.* at 1513.

36. *Id.*

37. *Id.* at 1513, n. 7.

38. *Id.*

39. *Id.* at 1513.

willing to substitute for one of the women on the Sabbath day.[40] The court concluded that the hotel violated Title VII because it did not make a good-faith attempt to resolve the conflict with the two employees in ways that would avoid a breach of the bargaining agreement.

A similar result was reached in *Drazewski v. Waukegan Development Center*,[41] in which an employer refused to consider shift swaps, part-time work, and other accommodations because they were not specifically provided for in the collective bargaining agreement. The court rejected the employer's motion for summary judgment because the collective bargaining agreement could provide a defense only when the proposed accommodations were clearly precluded by the agreement.[42]

The decisions in *Hacienda* and *Drazewski* suggest that, even after *Hardison,* a collective bargaining agreement may not be an impregnable defensive shield. Some courts may still require an employer to be creative in seeking out ways of avoiding a conflict between an accommodation and a bargaining agreement. In doing so, however, the employer may not bypass the union to bargain with individual employees over the rearrangement of their schedules; such action would violate national labor relations policy.[43]

---

40. *Id.*

41. 651 F. Supp. 754, 758–59 (N.D. Ill. 1986). *Accord* Boomsma v. Greyhound Food Management, Inc., 639 F. Supp. 1448, 1455-56 (W.D. Mich. 1986), *appeal dismissed,* 815 F.2d 76 (6th Cir. 1987).

42. 651 F. Supp. at 758–59. *Cf.* Cook v. Chrysler Corp., 779 F. Supp. 1016. In *Cook,* the employer was faced with a collective bargaining agreement that affected its ability to accommodate an employee who refused to work on the Sabbath for religious reasons. This agreement, however, was strict and offered no room for accommodation. Although the court questioned the extent of Chrysler's efforts to accommodate the employee, Chrysler did not merely point to the agreement as an excuse not to cooperate. *Id.* at 1024. Instead, it tried to accommodate the plaintiff within the confines of the agreement itself. Chrysler (1) checked the plaintiff's seniority status, (2) conferred with members of the plaintiff's church, and (3) attempted to obtain permission from the union to better accommodate the plaintiff. Although Chrysler was ultimately unsuccessful in its efforts to accommodate the plaintiff, the court held that it sought to accommodate in good faith and did not violate Title VII when it ultimately fired the plaintiff. *Id.* at 1025.

43. Turpen v. Missouri-Kansas-Texas R. Co., 736 F.2d 1022, 1027 (5th Cir. 1984). *Cf.* EEOC v. Arlington Transit Mix, Inc., 957 F.2d 219, 222 (6th Cir. 1991) (non-union employer is obligated to explore voluntary waiver of seniority rights with coworkers of plaintiff).

Interference in the Preferences of Other Employees

Even in a workplace that is not governed by a collective bargaining agreement, employees will have certain expectations and preferences regarding their job and shift assignments, location, and so forth. In the unionized workplace, the terms and conditions of employment are set by contract and are virtually inviolable under *Hardison.* Are non-unionized workers, who are employed at will, equally able to preserve their working conditions in the face of accommodation claims? The answer is not clear, since the lower courts have not agreed whether *Hardison* should be limited to the context of collective bargaining agreements.

In *Opuku-Boateng v. State of California,*[44] the Ninth Circuit held that the State was required to consider the types of scheduling changes between plaintiff and other employees that were rejected in *Hardison.* The court observed that, unlike in *Hardison,* the workplace was not unionized, and other employees would not be deprived "of any contractually-established . . . seniority rights or privileges."[45] Without the loss of contractual rights, the changes in shift schedules requested by the plaintiff were found to impose no more than a de minimis burden on other employees.[46]

In contrast, the Eleventh Circuit held in *Beadle v. Hillsborough Country Sheriff's Department,*[47] that *Hardison* should be read more broadly. The court accepted the nonunion employer's defense that scheduling changes among employees would create an undue hardship, holding that *Hardison* governed any "neutral rotating shift system" and not merely collectively bargained seniority systems.[48]

While the lower courts debate the wisdom of extending *Hardison* beyond its particular facts, one fact is clearly true for both the unionized

---

44. 95 F.3d 1461.

45. *Id.* at 1470.

46. *Id.* The court also noted that all employees would work an equal number of undesirable shifts, regardless of whether the plaintiff received an accommodation. *See also* Niederhuber v. Camden County Vocational, 495 F. Supp. 273, 279-280 (D.N.J. 1980), *aff'd,* 671 F.2d 496 (3d Cir. 1981) (distinguishing *Hardison* because it involved breach of an existing "seniority agreement").

47. 29 F.3d 589 (11th Cir. 1994), *cert. denied,* 514 U.S. 1128 (1995).

48. *Id.* at 593. *Accord* Eversly v. MBank Dallas, 843 F.2d 172, 175 (5th Cir. 1988). *See also* Murphy v. Edge Memorial Hosp., 550 F. Supp. 1185, 1189 (M.D. Ala. 1982) (undue hardship for non-union employer to deviate from neutral scheduling system, even if it was not based on seniority).

and non-union employer: The courts are reluctant to approve an accommodation that has a provable adverse impact upon other employees. The existence of a collective bargaining agreement may well make the employer's task easier in resisting an accommodation, but such agreements are not a prerequisite to proving that other workers will suffer economic consequences as a result of an accommodation. If adverse consequences are proved, the courts are prepared to find an undue hardship, even though the employer does not directly suffer the hardship.

In this category, the following burdens placed upon coworkers to accommodate another employee's religious practices have been deemed more than de minimis:

- requiring a coworker to switch shifts.[49]
- denying a coworker annual leave.[50]
- depriving a coworker of seniority rights contained in collective bargaining agreements.[51]
- requiring a coworker to perform a greater share of potentially hazardous work.[52]

Impact on Safety

The cost of accommodating an employee may be more than de minimis if the accommodation would impair safety at the workplace. As with other types of hardships, the employer is required to show that the risk is grounded in fact and not speculation. Unfortunately, the courts have been inconsistent when deciding safety cases. Some rigorously review the underpinnings of the employer's contentions, whereas others accept the employer's argument without close scrutiny.

---

49. TWA v. Hardison, 432 U.S. at 81 ("It would be anomalous to conclude that by 'reasonable accommodation' Congress meant that an employer must deny the shift and job preferences of some employees . . . in order to accommodate or prefer the religious needs of others"); Lee v. ABF Freight System, 22 F.3d at 1023.

50. Cooper v. Oak Rubber Co., 15 F.3d 1375, 1380 (6th Cir. 1994) (undue burden to deny annual leave); EEOC v. BJ Services Co., 921 F. Supp. 1509, 1514 (N.D. Tex. 1995) (undue burden to deny one vacation day to another employee).

51. TWA v. Hardison, 432 U.S. at 81.

52. Bhatia v. Chevron U.S.A., 734 F.2d 1382, 1384 (9th Cir. 1984) (plaintiff refused to shave, and therefore could not use a respirator; court held that the cost of plaintiff's requested accommodation was more than de minimis when it required plaintiff's coworkers to assume his share of potentially hazardous work).

In *Toledo v. Nobel-Sysco, Inc.*,[53] the Tenth Circuit panel was asked to determine whether Nobel-Sysco legally refused to hire the plaintiff as a truck driver solely because he took part in Native American religious ceremonies that required the use of peyote.[54] Nobel-Sysco claimed that it was unable to accommodate the plaintiff in any manner. It alleged that (1) hiring the plaintiff would violate Federal Department of Transportation regulations regarding drug use by truck drivers, (2) use of peyote is illegal and therefore would violate its own policies and its truck lease agreement, and (3) hiring a known drug user would expose it to unacceptably high liability risks.[55]

The court first rejected Nobel-Sysco's argument that federal regulations prohibited the hiring of the plaintiff. The regulations prohibited the operation of a truck if a driver possesses, drives under the influence of, or uses a substance that would render a him incapable of safely operating a vehicle. Since the plaintiff never used peyote while driving a truck or close in time to when he would be driving,[56] the regulations did not apply to his situation.[57]

The court next rejected Nobel-Sysco's argument that peyote was an illegal drug and would therefore violate its own policies and its lease agreements. It found that the use of peyote for religious reasons did not violate either federal law or state law in the states in which the plaintiff would have driven a truck.[58]

---

53. 892 F.2d 1481 (10th Cir. 1989), *cert. denied,* 495 U.S. 948 (1990).

54. Toledo was a member of the Native American Church. The use of peyote, a small spineless cactus that contains the hallucinogen mescaline, is the central and most sacred practice of the Church. *Id.* at 1484-85.

55. *Id.* at 1490.

56. The court interpreted the regulations as not prohibiting the use or possession of such substances while off duty. *Id.*

57. *Id. Cf.* Bhatia v. Chevron U.S.A., 734 F.2d at 1384 (undue burden to allow plaintiff to maintain current duties because company would risk liability for violating state occupational safety and health administration standards).

58. Toledo v. Nobel-Sysco, 892 F.2d at 1491. Bona fide religious use of peyote by Native Americans is exempted from criminal liability under the statutes of New Mexico and Colorado; federal regulation similarly exempted religious use of peyote by Native Americans from the provisions of the Controlled Substance Act of 1970. *Id.* These facts distinguish *Toledo* from Employment Div., Dept. of Human Res. v. Smith, 494 U.S. 872 (1990), in which the Supreme Court held that Oregon could constitutionally deny unemployment benefits to a Native American who was terminated because of peyote use. Unlike New Mexico and Colorado, Oregon did not exempt the religious use of peyote. *Id.* at 890.

Finally, the court considered Nobel-Sysco's argument that hiring the plaintiff would subject the company to greater tort liability. The court relied upon the scientific evidence introduced at trial that the amount of peyote ingested in religious ceremonies would have dissipated in 24 hours. It therefore found that requiring the plaintiff to take a day off after each use of peyote would "virtually eliminate the risk that the influence of peyote would cause an accident or be a factor in subsequent litigation."[59] Because Nobel-Sysco could have accommodated the plaintiff by requiring him to wait one day after a religious ceremony before driving a truck, the court found that the refusal to hire him violated Title VII's prohibition against discrimination based upon religion.[60]

A similar outcome is found in *Carter v. Bruce Oakley, Inc.*[61] The plaintiff was terminated because he refused to shave his beard in compliance with his employer's facial-hair policy. The company's justification for the policy was simply tradition—the previous president had started the policy and the current president decided to continue it. Evidence in support of the policy was virtually nonexistent. Nonetheless, the employer argued that wearing a beard was unsafe and projected an unprofessional appearance. The plaintiff countered that the face mask he wore on occasion fit properly even with a beard. The court held that the employer failed to establish how an accommodation would have posed a safety risk.[62]

At the other end of the spectrum, the district court in *EEOC v. Sambo's of Georgia, Inc.*,[63] seemingly accepted the employer's arguments without scrutiny. The plaintiff, a Sikh, applied for a restaurant-manager position at Sambo's. As a Sikh, he was prohibited from shaving his facial hair. Sambo's grooming policy prohibited facial hair except for neatly trimmed moustaches. The plaintiff refused to cut his beard and was refused hire.

In support of its position, Sambo's argued that the public prefers clean-shaven employees at restaurants because of concerns about sanitary conditions and that the no-beard policy was critical to keeping its customer base. Sambo's also alleged that the Georgia guidelines for restaurant inspections included penalties if a restaurant's employees displayed

---

59. Toledo v. Nobel-Sysco, 892 F.2d at 1492.
60. *Id.*
61. 849 F. Supp. 673 (E.D. Ark. 1993).
62. *Id.* at 676.
63. 530 F. Supp. 86 (N.D. Ga. 1981).

excessive growth of facial hair. The court accepted Sambo's arguments, and held that accommodating the plaintiff would impose an undue hardship because: (1) Sambo's public image and operation of its business would be harmed, (2) Sambo's risked noncompliance with restaurant sanitation regulations, and (3) accommodation would make it difficult to enforce grooming standards on other employees and would therefore affect employee morale and efficiency.[64] However, the court cited little or no evidence to support its conclusions concerning public attitudes towards beards and the affect upon employee morale. Furthermore, the state guidelines prohibited "excessive" facial hair, but not all facial hair. Given these factors, the court's lax approach to an employer's burden of proof should perhaps be viewed as an aberration.[65]

Violations of Law

An employer may establish that an accommodation poses a greater than de minimis cost if it would lead to a violation of law. In *Toledo,* the court found that accommodating the employee's use of peyote would not, in fact, have caused the employer to abet or condone an illegal act. However, it did not exclude the assertion of that defense in appropriate cases. One case in which this defense was properly asserted was *U.S. v. Board of Education.*[66] In that case, a school board claimed undue hardship when it failed to accommodate a teacher who insisted on wearing religious attire consistent with the beliefs of the Muslim religion. The school board refused to violate a Pennsylvania law that prohibited teachers from wearing religious clothing. The court held that the school board was not

---

64. *Id.* at 90.

65. *Cf.* Beadle v. City of Tampa, 42 F.3d 633 (11th Cir. 1995), *cert. denied,* 515 U.S. 1152 (1995), in which the police department refused to accommodate the plaintiff's refusal to work on his Sabbath. The department argued that granting the plaintiff shift exemptions would interfere with his training because it was important for new officers to experience a variety of training officers. The court agreed and stated that "[w]hen the employer's business involves the protection of lives and property, 'courts should go slow in restructuring [its] employment practices.'" *Id.* at 637, citing United States v. City of Albuquerque, 545 F.2d 110, 114 (10th Cir. 1976), *cert. denied,* 433 U.S. 909 (1977). *Beadle* and *Albuquerque* involved law-enforcement agencies in the public sector. For this reason, their acceptance of employer claims of safety hardships may not be readily transferable to the private sector.

66. 911 F.2d 882 (3d Cir. 1990).

required to expose itself and "its administrators to a substantial risk of criminal prosecution, fines, and expulsion from the profession."[67]

Economic or Monetary Hardships

The cost of accommodation may be measured in many different ways, some direct and some indirect. Some costs are not easily quantifiable, but nevertheless economic in their impact.[68] For example, an accommodation may interfere with the operation of a business through loss of productivity, a factor that may not be easily measured on an ad hoc basis. Before addressing the courts' treatment of these types of hardships, it is necessary to confront the issue of the relationship between an employer's size and the cost to be incurred.

The Relationship Between the Cost of the Accommodation and the Size of the Business—*Hardison* versus EEOC Guidelines

The EEOC's Guidelines on Discrimination Because of Religion contain a section devoted to the relationship between undue hardship and cost.[69] The discussion regarding cost is interesting for a number of reasons. First, this portion of the Guidelines is typically ignored by the courts in determining whether a particular accommodation poses an undue hardship. Second, the Commission requires a much higher cost than do the courts before an employer can successfully claim undue hardship.

The Commission states that it will determine whether a particular cost is more than de minimis by considering the identifiable cost of the accommodation:

> in relation to the size and operating cost of the employer, and the number of individuals who will in fact need a particular accommodation.[70]

---

67. *Id.* at 891. The court refused to state whether the result would be the same if the plaintiff presented sufficient evidence that enforcement of the statute was nonexistent. *Id.* Other cases involving potential violation of law include Bhatia v. Chevron, 734 F.2d at 1384 (state safety standards), and EEOC v. Sambo's, 530 F. Supp. at 89-90 (state restaurant guidelines).

68. Favero v. Huntsville Independent School District, 939 F. Supp. 1281, 1292 (S.D. Tex. 1996), *aff'd*, 110 F.3d 793 (5th Cir. 1997) ("An undue hardship may entail not only monetary concerns, but also an employer's burden in conducting its business").

69. 29 C.F.R. § 1605.2(e)(1).

70. *Id.*

The Commission further notes that:

> [C]osts similar to the regular payment of premium wages of substitutes . . . would constitute an undue burden. However, the Commission will presume that the infrequent payment of premium wages for a substitute or the payment of premium wages while a more permanent accommodation is being sought are costs which an employer can be required to bear as a means of providing a reasonable accommodation.[71]

Whether this is a fair reading of the law after *Hardison* is questionable. The *Hardison* case involved a very large employer, TWA, and actual costs of $150 for the payment of a substitute; only one employee in that litigation raised a Sabbath claim. Further, the payment of a substitute was necessary only for a short time before Hardison obtained sufficient seniority to remedy his scheduling problem without special assistance. Nonetheless, the Court declared that TWA would suffer more than de minimis costs by accommodating Hardison.[72]

It would appear from this holding that virtually any measurable cost will be deemed more than de minimis, even for a large, global company. Indeed, the size of the company would seem to have been irrelevant to the Court in *Hardison,* which would make the EEOC Guidelines wildly off the mark.

There is one caveat, however, to this interpretation. The final footnote to the majority opinion criticizes the dissent's conclusion that accommodating Hardison resulted in only a de minimis cost:

> [I]t fails to take account of the likelihood that a company as large as TWA may have many employees whose religious observances, like Hardison's, prohibit them from working on Saturdays or Sundays.[73]

Apart from the purely speculative nature of the observation,[74] the Court seems to be suggesting that the undue hardship did not arise solely out of

---

71. *Id.*

72. 432 U.S. at 84–85.

73. *Id.* at 84 n.15.

74. *See* 29 C.F.R. § 1605.2(c) (EEOC Guidelines state that employers may not assume that other employees will request a similar accommodation to a plaintiff); Nottelson v. Smith Steel Workers, 643 F.2d at 452 (employer may not speculate that an accom-

Hardison's individual circumstance, but out of the cost multiplied over a large workforce. The Third Circuit, in a decision issued shortly after *Hardison,* similarly questioned whether the Supreme Court's view of de minimis costs might not require an assessment of an accommodation's impact upon the entire workforce, rather than the financial consequences of a single plaintiff's accommodation.[75] In that context, the size of the employer and the nature of the accommodation would become relevant.

Consistent with this interpretation, several courts have decided undue hardship issues only after a consideration of the size of the workforce and the likely impact of the plaintiff's accommodation on the overall operations. For example, in *Brown v. General Motors Corporation*[76] and *Protos v. Volkswagen of America,*[77] the Eighth and Third Circuits, respectively, held that granting an employee time off on the Sabbath would not sufficiently interfere in the operations or finances of a large automobile plant to justify a finding of undue hardship. In contrast, one district court ruled that a small employer was not obligated to rearrange employee schedules to accommodate Sabbath observance; the court distinguished *General Motors* based on the disparity in size of the two workforces.[78]

These decisions give some support to the EEOC's statement that the size of the employer, as well as the amount of the cost, should be considered when deciding whether an accommodation would present an undue hardship. However, for the most part, the courts continue to ignore this aspect of the Guidelines; thus, the Guidelines might be viewed more as the EEOC's suggestion for how the law should be interpreted, rather than an accurate summary of the state of the law after *Hardison.*

Loss of Production or Business
The courts are generally sympathetic to businesses that prove that they would suffer a loss of production if employees are permitted to excuse themselves from work for religious reasons on a regular basis.

---

modation for one employee will necessarily be requested by others). See also the previous discussion in this chapter under the heading "Undue Hardships May Not Be Speculative."

75. Ward v. Allegheny Ludlum Steel Corp., 560 F.2d 579, 583 n.22 and 24 (3d Cir. 1977).

76. 601 F.2d 956, 959 (8th Cir. 1979).

77. 797 F.2d 129, 135 (3d Cir.), *cert. denied,* 479 U.S. 972 (1986).

78. Murphy v. Edge Memorial Hosp., 550 F. Supp. at 1192.

In *Cooper v. Oak Rubber Company*,[79] a Seventh-Day Adventist consistently refused to work on Saturday, her Sabbath. On occasion, however, the company scheduled full-production work for Saturdays. The plaintiff ultimately resigned to avoid termination, but then brought suit against the company. The employer proved that the machinery on which the plaintiff worked required seven employees for its operation and normally had to be overstaffed to cover for breaks, lunch periods, vacations, and other excused absences. If a machine was understaffed by even one worker, it could not operate. The court therefore found that the company's production needs required the attendance of all employees on full-production Saturdays and that the risk of a loss of production due to understaffing was an undue burden.[80]

A similar result was reached in *EEOC v. Caribe Hilton International*,[81] when one of three security doormen at a casino sought scheduling changes with coworkers for his Sabbath. Because of the possibility that plaintiff would not be able to find a substitute for all of his absences, the court found an undue hardship in the requested accommodation. It found that plaintiff's absence would leave the casino understaffed in a critical security function.[82]

This type of burden is obviously heightened if the employee performs critical duties that are not easily replaced.[83] If an employee's

---

79. 15 F.3d 1375 (6th Cir. 1994).

80. *Id.* at 1380. *See also* Cook v. Chrysler Corp., 981 F.2d 336, 339 (8th Cir. 1992) (undue burden for company to forgo using floater elsewhere to cover absence every Friday night); Lee v. ABF Freight System, 22 F.3d at 1023 (loss of production resulting from not replacing a worker can amount to undue hardship); Turpen v. Missouri-Kansas-Texas R. Co., 736 F.2d at 1027 (it is an undue hardship when understaffing would cause decreased efficiency); Stevenson v. Southport, Inc., 73 FEP 1789, 1792 (E.D. La. 1997) (loss of production caused by employee who refused to work on Saturdays was more than a de minimis cost). *Cf.* Protos v. Volkswagen of America, 797 F.2d at 135 (no undue burden found where company could not establish loss of production or understaffing).

81. 597 F. Supp. 1007 (D.P.R. 1984), *aff'd*, 821 F.2d 74 (1st Cir. 1987). *See also* EEOC v. BJ Services Co., 921 F. Supp. at 1515 (if plaintiff did not work Saturdays and a job was canceled, defendant would face losing work to competitors; this was greater than de minimis cost). *Cf.* EEOC v. Hacienda Hotel, 881 F.2d 1504, 1513 (9th Cir. 1989) (no undue hardship in requiring employer to seek shift swaps among maids in a hotel).

82. EEOC v. Caribe Hilton Int'l, 597 F.2d at 1011–12.

83. Smith v. United Refining Co., 21 FEP 1481, 1484 (W.D. Pa. 1980) (plaintiff was only employee with knowledge necessary for maintenance and repair work in plant).

absence will cause work not to be completed, then an undue hardship is likely to be found.[84] However, if the employee occupies a noncritical position among a large workforce, especially if substitutes are normally used, the courts may be much less receptive to the employer's complaints.[85] The courts will then require the employer to come forward with concrete proof that business will be lost or that production will be impaired. If an employer can avoid a drop in production resulting from an absence by engaging in reasonable advanced planning, its defense of undue hardship is likely to be rejected.[86]

In *EEOC v. Ilona of Hungary, Inc.*,[87] the Seventh Circuit rejected a claim by a Chicago beauty salon that granting unpaid leave to two Jewish employees (a manicurist and a skin-care specialist) on Yom Kippur was more than a de minimis cost. Both employees were partially booked for the Saturday in question when they requested an accommodation. Saturdays were traditionally the busiest day of the week for the salon, and it wanted a full complement of personnel available to serve its customers. The salon refused to accommodate the employees because it believed that rescheduling the clients would lead to lower revenue.[88] The court disagreed, concluding that any inconvenience or loss of revenue caused by the absence of the two employees could have been avoided if the salon rescheduled their appointments in advance.[89]

The decision in *Ilona* points up a distinction that the EEOC emphasizes in its Guidelines: repeated, regular absences by an employee (for Sab-

---

84. Wren v. T.I.M.E.-D.C., Inc., 595 F.2d at 445.

85. Protos v. Volkswagen, 797 F.2d at 135; Brown v. General Motors, 601 F.2d at 959-62.

86. Willey v. Maben Mfg., 479 F. Supp. 634, 637-38 (N.D. Miss. 1979) (employer had ample time to find a replacement for plaintiff, but failed to do so).

87. 108 F.3d 1569 (7th Cir. 1997).

88. *Id.* at 1574. The court noted that, although an employer's precarious financial condition may be relevant to determining undue hardship, in this case it was not a factor because the salon would not have suffered economically if it had provided a reasonable accommodation to the two employees. *Id.* at 1577.

89. *Id.* The EEOC's expert established that the salon, at times, generated equal or greater revenues on days it was not fully staffed. Other evidence included the salon's willingness to allow employees to take leave on Saturdays for nonreligious reasons and the failure of the salon to replace one of the terminated employees for nine months. *See also* Willey v. Maben, 479 F. Supp. at 637.

bath observances, for example) may pose a greater hardship than the kinds of sporadic absences that arise out of other religious observances.[90] *Hardison* was the result of an employee requiring regular absences. In those situations, an employer (especially a smaller employer) may find it more difficult to guarantee that the vacancy will always be covered and that the work will be performed. However, when an ad hoc request for leave is made (assuming adequate advance notice), the courts may be more skeptical of claims that a reasonable accommodation cannot be reached because of undue hardship.[91]

The Cost of Using Temporary Workers or Substitutes

One obvious alternative to having employees absent on religious leave is to schedule temporary replacements. While courts have compelled some employers to take this step, the expense may constitute an undue burden. Employers frequently argue, often with success, that temporary workers for skilled positions are not as efficient, produce less, and produce shoddier product—in other words, they are more costly than regular workers.

The most obvious and most readily quantifiable cost associated with the use of a substitute employee is the wage paid to the substitute. If the substitute's wage is not greater than what would be paid to the regular employee, then the employer cannot claim this cost as the basis for an undue hardship.[92] However, if the substitute or temporary employee would be paid more than a de minimis amount in excess of the regular

---

90. 29 C.F.R. § 1605.2(e)(1). Yom Kippur, for example, occurs only once a year.

91. *Compare* Niederhuber v. Camden County Vocational and Technical School, 495 F. Supp. at 279-80 (leave of absence for five to ten days per year by a teacher would not create undue hardship) *with* Favero v. Huntsville, 939 F. Supp. at 1292-94 (eight-day absence by school bus drivers in district that already had a shortage of drivers would create undue hardship). *See also* Ansonia Board of Education v. Philbrook, 479 U.S. 60, 70 (1986) (granting LWOP to teacher who missed approximately six days of work per year was reasonable); Wangsness v. Watertown School District, 541 F. Supp. 332 (leave of absence of eight days for a teacher did not constitute an undue hardship).

92. *See* Redmond v. GAF Corp., 574 F.2d at 904 ("[t]o pay replacement employees premium wages would not impose a cost on the defendant, for the regular warehouse employees were already receiving premium wages for their Saturday work"); *Protos,* 797 F.2d at 135 (no undue burden found when company employed roving absentee relief operators to be deployed as substitutes for absent employees at regular wages).

employee, then *Hardison* suggests a finding of undue hardship.[93] As one district court observed: "The courts have repeatedly held that paying additional wages to accomplish an accommodation is an undue burden."[94]

Quite apart from the payment of extra wages, the courts have also recognized that the use of substitutes, casuals, or transfers may result in other significant costs or reductions in efficiency and productivity. Although the results have been less uniform, the courts have tended to accept employer arguments that these "costs" are more than de minimis.

In *Cook v. Chrysler Corporation*,[95] plaintiff was a Seventh-Day Adventist who worked on an assembly line for Chrysler. He was terminated after he refused to work on his Sabbath (Saturday), a regular work day for his shift.[96] The court of appeals upheld the district court's finding that the cost of accommodating Cook was more than de minimis. Specifically, the court found that the use of floaters reduced efficiency and adversely affected the quality of Chrysler's product because greater repairs were required on the final product.[97] The court also found that replacing Cook every Friday night meant that Chrysler either had to hire another floater or transfer one from another assignment; the cost of either option was more than de minimis.[98]

The nonwage costs associated with the use of a substitute employee was also one of the factors in *Lee v. ABF Freight System*.[99] There, a truck driver would not work on Saturdays and suggested a substitute "foreign"

---

93. 432 U.S. at 84.

94. Favero v. Huntsville, 939 F. Supp. at 1291. *See* Cooper v. Oak Rubber Co., 15 F.3d at 1380 (undue burden to require company to hire additional full-time worker, even though company hired an additional eighteen employees one month after the plaintiff resigned); Cook v. Chrysler Corp., 981 F.2d at 339 (hiring a floater for every Friday night is undue burden); Lee v. ABF Freight System, 22 F.3d at 1023 ("cost of hiring an additional worker" for Sabbath observance may be more than de minimis; "function[ing] as part-time employee but receiv[ing] full-time benefits" results in significant costs).

95. 981 F.2d 336 (8th Cir. 1992).

96. Employees at the plant worked pursuant to a collective bargaining agreement that contained a seniority system governing transfers and shift changes.

97. *Id.* at 339.

98. *Id. But see* Protos v. Volkswagen of America, 797 F.2d at 135 (although plaintiff could not work any Saturday, no undue burden found when company used roving substitutes at regular wages for every shift, and plaintiff's evidence was more credible than company's regarding efficiency, production, quality, and morale).

99. 22 F.3d 1019 (10th Cir. 1994).

driver. However, the court noted that the cost of bringing the substitute driver from another city was more than de minimis.[100] The monetary cost of transferring an equipment operator from another location was similarly one of the bases for an undue hardship finding in *EEOC v. BJ Services Company*.[101]

When the work is unskilled, however, employers have a much more difficult time establishing undue hardship because of a loss of efficiency in the use of replacement workers. In *Redmond v. GAF Corp.*,[102] the company rarely scheduled Saturday work[103] that conflicted with Redmond's religious practices.[104] When Redmond was assigned to work a Saturday, he refused and was terminated. The factual record revealed that the company had many employees from which it could have requested assistance, that Saturday work was unusual, and that the work was unskilled, so that any employee could perform it in a satisfactory manner.[105] The court held that the corporation failed to establish that it would suffer any undue hardship in accommodating Redmond.[106]

The courts are similarly unsympathetic to the defense of lost efficiency in the use of substitutes when the employer maintains a pool of substitutes or "casuals" who are regularly used for nonreligious absences.[107] Employers who normally permit employees to trade shift assignments are also less likely to persuade a court of inefficiencies in per-

---

100. *Id.* at 1023–24.

101. 921 F. Supp. at 1514. The court found that it would cost $200 per day for each substitute for work whose normal wage cost was less than $120. The court was also persuaded (like the court in *Cook v. Chrysler*) that, if the substitutes used in place of plaintiff did not possess his skills, there would be a loss in production because of decreased efficiency. *Id.*

102. 574 F.2d 897 (7th Cir. 1978).

103. In 1973, this work was scheduled for plaintiff's position only five times. *Id.* at 903–904.

104. Redmond was a Jehovah's Witness, and led a Bible-study class on Saturday mornings.

105. The court further distinguished the facts of *Hardison* by noting that the payment of premium wages for a substitute did not impose a cost upon the corporation because all employees received premium wages for Saturday work, and no union or collective bargaining agreement presented any problem with rearranging work schedules. *Id.* at 903–04.

106. *Id.* at 904.

107. *Protos v. Volkswagen*, 797 F.2d at 135.

mitting a shift swap for religious reasons.[108] However, even when an employer routinely uses substitutes, it can avoid this type of accommodation if the facts of a particular case support an argument that it will be unable to complete work or will suffer an overall drop in efficiency of operations. This problem is exemplified in *Favero v. Huntsville Independent School District*,[109] in which two school-bus drivers requested eight consecutive days of religious leave. The school district cited chronic understaffing and the schedules of other drivers in granting only five days of leave. One of the forms of accommodation proposed by the plaintiffs was the use of supervisors and/or mechanics as substitute drivers, since they had been used as substitutes in the past. The court concluded, however, that the use of supervisors or mechanics during the week in question would create an undue hardship. Because of the shortage of drivers generally, the use of supervisors and mechanics as substitutes had already caused the latter employees to neglect their regular duties. The additional strain created by the plaintiffs' absences would have exacerbated the negative impact on those other operations.[110] The resultant loss of efficiency was deemed more than de minimis.[111]

Employee Objections to Specific Assignments

In some instances, an employee may object on religious grounds to the subject matter of certain work assignments and request that he or she be excused from those assignments. One possible accommodation is to transfer the employee to a new job. Another possibility is to allow employees to swap particular assignments with coworkers. In the following two cases, the courts were presented with similar fact situations, but reached different conclusions.

In *Haring v. Blumenthal*,[112] the plaintiff was employed by the Internal Revenue Service and applied for a promotion to the position of reviewer in the Exempt Organizations Division. The reviewers were authorized to issue final favorable rulings regarding the tax-exempt status

---

108. Smith v. Pyro, 827 F.2d 1081, 1089 (6th Cir. 1987), *cert. denied,* 485 U.S. 989 (1988).

109. 939 F. Supp. 1281.

110. *Id.* at 1292.

111. *Id.* at 1294.

112. 471 F. Supp. 1172 (D.D.C. 1979).

of organizations. Two reviewers supervised eight to twelve tax-law spe-cialists. The IRS denied the plaintiff a promotion because he refused, based upon his religious beliefs, to work on applications from organiza-tions favoring the right to an abortion. The plaintiff introduced evidence that less than 2 percent of the reviewer's workload would have involved such organizations.

The court found that the inability to perform the small percentage of work objected to by the plaintiff could be accommodated by the IRS with de minimis cost, even though it required another person to do the work.[113] The court rejected the IRS's argument that accommodation would have led to an inefficient use of resources because it believed that the agency should have no problem on a "mechanical level" rearranging the work as necessary.[114] The court warned, however, that if the plaintiff's objections to specific work grew to encompass a significant portion of his workload, the IRS would be unable, without undue hardship, to accom-modate his beliefs.[115]

The opposite result was reached in *Ryan v. United States Department of Justice*.[116] The plaintiff was in charge of domestic security and terrorism at the FBI's office in Peoria, Illinois. He refused, based upon his religious beliefs, to investigate groups with pacifist agendas, even when they destroyed government property. When assigned to investigate such a group, the plaintiff chose formal disobedience rather than requesting reas-signment or accepting a job swap with another agent.[117] In turn, he was terminated for insubordination.

The FBI considered different types of accommodation short of disci-pline—doing nothing, moving him to another office, or assigning him different work. The FBI rejected doing nothing, because disobedience was inconsistent with the mission of the FBI. The agency rejected reassign-ment to another office because of the costs involved, including undermin-ing the authority of the special agent in charge and the potential effects

---

113. *Id.* at 1180.

114. The court stated "[t]he applications for exemption which plaintiff refuses to handle could clearly be processed without undue hardship or burden . . . , or any signifi-cant expense or loss of time, by another reviewer." *Id.* at 1180.

115. *Id.* at 1182.

116. 950 F.2d 458 (7th Cir. 1991), *cert. denied,* 504 U.S. 958 (1992).

117. Ryan also refused to participate in related matters in the future.

on morale. The FBI did not actively consider reassigning the plaintiff within the Peoria office, because it was too small (with only five agents). In direct contradiction of *Haring,* the court stated, "It is difficult to create special work within a field office where other agents are required to handle all work that is assigned to them."[118] The court's decision accordingly paid no attention to the percentage of plaintiff's work that was devoted to investigating pacifist groups. Instead, it noted his unwillingness to swap assignments with other agents, concluding that the FBI could not accommodate the plaintiff without undue hardship:

> With good will all around, and flexibility on the part of Ryan's fellow agents, it just might be possible to make a go of it. Title VII does not, however, compel the FBI to attempt this. . . . Compelled, as it is by Title VII, to have one rule for all of the diverse religious beliefs and practices in the United States, the FBI may choose to be stingy with exceptions lest the demand for them overwhelm it."[119]

The court seems to have been influenced by the plaintiff's own intransigence in declining work[120] and the FBI's need—as a paramilitary organization—to maintain discipline.[121] However, the ease with which the court accepted the FBI's decision that an office with five agents was too small to allow the reassignment of work is questionable. In both the private and public sectors, it is not unusual for employees to recuse themselves from matters for which they have financial or familial interests. Moreover, the court's statement that exceptions to work assignments should be infrequently granted, lest those exceptions overwhelm the agency, misses the mark. Speculative fears of the inability to accommodate other employees is not a factor the court should consider. Providing an accommodation does not mean easier or less work; here, it could have meant different work during the few situations in which the conflict arose.

---

118. *Id.* at 462.

119. *Id.*

120. Ryan did not affirmatively seek an accommodation; in the court's view, he sought the FBI's capitulation by simply rejecting all objectionable assignments. *Id.* at 461. *Cf.* HERMAN MELVILLE, BARTLEBY THE SCRIVENER.

121. The court noted that although it is difficult for any organization to accommodate employees who are choosy about assignments, it is particularly difficult for paramilitary organizations. *Id.* at 462.

The decision in *Haring* has been cited approvingly by other courts and, in our view, probably represents a more accurate statement of the general rule regarding the accommodation of particular work assignments than does *Ryan*.

Administrative Costs

Administrative costs expended by employers to accommodate an employee's religious beliefs are usually viewed as de minimis. The EEOC Guidelines, for example, provide that "the Commission will presume that generally, the payment of administrative costs necessary for providing the accommodation will not constitute more than a de minimis cost."[122]

The courts similarly have required employers to undertake significant administrative efforts at accommodation:

- arranging or assisting shift or schedule swaps,[123] and
- keeping track of charitable contributions from employees who object to paying union dues.[124]

Of course, if such administrative costs become quantifiably large, the courts will declare them greater than de minimis and therefore not mandatory.

Disruption in the Workplace Caused by Proselytizing Employees

In the evolving area of workplace harassment, employers have been confronted by employees who believe that they should share their religious beliefs with coworkers, while those coworkers have sometimes objected to

---

122. *See* EEOC Guidelines on Discrimination Because of Religion, 29 C.F.R. § 1605.2(e)(1).

123. *See* Smith v. Pyro, 827 F.2d at 1089 (no undue hardship for personnel department to post on bulletin board or company newsletter that plaintiff sought a shift swap); Opuku-Boateng v. State of California, 95 F.3d 1461 (no undue hardship for employer to prepare tentative twelve-month schedule, determine number of days plaintiff scheduled for Sabbath work, and determine how many coworkers were willing to trade shifts); EEOC v. J.P. Stevens and Co., 740 F. Supp. 1135, 1138-39 (M.D.N.C. 1990) (company should assist with advertising need for swap). *See also* TWA v. Hardison, 432 U.S. at 78 (recognizing TWA's efforts to approve shift swaps and otherwise accommodate employee).

124. *See* Burns v. Southern Pac. Transp. Co., 589 F.2d at 407 (rejecting argument that administrative costs in keeping track of charitable contributions would be more than de minimis).

the religious message they hear or the manner in which it is communicated. In the private sector, the courts have tended to require employers to strike a careful balance between the two groups—an employee has a right to voice his or her religious opinions, but only if the proselytizing does not have a negative impact on the workplace.[125] Although there are few court decisions addressing religious speech in the private sector, it appears that there are two circumstances in which an employer can restrict employee proselytizing.

First, the employer can squelch the activity if it has evidence that an employee's religious proselytizing causes the workplace to be less productive—perhaps because the employee spends time talking when he or she should have been working or perhaps because his or her comments distract coworkers from their work.[126]

Second, if an employer receives complaints from other workers that the religious proselytizing is offensive to them, it may place restrictions on the employee. The employer is not required to face a potential religious harassment lawsuit by the employees subjected to the proselytizing.

The following cases exemplify these two principles:

- An employee took a religious vow to wear a graphic anti-abortion button "until there was an end to abortion or until [she] could no longer fight the fight."[127] The button caused immediate and emotional reactions from her coworkers. Some employees refused to attend meetings where this worker would be present, and management was able to document a 40 percent decrease in productivity during the times she wore the button. The company offered her several options, including wearing the button with a covering over it. Since she would still be wearing the button, she would be fulfilling her vow without offending other employees. The Eighth Circuit Court of Appeals held that the company had

125. Proselytizing raises a host of constitutional issues in the public workplace, which are discussed in Chapter 11.

126. *See* Gillard v. Sears, Roebuck & Co., 32 FEP 1274, 1276 (E.D. Pa. 1983) (employer not required to permit employee to read Bible during working hours); Tucker v. State of California Dept. of Educ., 97 F.3d 1204, 1211 (9th Cir. 1996) (rejecting a state agency's prohibition of religious advocacy because it did not have tangible evidence that the speech interfered with the efficiency of the workplace).

127. Wilson v. U.S. West Communications, 58 F.3d 1337, 1339 (8th Cir. 1995).

met its burden to offer a reasonable accommodation and that
allowing the button without limitation would have created an
undue hardship.[128]

- A supervisor "impose[d] personally and directly on fellow employees, invading their privacy and criticizing their private lives" by
sending them letters suggesting that they "go to God and ask for
forgiveness" for their sins.[129] The supervisor claimed a religious
motivation for her missives, while the coworkers expressed out-
rage over their treatment. The company fired the supervisor for a
"serious error in judgment," and the Fourth Circuit Court of
Appeals held that the company's actions did not violate Title VII.

Although the courts are willing to uphold employer claims of
undue hardship when confronted by a disruptive proselytizer in the
workplace, they also are cautious in doing so. As with other kinds of
hardship, an employer must have actual evidence that the religious discussions are disruptive to other workers; it should not hypothesize about
the "potential effect" the comments might have on a coworker.[130] Moreover, if an employer fails to determine whether the employee complaints
are "reasonable and legitimate" before restricting the religious speech of
a worker, it runs the risk of being found liable for discriminating against
the proselytizer.[131]

Impact of Proselytizing on an Employer's Customers

Closely related to the above issue is the employee who directs his or her
proselytizing towards the employer's customers. In such cases, the
employer's immediate reaction usually is to demand a cessation of the
activity for fear that it will adversely affect customer relations.[132]

---

128. *Id.* at 1341–42.

129. Chalmers v. Tulon Co., 101 F.3d 1012, 1015, 1021 (4th Cir. 1996), *cert.
denied,* 118 S.Ct. 58 (1997).

130. Brown v. Polk County, Iowa, 61 F.3d 650, 657 (8th Cir. 1995) (en banc), *cert.
denied,* 516 U.S. 1158 (1996) (although a case involving a public employer, the Court of
Appeals rejected the state agency's actions under Title VII in part because of a lack of evidence that coworkers had actually been injured).

131. *Id.*

132. When proselytizing occurs in the public-sector workplace and is directed
towards the public, the Establishment clause of the First Amendment becomes an issue.
Cases involving proselytizing in the public sector are discussed in Chapter 11.

However, courts have reached opposite conclusions in two seemingly identical cases. In *Johnson v. Halls Merchandising*,[133] a retail business hired a new employee who, when talking with customers, often prefaced her sentences with "in the name of Jesus Christ of Nazareth." The company soon fired her. The district court dismissed her claim in a short opinion that concluded that a retail business could not allow an employee to make this type of statement to customers because it might offend the beliefs of some customers and therefore cost the company business. The court held that the store could not accommodate her religious speech without undue hardship on the conduct of the business.[134]

In *Banks v. Service America Corp.*,[135] two men worked in the cafeteria of a manufacturing plant. As people passed through the line, they would make comments such as, "God bless you" and "Praise the Lord" to the customers. The employer argued that because several customers expressed irritation about the religious comments, the company could not allow them to continue. The district court held, however, that, while there was evidence that the plaintiff's comments were not well-received by some customers, these comments were received from less than 1 percent of the people who passed through the cafeteria. The court also noted that the fear that customers would "boycott" the cafeteria "and bring sack lunches from home to avoid plaintiffs' religious speech—and that Service America would sustain a material loss on account of that activity—is more hypothetical than real."[136] The court held that, because "the fast food service encounter . . . is a fleeting and spontaneous one," the employer could not establish that it would suffer undue hardship if it allowed the religious comments to continue.[137]

The lack of agreement between these courts makes it impossible to articulate a generally applicable rule. However, the courts will probably look at several factors in deciding whether employee proselytizing can be accommodated. First, the courts will ask whether the proselytizing is directed at or audible to customers (as opposed to coworkers). If so, the nature of the business is critical: Do the company's employees have close contact with the customers, as does a salesperson in a retail store, or are

---

133. 49 FEP 527 (W.D. Mo. 1989).
134. *Id.* at 529.
135. 952 F. Supp. 703 (D. Kan. 1996).
136. *Id.* at 710.
137. *Id.* at 711.

the employees' contacts with customers minimal, such as a food-service worker who quickly prepares a customer's food order? Next, the courts will assess how explicit or provocative the employee's comments are. Finally, the employer will be required to prove how and if the proselytizing affected customer relations.

Summary

- An undue hardship arises whenever an employer is required to incur a greater than de minimis cost.
- An employer may not speculate as to the costs or hardships involved in an accommodation. Concrete proof of the costs and hardships is necessary.
- Routine administrative costs involved in an accommodation are considered de minimis.
- Costs arising out of the payment of additional wages to temporary or substitute employees are deemed greater than de minimis, unless the employer routinely uses temporary or substitute workers for nonreligious reasons.
- A measurable loss in productivity resulting from an employee's absence or from the use of temporary or substitute workers is deemed a greater than de minimis cost.
- The following accommodations create undue hardships and are therefore deemed unreasonable:
  1) an accommodation that requires the employer or union to breach nondiscriminatory seniority provisions of a collective bargaining agreement;
  2) an accommodation that causes other employees to suffer a loss or diminution of their job rights;
  3) an accommodation that impairs or endangers workplace safety;
  4) an accommodation that requires the employer to violate public law.
- An employer is not required to permit religious proselytizing by employees at the workplace if doing so causes a loss of productivity or if it will subject the employer to claims of religious harassment by other employees. In those circumstances, accommodating the proselytizer will create an undue hardship.

CHAPTER 10

Accommodating Employee Objections to the Payment of Union Dues

As previously explained, the nondiscrimination provisions of Title VII extend to labor unions, and unions are frequently sued, along with employers, in accommodation lawsuits. A union will often be made a defendant when it refuses to consent to a waiver of the terms of a collective bargaining agreement in order to permit an accommodation. Since *Trans World Airways, Inc. v. Hardison,*[1] unions have generally prevailed in such litigation; those cases are discussed in Chapter 9.

There is one additional area of dispute, however, that pits employees directly against their unions: employees who oppose the payment of union dues or fees because doing so is contrary to their religious beliefs. The courts have held that this conflict is also subject to the accommodation requirements of Title VII.

Title VII

The National Labor Relations Act (NLRA) permits employers and unions to negotiate "union security clauses" in their collective bargaining agreements.[2] These clauses typically require employees to pay dues or compara-

---

1. 432 U.S. 63 (1977).
2. 29 U.S.C. §§ 158(a)(3), 186(b). These clauses are not permitted in "right to work" states. 29 U.S.C. § 164(b). *See also* 45 U.S.C. § 152 (union security provision of the Railway Labor Act).

ble fees to the union as a condition of employment. Because there are some religions whose tenets preclude membership in or support of unions, security clauses in collective bargaining agreements must be reconciled with Title VII. To the extent that such clauses come into conflict with an employee's religious beliefs, the NLRA must yield to Title VII: "The union security provisions of [the NLRA] do not relieve an employer or a union of the duty of attempting to make reasonable accommodation to the individual religious needs of employees."[3]

When an employee complains that his or her religious beliefs conflict with a union security clause, both the employer and union become potential defendants. Most union security clauses require the employer to terminate an employee who fails to pay union dues or fees. If the employer does so without attempting to reach an accommodation, it may be sued under the same provisions of Title VII that apply to any other discriminatory discharge.[4] To the extent that a union requests or causes the termination, it too can be held liable under a separate provision of Title VII:

It shall be an unlawful employment practice for a labor organization —

(1) to exclude or to expel from its membership, or otherwise to discriminate against, any individual because of his race, color, religion, sex, or national origin; . . .

(3) to cause or attempt to cause an employer to discriminate against an individual in violation of this section.[5]

The courts have responded with virtual unanimity to employees who assert that their religious views prohibit their membership in or contribution to a union. They have held repeatedly that Title VII requires both employers and unions to make an effort to reach a reasonable accommodation with respect to this dues issue *and* that one such reasonable accommodation is to have an objecting employee pay the equivalent of dues to a

---

3. McDaniel v. Essex Intern., Inc., 571 F.2d 338, 343 (6th Cir. 1978). *Accord* Nottelson v. Smith Steel Wkrs. D.A.L.U. 19806, 643 F.2d 445, 450-51 (7th Cir.), *cert. denied,* 454 U.S. 1046 (1981).

4. 42 U.S.C. §§ 2000e(j), 2000e-2(a).

5. 42 U.S.C. § 2000e-2(c).

charity.[6] The EEOC's regulations similarly provide that a labor organization should accommodate an objecting employee by "permitting him or her to donate a sum equivalent to dues to a charitable organization."[7]

In all of the reported cases, unions have opposed this form of accommodation with three main arguments. First, unions argue that Title VII's accommodation principle must defer to the Congressional policy expressed in the NLRA that unions are entitled to financial support through union security clauses. Second, unions point to the Supreme Court's holding in *TWA v. Hardison* that an employer cannot be compelled to violate a collective bargaining agreement as the price of an accommodation. Third, they argue that the loss of dues constitutes an undue hardship. Each of these arguments has been rejected repeatedly by the courts.

As to the perceived clash between Title VII and the NLRA, the courts have been unsympathetic to the unions' pleas for financial protection. The Congressional policy against discrimination takes precedence over the union security provisions of the NLRA.[8]

The courts similarly have found the undue-hardship defense to be of very limited value. Although the courts recognize that unions may avail themselves of an undue-hardship defense,[9] *Hardison* has been distinguished because it involved an accommodation that "required abrogation of the rights of other employees under a bona fide seniority system[.]"[10] In the case of religious objections to union dues, union members (other than the objector) have not been shown to be burdened by the payment of a dues equivalent to a charity. Other members are not required to give up any contractual rights as the cost of permitting an accommodation,[11] and

---

6. Intern. Assn. of Machinists v. Boeing Corp., 833 F.2d 165 (9th Cir. 1987), *cert. denied,* 485 U.S. 1014 (1988); Tooley v. Martin-Marietta Corp., 648 F.2d 1239 (9th Cir.), *cert. denied,* 454 U.S. 1098 (1981); Nottelson v. Smith Steel Wkrs., 643 F.2d at 451-52; McDaniel v. Essex, 571 F.2d at 343-44; EEOC v. Davey Tree Surgery Co., 671 F. Supp. 1260 (N.D. Cal. 1987). *Cf.* Yott v. North American Rockwell Corp., 602 F.2d 904 (9th Cir. 1979), *cert. denied,* 445 U.S. 928 (1980) (employee who refused to pay dues equivalent to a charity was properly discharged).

7. 29 CFR § 1605.2(d)(2).

8. *See, e.g.,* Nottelson v. Smith Steel Wkrs., 643 F.2d at 450-51.

9. McDaniel v. Essex Intern., 571 F.2d at 344.

10. Nottelson v. Smith Steel Wkrs., 643 F.2d at 452.

11. *Id.*

the cost to a union of losing one employee's (or a few employees') dues has been found, as a factual matter, to have only a de minimis impact.[12] As one court observed, the loss of one employee's dues would cause other members to have to pay only an additional two cents per month.[13] These courts have also refused to credit union speculation that one accommodation will incite other employees to do the same, causing a far larger loss of dues; as with any other type of accommodation, the courts are unwilling to consider hypothetical hardships as a basis for rejecting a proposed accommodation.[14]

In addition to situations in which an employee's religious beliefs prevent membership in or support of a union per se, there have been a few cases in which an employee has raised religious objections to the policies of a particular union and has objected to paying dues money to support those policies. For example, employees who oppose abortion have objected to paying dues or fees to a union that supports a woman's right to an abortion.[15] The courts have held that these types of objections are equally recognizable under Title VII:

> The fact that [plaintiff] does not harbor a per se religious objection to labor unions is not dispositive. In order to invoke the employer's duty to offer a reasonable accommodation, it is sufficient that the employee establishes that he holds a sincere religious belief that conflicts with an employment requirement.[16]

In these cases, the courts have also held that charitable payments equivalent to dues constitute a reasonable accommodation and that an employer or union unwilling to accept this accommodation violates Title VII.[17]

---

12. *See, e.g.,* Nottelson v. Smith Steel Wkrs., 643 F.2d at 452; Burns v. Southern Pac. Transp. Co., 589 F.2d 403 (9th Cir. 1978), *cert. denied,* 439 U.S. 1072 (1979).

13. Burns v. Southern Pac. Transp., 589 F.2d at 407.

14. *Id.;* Nottelson v. Smith Steel Wkrs., 643 F.2d at 452; EEOC Dec. No. 81-33, 27 FEP 1834, 1836 (1981).

15. EEOC v. University of Detroit, 904 F.2d 331 (6th Cir. 1990); EEOC v. American Federation of State, County and Municipal Employees, 937 F. Supp. 166 (N.D.N.Y. 1996) (objections to union's positions on abortion and the death penalty).

16. EEOC v. University of Detroit, 904 F.2d at 335.

17. *Id. Accord* EEOC v. AFSCME, 937 F. Supp. 166.

What if an employee refuses to accept equivalent payments to a charity as an accommodation? The courts and the EEOC view the charitable contribution as a reasonable accommodation. The EEOC's "Policy Statement on Religious Accommodation Under Title VII Based on Objections to Unionism" states that the "charitable substitution is the only accommodation the employer/union need offer."[18] The one exception to this rule is if the employee has religious objections to paying money to a particular charity designated by an employer or a collective bargaining agreement. In that event, the EEOC suggests exploring whether there is another charity that is acceptable to the employee, employer, and union.[19]

If an employee resists paying a charitable substitute for reasons that are not based on religious objections, then the principles of *Ansonia Board of Education v. Philbrook*[20] take hold: Neither the employer nor the union is obligated to offer more than the one reasonable accommodation that has already been offered. In the few judicial decisions to address this issue, the employee has lost; the courts have found the charitable contribution to be a reasonable accommodation and the employee's suggested alternatives to create an undue hardship.[21]

National Labor Relations Act

In 1980, Congress amended Section 19 of the NLRA to state the following:

> Any employee who is a member of and adheres to established and traditional tenets or teachings of a bona fide religion, body, or sect which has historically held conscientious objections to joining or financially supporting labor organizations shall not be required to join or financially support any labor organization as a condition of employment; except that such employee may be required in a contract between such employees' employer and a labor organization in

---

18. Reprinted at Appendix B.

19. *Id.*

20. 479 U.S. 60 (1986).

21. Yott v. North American Rockwell, 602 F.2d 904; Stern v. Teamsters Local 200, 626 F. Supp. 1043 (E.D. Wis. 1986).

lieu of periodic dues and initiation fees, to pay sums equal to such dues and initiation fees to a nonreligious organization charitable fund exempt from taxation under section 501(c)(3) of Title 26, chosen by such employee from a list of at least three such funds, designated in such contract or if the contract fails to designate such funds, then to any such fund chosen by the employee. If such employee who holds conscientious objections pursuant to this section requests the labor organization to use the grievance-arbitration procedure on the employee's behalf, the labor organization is authorized to charge the employee for the reasonable cost of using such procedure.[22]

Although this provision adopted the principle of equivalent charitable contributions that was previously embraced by the courts under Title VII, the NLRA is significantly more restrictive than the judicially crafted standard. The NLRA requires that a religion be "bona fide" and that it have "established and traditional" tenets opposed to financial support for labor organizations. This restriction deviates considerably from the much broader definition of religion used in Title VII cases and under the First Amendment.[23] The NLRA also requires that the charity option be incorporated in a contract between the employer and union. Finally, the NLRA limits the kinds of charities to which the alternative contribution can be made.

The validity of this provision of the NLRA is in serious doubt. In 1990, the Sixth Circuit declared the statute unconstitutional, and the Supreme Court refused to review the decision. In *Wilson v. National Labor Relations Board,*[24] the Court of Appeals confronted a decision by the NLRB that an employee who offered to pay the equivalent of union dues to a charity was not entitled to the protection of Section 19 because he was not a member of a "bona fide religion, body, or sect" and because his religious objections to unions were based on personal convictions.

The Court of Appeals concluded that Section 19 is unconstitutional because it differentiates among religions; adherents of some religious

---

22. 29 U.S.C. § 169, reprinted at Appendix E.
23. See Chapter 3.
24. 920 F.2d 1282 (6th Cir. 1990), *cert. denied,* 505 U.S. 1218 (1992).

beliefs are entitled to the statute's protection, while other religious adherents are not protected. Members of "bona fide" religions are granted a statutory benefit, while members of religions that do not fit the statute's narrow description are denied the benefit. Failing to find any compelling interest in such discrimination, the court declared the law violative of the Free Exercise clause of the First Amendment.[25] It also found the law to be an unconstitutional establishment of religion, since it advances some religious beliefs over others and unnecessarily entangles the government (the NLRB and the courts) in interpreting religious doctrine in order to determine what is "bona fide."[26]

Prior to *Wilson,* several courts endeavored to reconcile Section 19 with Title VII.[27] None of these courts had addressed the constitutionality of Section 19. Since the decision in *Wilson,* the courts have been silent with respect to Section 19. Perhaps *Wilson* has nudged this provision into a well-deserved oblivion. As long as *Wilson* remains unchallenged, employers and unions should assume that the more lenient standards established under Title VII for the payment of dues equivalents by religious objectors will apply.

Summary

- Employees who have religious objections to the payment of union dues or to association with a labor union are entitled to an accommodation that permits the employees to pay the equivalent of dues to a charity. Such an accommodation is deemed reasonable and no other accommodation by the employer or the union is necessary.

---

25. *Id.* at 1287, relying on Larson v. Valente, 456 U.S. 228 (1982).

26. *Id.* at 1287-88.

27. EEOC v. Davey Tree Surgery Co., 671 F. Supp. 1260; International Assn. of Machinists v. Boeing Co., 662 F. Supp. 1069 (W.D. Wash. 1986), *aff'd,* 833 F.2d 165 (9th Cir. 1987), *cert. denied,* 485 U.S. 1014 (1988); Stern v. Teamsters General Local Union No. 200, 626 F. Supp. 1043 (E.D. Wis. 1986).

◉ CHAPTER 11

Religion in the Public Sector Workplace

Although public-sector employers are subject to Title VII, public employees have one additional protection that is not available to their private-sector counterparts: the First Amendment. To the extent that a Title VII "failure to accommodate" claim is made, the rules governing those claims have already been addressed in preceding chapters; for the most part, the general principles governing religious accommodation are the same in both the public and private sectors. However, claims for relief under the First Amendment present quite different issues. That Amendment prohibits government from passing any law "respecting the establishment of religion, or prohibiting the free exercise thereof. . . ." Because of the restraints that the First Amendment places on government action, public employees complaining of religious discrimination or seeking religious accommodation will often assert a constitutional claim in addition to a Title VII claim.

This chapter is devoted to the constitutional and statutory issues that affect public-sector employers and employees. The next chapter discusses the statutes and regulations that are peculiar to the federal workplace.

The First Amendment's Prohibition against the Establishment of Religion

In order to understand the types of claims typically asserted in public-sector cases, it is necessary to also understand the development of the relevant First Amendment standards and the way in which they have changed over time.[1]

The law governing establishment of religion has sometimes proved difficult to apply, although the conceptual framework for analyzing these cases has remained constant for more than a quarter-century. The Court's current standard for judging Establishment clause violations was enunciated in *Lemon v. Kurtzman*.[2] It has been oft-criticized, including by some of the Justices,[3] but has not been replaced. The Court has summarized that standard as follows:

> The Establishment Clause forbids the enactment of any law "respecting an establishment of religion." The Court has applied a three-pronged test to determine whether legislation comports with the Establishment Clause. First, the legislature must have adopted the law with a secular purpose. Second, the statute's principal or primary effect must be one that neither advances nor inhibits religion. Third, the statute must not result in an excessive entanglement with religion. State action violates the Establishment Clause if it fails to satisfy any of these prongs.[4]

Under this test, government may neither endorse nor disapprove of religion.[5]

In the employment context, litigation often arises out of the conflict between the Establishment clause and the Free Exercise clause. For example, proselytizing in the governmental workplace has proved to be a vexing problem. On the one hand, employees have asserted that proselytizing is an essential component of their faith that cannot be infringed. Employers, in response, argue that proselytizing in governmental offices can itself give the appearance (to the public or to other employees) that the govern-

---

1. The history of Supreme Court litigation involving the Free Exercise and Establishment clauses of the First Amendment is long and complicated—and beyond the purview of this book. We discuss this Supreme Court precedent only to the limited extent necessary to understand its impact on employment decisions in the public workplace.

2. 403 U.S. 602 (1971).

3. *See, e.g.,* Wallace v. Jaffree, 472 U.S. 38, 112 (1985) (Rehnquist, J., dissenting); Edwards v. Aguillard, 482 U.S. 578, 610 (1987) (Scalia, J., dissenting).

4. Edwards v. Aguillard, 482 U.S. at 582-3 (citations omitted).

5. *See* Wallace v. Jaffree, 472 U.S. at 70.

ment is supporting or promoting particular religious views. In other words, employers complain that, if they do not ban or curtail the proselytizing, they will be accused of violating the Establishment clause. The courts have not developed a uniform view as to how to treat such cases, resulting in divergent decisions. However, before addressing those cases in detail, it is necessary to explain the Supreme Court's interpretation of the Free Exercise clause, as applied to workplace issues.

The First Amendment's Protection of the Free Exercise of Religion

In *Sherbert v. Verner*,[6] the unemployment compensation law of South Carolina required out-of-work employees to make themselves available for suitable work; persons who, without good cause, refused to accept work could be denied benefits. The state had denied unemployment compensation benefits to the plaintiff, whose membership in the Seventh-Day Adventist Church precluded her from accepting work assignments on Saturdays. The denial was based on her refusal to take jobs requiring her to work on Saturdays. The Supreme Court reversed the state's action, holding that the unemployment compensation law placed a burden on the religious practices of Sabbatarians that could only be constitutional if it was supported by a "compelling state interest."[7] A mere "rational relationship" between the law and some "colorable state interest" would not be sufficient.[8] The Court found no compelling interest underpinning the South Carolina law and struck it down.

In *Wisconsin v. Yoder*,[9] the Supreme Court held that even laws that do not directly regulate religious practices are unconstitutional if they unduly burden the free exercise of religion and are not supported by a compelling governmental interest.[10]

The Supreme Court further refined this constitutional test in *Thomas v. Review Board of Indiana Employment Security*.[11] In that case, a Jehovah's

---

6. 374 U.S. 398 (1963).

7. *Id.* at 406. *See also* Frazee v. Illinois Dept. of Employment Sec., 489 U.S. 829 (1989).

8. 374 U.S. at 406.

9. 406 U.S. 205 (1972).

10. In *Yoder*, the Court concluded that the State of Wisconsin's interest in universal education did not overcome the Amish community's opposition on religious grounds to the State's mandatory education program for children.

11. 450 U.S. 707 (1981).

Witness quit his job rather than work in armaments production. He asserted that his religious beliefs precluded him from building military weapons. The State of Indiana denied unemployment benefits to Thomas because he had voluntarily terminated his own employment, even if it was guided by religious belief. The Supreme Court reversed, holding that

> Where the state conditions receipt of an important benefit upon conduct proscribed by a religious faith, or where it denies such a benefit because of conduct mandated by religious belief, thereby putting substantial pressure on an adherent to modify his behavior and to violate his beliefs, a burden upon religion exists. While the compulsion may be indirect, the infringement upon free exercise is nonetheless substantial.[12]

The Court then stated that such an infringement could only be constitutional if the State could show that

> it is the least restrictive means of achieving some compelling state interest.[13]

The state failed to persuade the Court that it satisfied this test.

The Supreme Court subsequently reaffirmed this version of the compelling interest test, but emphasized that the burdens on religion must be "substantial" to rise to the level of a constitutional conflict.[14] The courts have identified a substantial burden as one that creates more than a mere inconvenience; it must also affect a *central* religious tenet or belief.[15] The

---

12. *Id.* at 717-18. The Court emphasized that the First Amendment protects only religious beliefs and not personal philosophies. However, it concluded that Thomas' opposition to armaments production was based on his religious principles.

13. *Id.* at 718. The Court also rejected Indiana's argument that the payment of benefits would constitute an endorsement of Thomas' religion, in violation of the Establishment clause. The Court held that ensuring the rights of free exercise by an individual cannot be equated with an unconstitutional endorsement of that person's religious beliefs.

14. Hernandez v. C.I.R., 490 U.S. 680, 699 (1989). *See also* Genas v. State of New York Department of Correctional Services, 75 F.3d 825, 831 (2d Cir. 1996).

15. Hernandez v. C.I.R., 490 U.S. at 699; Fruchter v. Sossei, 68 FEP 59, 62 (S.D.N.Y. 1995). Some courts have held that a "central" religious practice or tenet is one that the faith mandates. *See, e.g.,* Bryant v. Gomez, 46 F.3d 948, 949 (9th Cir. 1995). Other courts have rejected this interpretation and have permitted plaintiffs to claim constitutional protection for activities that are optional under their religions. *See, e.g.,* Blanken v. Ohio Dept. of Rehabilitation, 72 FEP 887 (S.D. Ohio, 1996).

following are examples of cases in which work restrictions were found to be insubstantial and therefore constitutional:

- An employee who is permitted to work alternative hours to make up for absences on Sabbath can be compelled to maintain a detailed diary of absences and make-up days; although other employees did not have to keep a diary, it did not preclude the accommodation of taking Sabbath days off and represented only an inconvenience.[16]

- When the City of Los Angeles undertook an investigation of an assistant police chief accused of injecting his religious views into his employment decisions and practices, he protested that the investigation chilled his religious rights. The Ninth Circuit Court of Appeals disagreed, holding that the investigation was properly limited in scope and that the chief had failed to demonstrate how he was actually burdened in his religious practices.[17]

- A state court could prevent a bailiff from reading his Bible and evangelizing while in court and while in the court's public areas. The reviewing federal court affirmed the state court's decision, concluding that the reading of the Bible in court was not a central religious belief or practice and that the bailiff had other opportunities to read and evangelize while not working.[18]

The compelling interest test remained the prevailing test under the Free Exercise clause for several decades. The status quo came to an end in 1990, when the Supreme Court decided *Employment Division, Department of*

---

16. Fruchter v. Sossei, 68 FEP 59.

17. Vernon v. City of Los Angeles, 27 F.3d 1385 (9th Cir.), *cert. denied,* 513 U.S. 1000 (1994).

18. Kelly v. Municipal Court of Marion County, 852 F. Supp. 724, 730-31 (S.D. Ind. 1994). *Cf.* Brown v. Polk County, Iowa, 61 F.3d 650 (8th Cir. 1995) (en banc), *cert. denied,* 516 U.S. 1158 (1996). In *Brown,* the majority held that the employer (a county government) would suffer no undue hardship when a supervisor infrequently opened staff meetings with voluntary prayers by employees. The four dissenting judges analyzed the issue differently. They took the view that the county should be able to discipline the supervisor for permitting the prayers, since he had ample opportunity during the day to engage in prayer without involving other employees; the dissenting judges found that the supervisor did not confront a substantial burden in having to find alternative prayer opportunities.

Human Resources v. Smith.[19] There, the State of Oregon denied unemployment benefits to two American Indians who were fired from their jobs because of their use of the drug peyote in Indian religious ceremonies. The State pointed to a law that defined peyote as a "controlled substance" and criminalized its possession; the employees were denied unemployment benefits because use of the drug was determined to constitute misconduct justifying the termination of their employment. The Supreme Court upheld the state's actions in this case and, in so doing, rejected the employees' argument that the state failed to establish a compelling governmental interest to justify the refusal to accommodate their religious needs. The Court held that if the object of a law is to regulate religion and if the regulation places a substantial burden on religious practices, then the compelling-interest test should be applied. However, if religion is only incidentally affected by a "neutral, generally applicable law," then the government is not obligated to prove the existence of a compelling interest as a justification for its actions.[20]

The lower courts have extended *Smith* to noncriminal laws that have general applicability, including rules governing the workplace.[21] The *Smith* rule has been summarized as follows:

> a neutral law of general applicability that incidentally impinges on religious practice will not be subject to attack under the free exercise clause. However, the Court left open the viability of free exercise attacks on government actions that directly regulate religious belief or religious-based conduct. . . . [22]

---

19. 494 U.S. 872 (1990).

20. *Id.* at 881-85. The Court majority expended considerable effort to distinguish *Sherbert, Yoder* and other cases that involved statutes that seemed to be neutral as to religion as written. A concurring opinion by Justice O'Connor takes the majority to task for misconstruing that precedent; she would have applied the compelling-interest test and would then have concluded that Oregon's criminalization of peyote was such an interest. 494 U.S. at 890-907.

21. *See, e.g.,* Ryan v. U.S. Dept. of Justice, 950 F.2d 458 (7th Cir. 1991), *cert. denied,* 504 U.S. 958 (1992) (employee refusal to carry out work assignments); Cornerstone Bible Church v. City of Hastings, 948 F.2d 464 (8th Cir. 1991) (zoning regulations that affect churches); Genas v. State of New York, 75 F.3d 825 (accommodation of work schedules for prison guards).

22. Cornerstone Bible Church v. City of Hastings, 948 F.2d at 472 (citations omitted).

This dichotomous approach to Free Exercise claims did not go unchallenged for long. In 1993, Congress passed the Religious Freedom Restoration Act (RFRA), which had the explicit purpose of restoring the "compelling interest test as set forth in Sherbert v. Verner . . . and Wisconsin v. Yoder . . . and to guarantee its application in all cases where free exercise of religion is substantially burdened" and providing "a claim or defense to persons whose religious exercise is substantially burdened by government."[23] The new law also explicitly stated that its purpose was to reverse the effects of the *Smith* decision by restoring the compelling interest test to all claims under the Free Exercise clause.[24] The new standard (or rather the return to the *Sherbert/Yoder* standard) was defined as follows:

(a) **In general.** Government shall not substantially burden a person's exercise of religion even if the burden results from a rule of general applicability, except as provided in subsection (b).

(b) **Exception.** Government may substantially burden a person's exercise of religion only if it demonstrates that application of the burden to the person—

(1) is in furtherance of a compelling governmental interest; and

(2) is the least restrictive means of furthering that compelling governmental interest.[25]

The law was made applicable to all branches of the federal and state governments, including all subdivisions of the state governments.[26] It applied to all federal and state laws and to the implementation of those laws, including laws adopted prior to the passage of RFRA.[27]

The passage of RFRA ensured that all public workplace rules affecting religion would be decided under the same constitutional standard, regardless of whether the rule was intended to regulate religious practices or was a neutral rule of general applicability.

---

23. 42 U.S.C. § 2000bb(b), reprinted at Appendix G. *See* Rodriguez v. City of Chicago, 69 FEP 993, 996 (N.D. Ill. 1996) and cases cited therein.

24. 42 U.S.C. § 2000bb(a).

25. *Id.* at § 2000bb-1.

26. *Id.* at § 2000bb-2.

27. *Id.* at § 2000bb-3.

However, the Supreme Court once again had the last word. In 1997, the Supreme Court declared RFRA unconstitutional, as applied to the states, in *City of Boerne v. Flores*.[28] The Court held that, in passing RFRA, Congress had not merely sought to enforce the First Amendment, but had redefined the scope of the substantive rights under that Amendment; in doing so, Congress's imposition of RFRA on the states exceeded its constitutional powers.[29] The decision in *Boerne* restores *Smith* as the prevailing law on "neutral" governmental regulations that have a substantial impact on religious practices.

In light of the decision in *Boerne,* one might surmise that RFRA has been consigned to the status of historical curiosity. However, as discussed in the next chapter, the federal government has decided (through White House "Guidelines on Religious Exercise and Religious Expression in the Federal Workplace")[30] that it will adhere to the RFRA standards. This means that the constitutional standards governing state employees may be different from the standards regulating federal employees. While the same compelling interest test applies to federal and state employers when the government directly tries to regulate religious practices, different standards apply to neutral work rules that only incidentally affect religion. A *state's* neutral rules will be adjudged under the standards of *Smith,* whereas a comparable *federal* rule may remain subject to the compelling-interest test of *Sherbert / Yoder / Thomas*.[31]

Work Rules that Directly Regulate Religious Practices

The compelling interest test applies to all work rules (state or federal) that have the objective of regulating religion. The decision in *Smith* did not purport to change the constitutional analysis for such regulations if they result in substantial burdens on religious beliefs or practices.

---

28. 117 S.Ct. 2157 (1997).

29. *Id.*

30. The full text of the Guidelines is reprinted at Appendix H.

31. We use the word "may" with respect to federal employment because the holding in *City of Boerne* only decided the impact of RFRA on state (as opposed to federal) governments and because the White House Guidelines state that they do not create any new rights or causes of action. It is therefore uncertain whether an aggrieved federal employee could bring suit based on an employer's deviation from the Guidelines.

As one might expect, there are relatively few workplace rules that are promulgated with the intention of restricting religious beliefs or behavior. In the few decided cases, the courts generally have supported an employer's efforts in this respect and have found a justifying governmental interest. These cases break down into two main categories: regulation of religious clothing and regulation of employee proselytizing. In both instances, employers have prevailed because they could show that their regulations were necessary to avoid an establishment-of-religion problem. That is, employers have successfully contended that they needed to restrain religious activities in order to preserve the "appearance of religious neutrality" in public offices.[32]

In effect, the government may rely upon the Establishment clause of the First Amendment as a defense to claims that it is interfering in the free exercise of religion. The preservation of religious neutrality, as required by the Establishment clause, becomes a compelling governmental interest that justifies the infringement of an employee's freedom to practice religion in the public workplace.

Regulation of Religious Clothing

The State of Oregon has a law that prohibits public-school teachers from wearing religious dress while working.[33] When a Sikh teacher challenged the law (after revocation of her teaching certificate for noncompliance with the law), the Oregon Supreme Court affirmed the law and the action against the teacher.[34] The court concluded that "a rule against such religious dress is permissible to avoid the appearance of sectarian influence, favoritism, or official approval in the public school."[35] The U.S. Supreme Court dismissed the teacher's appeal for want of a substantial federal question, leaving the Oregon decision intact.

Several years later, a similar challenge was made against Pennsylvania's religious "garb" statute, which was even broader than the Oregon law. The Pennsylvania statute prohibited teachers from wearing any

---

32. United States v. Bd. of Education for School District of Philadelphia, 911 F.2d 882, 889 (3d Cir. 1990).

33. Or. Rev. Stat. § 342.650.

34. Cooper v. Eugene School District No. 4J, 301 Or. 358, 723 P.2d 298 (1986), *appeal dismissed,* 480 U.S. 942 (1987).

35. 723 P.2d at 308.

"dress, mark, emblem or insignia indicating the fact that such teacher is a member or adherent of any religious order, sect or denomination."[36] The law also provided that a teacher violating the rule must be suspended for one year for the first infraction and must be permanently disqualified from teaching in the school for the second violation; a public-school director who fails to enforce this rule can be prosecuted for a misdemeanor and can be barred from being a director of public education in the state for five years in the event of a second conviction.[37] The U.S. Department of Justice sued the City of Philadelphia and the State of Pennsylvania under Title VII, claiming that enforcement of the "garb" law violated the right of teachers to have their religious practices accommodated.

The Third Circuit Court of Appeals rejected the Justice Department's arguments and upheld the state law.[38] The Court found that the law was a narrowly tailored effort to ensure religious neutrality in the public school system and that this objective was a compelling governmental interest.[39] The Court further concluded that officials of the Board of Education would be subjected to an undue hardship if they were forced to violate this valid statute:

> forcing an employer to sacrifice a compelling state interest would undeniably constitute an undue hardship.[40]

The Oregon and Pennsylvania decisions make it clear that the courts are willing to tolerate a policy of suppressing certain religious

---

36. 24 Pa. Stat. Ann. § 11-1112.

37. *Id.*

38. United States v. Board of Educ., 911 F.2d at 893-94.

39. *Id.* at 893.

40. *Id.* at 890. The court noted that the hardship was even more onerous in view of the law's threat of criminal prosecution against school board officials who failed to enforce the law. *Id.* at 891.

The outcome in *Board of Education* must be contrasted with the decision in *EEOC v. Reads, Inc.,* 759 F. Supp. 1150 (E.D. Pa. 1991), in which an applicant for a school-counselor position was not hired because she wore various head coverings in compliance with her Muslim faith. The court declined to apply the Pennsylvania Garb law because it found an absence of evidence that the counselor's head coverings were perceived as religious clothing. Absent that perception, the court concluded that the counselor was entitled to the protection of Title VII's accommodation provisions.

activities in the public workplace if failure to do so would expose the state to an establishment-of-religion claim.

Employer Bans on Proselytizing

Whereas the Oregon and Pennsylvania cases involved duly promulgated laws regulating religion, most other cases that have addressed clashes between the Establishment and Free Exercise clauses have arisen out of ad hoc decisions by government officials to prevent an employee's religious activities on the ground that they breached or gave the appearance of breaching the government's religious neutrality. Most of these cases have involved expressions of religious belief or proselytizing at work.

For many Americans, religion is a purely private matter, to be practiced in houses of worship or at home. For others, however, this view directly contradicts the core teachings of their religious belief system. Some religions direct their adherents to "spread the Gospel wherever the opportunity presents itself;"[41] to encourage others to "accept God;"[42] or to be a "living witness" to their beliefs.[43] These people believe that they are compelled by their faith to encourage others to consider their beliefs. Since they spend much of their day at work, they often share their religious views at the workplace.

Most people view the government workplace as a religion-free zone, largely because of their understanding of the Establishment clause of the First Amendment. However, some courts have taken a less absolutist view of the First Amendment and have held that the context in which proselytizing occurs will determine its legality.[44] Specifically, a number of courts have concluded that the boundaries of permissible religious conduct will depend on whether the employee shares his or her religious beliefs solely with coworkers or whether those beliefs are directed towards members of the public.

---

41. Spratt v. County of Kent, 621 F. Supp. 594 (W.D. Mich. 1985), aff'd, 810 F.2d 203 (6th Cir. 1986), cert. denied, 480 U.S. 934 (1987).

42. Chalmers v. Tulon Co., 101 F.3d 1012, 1015 (4th Cir. 1995), cert. denied, 118 S.Ct. 58 (1997).

43. Wilson v. US West Communications, 58 F.3d 1337, 1339 (8th Cir. 1995).

44. As discussed in the next chapter, the White House Guidelines on religion take a similar view.

Employees Who Share Their Religious Views with the Public

As seen in the religious-clothing cases, the courts are especially sensitive to the religious activities of employees in public schools and have been hostile to employees' insistence that they be able to express their religious views openly in that context. The following cases exemplify this hostility:

- A school district could properly refuse to renew a substitute teacher's contract in part because he "interjected . . . religious-oriented materials into portions of [his] classroom presentation."[45] The teacher's activities included distributing Biblical pamphlets to students and telling students that he did not believe in evolution. The Seventh Circuit held that the employer had no obligation to accommodate the teacher's religious activities and that it did not discriminate on the basis of religion when terminating the teacher.

- The Tenth Circuit came to the same conclusion in a case involving somewhat more passive activities by a teacher.[46] A fifth-grade public-school teacher had kept a Bible on his desk and two other religious books in his classroom library; he also read from his Bible during a fifteen-minute silent reading period in the classroom. He did not overtly engage in proselytizing or the teaching of religion. The Court of Appeals nevertheless affirmed the school's directive that he remove the Bible and other books and that he refrain from religious activities in front of the students "to avoid the appearance of teaching religion".[47] The court also found that the school's policy did not constitute an anti-Christian establishment of religion, since the policy had a secular purpose and

---

45. Helland v. South Bend Community School Corp., 93 F.3d 327, 329 (7th Cir. 1996), *cert. denied,* 117 S.Ct. 769 (1997). The employee's proselytizing was only one of several factors that led to his discharge; he was also cited for failing to follow lesson plans and failing to control his students. The court found that these other factors were not pretexts.

46. Roberts v. Madigan, 921 F.2d 1047 (10th Cir. 1990), *cert. denied,* 505 U.S. 1218 (1992).

47. 921 F.2d at 1050, 1056-58.

did not have the primary effect of endorsing or disapproving any particular religion.[48]

■ When students complained that a public university professor had injected his religious views into his course work on exercise physiology and had organized an "optional class" on the topic of "Evidences of God in Human Physiology," in which he taught that humans were created by God and were not the product of evolution, the Eleventh Circuit upheld the university's directive that such activities cease.[49] The court concluded that the professor's ability to practice his religion was not impeded and that the appearance of proselytizing by the professor gave rise to a potential violation of the Establishment clause of the First Amendment.[50]

■ The Ninth Circuit similarly affirmed that discussions of religion by teachers are sanctionable, even if they occur outside of the classroom.[51] When a biology teacher refused to teach evolution as a scientific fact, the school district instructed him to cease all discussions of religion, even those initiated by students outside of the classroom. The teacher protested the forced teaching of evolution and the restrictions on his religious speech, but the Court of Appeals upheld the school district because of the likelihood that

---

48. *Id.* at 1053-56. The court's ruling was based on the totality of the teacher's conduct. It is therefore not clear whether the same result would necessarily have been reached if the teacher's only activity was to keep a Bible on his desk. The dissenting opinion raised this point, concluding that the plaintiff's activities were too passive to rise to the level of a constitutional problem, since he did not read the Bible aloud or discuss its contents with his students. The dissenting judge also noted that none of the students or students' parents had complained of religious intimidation or coercion in the teacher's activities. *Id.* at 1059.

49. Bishop v. Aronov, 926 F.2d 1066 (11th Cir. 1991), *cert. denied,* 505 U.S. 1218 (1992).

50. The court made clear that the professor was free to organize extracurricular programs on campus in which he could discuss his religious views. The prohibition against his activities only extended to his course work and to the after-class meetings that were intended as an adjunct to his course work. *Id.* at 1075-76. The court also held that the university's actions did not violate the *Lemon v. Kurtzman* standards, since it acted with the secular purpose of maintaining religious neutrality in the classroom. *Id.* at 1077.

51. Peloza v. Capistrano Unified School District, 37 F.3d 517 (9th Cir. 1994), *cert. denied,* 515 U.S. 1173 (1995).

students would equate his views with those of the school.[52] The court concluded that the teacher's expressions of religious views would create an establishment of religion within the meaning of *Lemon v. Kurtzman.*

The courts have also shown considerable concern over employee proselytizing in the law enforcement context. Employees in that sector have unusual influence over members of the public; sometimes they literally have a captive audience. Jails and prisons are the most obvious examples—inmates are subject to the authority of their guards and are given strong incentives to agree with the directions given them by government employees. These factors have caused courts to reject discrimination claims filed by government workers involved in various aspects of law enforcement when their employers have attempted to squelch proselytizing activities:

- When a juvenile-outreach counselor used explicitly religious philosophy (which he termed a "Christian perspective") in counseling juveniles in trouble with the law, his employer instructed him to cease the practice. When he refused to follow these instructions, he was fired. The district court held that neither Title VII nor the First Amendment protected the counselor.[53] While the counselor could use religious principles in his counseling—for example, the need to refrain from stealing or the benefits of honoring one's parents—he could not engage in the type of explicitly religious sermonizing that he had previously used because it "would impermissibly entangle the Juvenile Court in religion."[54]

- A county-court bailiff often read his Bible while on duty in the courtroom and in the public-reception area. He also volunteered his religious beliefs to prisoners who were in a holding cell as they waited to appear before the judge. The federal district court held

---

52. The dissenting judge's opinion focused on the distinction between the teaching of religion per se and teaching *about* religion. The dissent also argued that the school district went too far in preventing the teacher from engaging in student-initiated discussions during non-teaching times. *Id.* at 525-26.

53. Langlotz v. Picciano, 683 F. Supp. 1041 (E.D. Va. 1988), *aff'd,* 905 F.2d 1530 (4th Cir. 1990).

54. *Id.* at 1049.

that the county had properly discharged the bailiff.[55] The court noted that the bailiff could have easily avoided forcing members of the public to be confronted by his religious beliefs (for example, he could read the Bible in private offices when he was not needed for public duties).

■ A county social worker often used religion in his counseling sessions with inmates. He read the Bible with the inmates, prayed with them, and addressed spiritual issues. He went so far as to exorcise demons. The county repeatedly warned him about his "counseling" methods and ultimately discharged him for his refusal to change his practices. The federal district court held that the employee did not have a claim under Title VII because any effort to accommodate him would have caused an undue hardship (that is, would have breached the government's obligation to maintain religious neutrality).[56] As to the employee's First Amendment claim, the court held that "plaintiff's free exercise rights must be limited to the extent that his conduct would infringe upon the establishment clause or constitutional rights of others. . . ."[57]

One final decision, consistent with the foregoing precedent, was issued by the Seventh Circuit in a case that involved a Veterans Administration chaplain who was hired to provide nondenominational counseling to residents of a VA hospital, many of whom were psychiatric patients. When he repeatedly ignored instructions not to engage in proselytizing among the patients, he was discharged. The Seventh Circuit found no violation of the plaintiff's Free Exercise rights, since he had "no absolute constitutional right to conduct religious services and offer religious counsel in a government institution."[58] The court held that the VA was constitutionally justified in preventing a violation of the Establishment clause that would arise from employee proselytizing.

If there is one thematic thread running through the foregoing public sector cases, it is that they all involved captive audiences of one sort or another (classrooms, jails, hospitals). In all of these cases, the result has

55. Kelly v. Municipal Ct. of Marion Count, 852 F. Supp. 724 (S.D. Ind. 1984).

56. Spratt v. County of Kent, 621 F. Supp. 594.

57. *Id.* at 601.

58. Baz v. Walters, 782 F.2d 701, 708-09 (7th Cir. 1986).

been the same: A public employee may not target that audience with religious proselytizing. The employee cannot preserve those on-the-job religious practices under the Free Exercise clause if it would create the reasonable appearance that the governmental employer was no longer neutral with respect to religion. The government cannot be required to accommodate an employee's religious practices if doing so would reasonably suggest that the government endorses those practices; in the context of Title VII, such an accommodation would constitute an undue hardship.

Employees Who Share Their Religious Views with Coworkers

While public sector employees have had little success in court when claiming a right to share their religious beliefs with members of the public, the courts have been more accepting of employee proselytizing that has been directed solely toward coworkers. The courts have held that a public employer can institute narrow restrictions on employees' religious activities in the workplace, but that public employees must be allowed some degree of personal freedom in this area, as long as the public is not targeted and there is no disruption of the workplace.

As the Ninth Circuit held in *Tucker v. State of California Department of Education,* government employees do not lose their First Amendment rights simply because they receive the benefit of public employment.[59] In a well-organized discussion, the court extensively analyzed both the government's and the employee's interests in cases involving proselytizing and other religious practices in the public sector workplace.

Tucker was a computer analyst for the California Department of Education who decided that his religious beliefs required him to give God credit for any work he performed. Acting upon this belief, he developed a software program to be used throughout the Department in which he inserted his name, followed by "Servant of the Lord Jesus Christ." He also included the acronym "SOTLJC" on the label to the program and other materials that he circulated. The agency reacted by not merely banning the circulation of religious statements and acronyms on official department work, but by also prohibiting employees from (1) engaging in "any religious advocacy, either written or oral, during the work hours or in the workplace," and (2) storing or displaying "any religious artifacts, tracts,

---

59. 97 F.3d 1204 (9th Cir. 1996), citing Pickering v. Board of Education, 391 U.S. 563 (1968).

information or other materials in any part of the workplace other than in their own closed offices or defined cubicles." Tucker sued under the state and federal constitutions and under Title VII. Tucker did not dispute the lawfulness of the department's ban on his use of the "SOTLJC" acronym on official work. He did, however, contest the remainder of the agency's ban on religious advocacy and religious displays.

The court of appeals noted that the government's restrictions on speech might have been constitutional if they were directed at teachers or other Department of Education employees who were addressing the public.[60] However, the bans on religious activities that grew out of Tucker's conduct were focused solely on an office that performed no educational function and barred speech that was directed solely to coworkers. In that context, the court found the suppression of religious advocacy to be unconstitutionally broad. The court further noted that

> there is a legitimate state interest in preventing displays of religious objects that might suggest state endorsement of religion. The state has a legitimate interest, for example, in preventing the posting of Crosses or Stars of David in the main hallways, by the elevators, or in the lobbies, and in other locations throughout buildings. Such a symbol could give the impression of impermissible government support for religion. . . . However, banning the posting of *all* religious materials and information in *all* areas of any office building except in employees' private cubicles simply goes too far. It is not a reasonable means of achieving the state's legitimate ends.[61]

What makes *Tucker* especially instructive is its consideration of each of the arguments put forward by the Education Department for its actions. Its analysis provides a road map to navigate similar cases in the future. The court noted that the government cited five bases to support the constitutionality of its ban on religious advocacy:

1. promoting the efficiency of the workplace;
2. protecting the "liberty interests" of other employees not to be subjected to religious advocacy;

---

60. *Id.* at 1213.
61. *Id.* at 1216, emphasis in original.

3. "meeting the expectations of the taxpayers that their tax dollars are being used to support legitimate state business and not to promote religion;"

4. fulfilling its duty to comply with the Establishment clause of the United States Constitution; and

5. fulfilling its duty to comply with the religion clauses of the California Constitution.[62]

As far as the alleged need to promote efficiency, the agency had relied primarily on the fact that Tucker's supervisor had spent "hundreds of hours" addressing his religious conduct. The court held that the time spent by a supervisor on a religious accommodation issue is not evidence of disruption in the workplace. It was simply part of the supervisor's duties to deal with personnel issues of this kind. Moreover, the court noted the absence of evidence of any "disruption in general" caused by Tucker's actions.

Lack of evidence similarly led to the rejection of the agency's claims that it needed to protect the interests of other employees and taxpayers. There was no evidence that coworkers had complained about Tucker's religious speech and no evidence that any members of the public had been exposed to Tucker's activities. The court declined to permit speculation about the impact on other employees or the public to justify an infringement on religious speech.

The government's primary defense was that it had a compelling interest in avoiding an unconstitutional establishment of religion under both the United States and California constitutions. However, the court observed that such an argument depends upon proof of a "plausible fear" that the public would reasonably perceive the speech as being endorsed by the government. The court found, to the contrary, that "[w]hat Tucker discusses in his cubicle or in the hallway with other computer analysts clearly would not appear to any reasonable person to represent the views of the state."[63]

---

62. *Id.* at 1211.

63. *Id.* at 1213. The conclusion under the State constitution was similar: "The state has cited no case that supports its argument that the California Constitution justifies the Department of Education's banning the advocacy of religion in private discussions between coworkers in the Child Nutrition and Food Distribution Division." *Id.* at 1214.

As to the agency's ban on the display of religious artifacts and symbols, the court noted that the "government has a greater interest in controlling what materials are posted on its property than it does in controlling the speech of the people who work for it, especially when its employees are engaged in private conversation among themselves."[64] Nevertheless, while the state can legitimately ban or regulate displays in various public parts of a government building,[65] the ban on all displays in all places was overbroad, especially when employees are permitted to post expressive materials in the building that do not relate to religion.[66]

In *Brown v. Polk County, Iowa,*[67] the Eighth Circuit came to conclusions similar to those reached in *Tucker,* with the court criticizing the employer's overly broad proscriptions and speculation, rather than proof, as to undue hardship. In *Brown,* the director of a county data-processing department had been fired for occasionally opening staff meetings with religious prayers and by keeping a Bible and religious artifacts at his desk; on occasion, he had also discussed religion with employees. In addition, the plaintiff had his secretary type his Bible-study notes and had also opened the offices early so that the premises could be used for morning prayers.

The court majority (over a vigorous dissent) agreed that the county could ban the latter two activities, since it involved the misuse of government premises and government employees.[68] However, the court reversed the discharge because of the county's reliance on a policy that directed the plaintiff to "cease any activities that *could be considered* to be religious proselytizing, witnessing, or counseling."[69] The court dismissed the county's arguments that the supervisor's prayers and religious artifacts violated the Establishment clause and that accommodating his conduct would create an undue hardship because of the potential disruption he would cause among employees.

---

64. *Id.* at 1214.

65. For example, the state could limit all employee notices to designated bulletin boards.

66. *Id.* at 1215-16.

67. 61 F.3d 650 (8th Cir. 1995).

68. *Id.* at 656.

69. *Id.* at 658-59 (emphasis in original).

As in *Tucker,* the court observed that there was no evidence that other employees had complained about his conduct. In the absence of such evidence, the court held that the county was merely speculating as to undue hardship in the event that it tried to accommodate his religious activities.[70]

In reaching this conclusion, the court did not address the possibility that subordinates would not complain about the activities of the head of a department, even if those activities did cause distress. The court ignored the inherent coercive power that resides within the authority of any high-ranking supervisor. The dissenting judge, however, recognized this problem and would have upheld the county's actions because its directive to plaintiff would not have prevented him from privately engaging in prayer or other religious activities during the course of the workday. As stated in the dissenting opinion, "the balance of interests tips in the County's favor in this case, primarily given Brown's status as a supervisor of fifty employees."[71]

As to the county's concerns that the supervisor's actions would create religious harassment or intimidation, the court held that the county's broad ban on any proselytizing or other religious activities by the plaintiff was not narrowly tailored to meet this objective. While a more narrowly drawn prohibition against intimidation or harassment would be constitutional, the court held that the breadth of the county's ban on the plaintiff's activities "exhibited a hostility to religion that our Constitution simply prohibits."[72]

Although there are relatively few cases of proselytizing by public employees, the decisions in *Tucker* and *Brown* suggest that employees who confine their religious activities to the workplace (that is, do not address their beliefs to the public) and who do not engage in practices

---

70. *Id.* at 655. The court found that the county had made no effort to accommodate the plaintiff's activities.

71. *Id.* at 660. The majority opinion also failed to recognize that an establishment of religion is not dependent upon whether the audience likes or abhors the message being conveyed. An "establishment" occurs whenever the government's actions lead to a reasonable perception that it has endorsed, supported, or opposed religious beliefs. A constitutional violation can occur even when (or especially when) the target audience is receptive to the religious message.

72. *Id.* at 658-59.

that are disruptive, intimidating or harassing will be given some leeway by the courts.

Work Rules that Are Neutral with Respect to Religion

The foregoing discussion focused on laws or management decisions in the public sector that directly target religious practices. However, there are also numerous situations in which neutral work rules have a restrictive impact on religious practices. Since the decision in *Smith,* state employers do not face the burden of justifying neutral work rules under the compelling interest test. Nevertheless, these employers must still satisfy the accommodation requirements of Title VII.

For the most part, the courts have approved the same types of accommodations for public sector employees as are found in the private sector. Shift swaps, voluntary changes in work assignments, and similar accommodations have been applied approvingly in both sectors. The standard of undue hardship enunciated in *TWA v. Hardison* has also been applied to the public sector workplace. Rather than repeat this discussion of accommodation precedent, we refer the reader to Chapters 6 through 9, which cover these topics and which cite both public and private sector cases.

However, there have been a few cases in the public sector in which the courts have expressed a greater reluctance to impose accommodations on an unwilling employer; these cases have involved law-enforcement/public-safety functions. The Seventh, Tenth and Eleventh Circuits, in particular, are sensitive to law-enforcement functions that require a significant degree of management flexibility and/or operate on a 24-hour-per-day basis.

In *Beadle v. Hillsborough County Sheriff's Office,*[73] a Seventh-Day Adventist who worked as a prison guard refused to work on Saturdays. The Sheriff's department permitted him to arrange voluntary shift swaps with other employees. However, on occasions when he was unable to do so, he insisted that the department assist him in finding another employee to work a Saturday shift. The department refused and ultimately fired the plaintiff when he failed to report for work after being unable to locate replacements for several shifts. The Eleventh Circuit Court

---

73. 29 F.3d 589 (11th Cir. 1994), *cert. denied,* 514 U.S. 1128 (1995).

of Appeals noted that the Sheriff's office maintained a neutral rotating-shift system that, to a limited extent, accommodated plaintiff's needs. The Court also approved of the shift swaps as an added accommodation. In light of these accommodations, the Court concluded that forcing any additional accommodations on the employer (such as requiring it to locate replacements for plaintiff) would constitute an undue hardship.[74]

This decision was not the last one to involve Mr. Beadle and the Eleventh Circuit. He next applied for and obtained a job with the police department in Tampa, Florida, which was aware of his pending suit against the Hillsborough County Sheriff's department. During his training, he advised his superiors that he could not work Saturdays and requested that he be assigned to a particular training officer who did not work Saturday shifts. The department declined and Beadle resigned. He later sued, claiming constructive discharge. In *Beadle v. City of Tampa*,[75] the Court of Appeals held that acceding to Beadle's demand for a change in assignment would constitute an undue hardship:

> The Tampa Police Department is a twenty-four hour a day, seven-day a week, three hundred sixty-five day a year agency that must allocate work schedules among over nine hundred employees. More importantly, the Department is charged with protecting the health, safety, and welfare of its citizenry. . . . When the employer's business involves the protection of lives and property, "courts should go slow in restructuring [its] employment practices."[76]

This same solicitousness for law enforcement is found in the Seventh Circuit's decision in *Ryan v. U.S. Department of Justice*.[77] In that case, an FBI agent refused to work on certain investigations for sincerely held reli-

---

74. *Accord* Genas v. New York Dept. of Correctional Services, 75 F.3d 825, 832-33 (2d Cir. 1996). The Second Circuit Court of Appeals held that the New York Department of Corrections had no obligation to accommodate a guard's Sabbath needs beyond the neutral assignment system under a collective bargaining agreement and the permission of voluntary shift swaps.

75. 42 F.3d 633 (11th Cir.), *cert. denied,* 515 U.S. 1152 (1995).

76. *Id.* at 637, quoting United States v. City of Albuquerque, 545 F.2d 110, 114 (10th Cir. 1976), *cert. denied,* 433 U.S. 909 (1977). The *Albuquerque* case involved a firefighter who failed to avail himself of shift swaps with other employees and failed to report to work on his Sabbath when a request for unscheduled leave was denied.

77. 950 F.2d 458 (7th Cir. 1991).

gious reasons. Ryan declined to swap assignments with another agent, but simply requested that he not be given the offending investigatory assignments; when he continued to receive those assignments, he refused to carry them out. In affirming his termination, the Circuit Court observed:

> It is difficult for any organization to accommodate employees who are choosy about assignments; for a paramilitary organization the tension is even greater. . . . With good will all around, and flexibility on the part of Ryan's fellow agents, it just might be possible to make a go of it. Title VII does not, however, compel the FBI to attempt this. Legal institutions lack the sense of nuance that will tell an experienced agent how far the rules may be bent without injury to the FBI's mission.[78]

A final case showing judicial solicitousness for law enforcement is *Blanken v. Ohio Department of Rehabilitation*.[79] The plaintiff was employed in the food-service area of a correctional facility; in that position, he supervised approximately thirty inmates. As a Native-American, he refused to cut his hair on religious grounds and brought an action under RFRA to enjoin the prison from enforcing a policy restricting the hair length of male employees, but not female employees. Even under the heightened standard of the compelling interest test of RFRA, the court found sufficient justification for the policy and granted summary judgment to the defendants.

Whether the foregoing cases would have been decided differently in the private sector or in a non-law enforcement context is difficult to say.[80] However, the courts' reluctance to interfere in law enforcement assignments and regulations suggests that this is one area in which employees should expect a less liberal interpretation of Title VII and in which

---

78. *Id.* at 462.

79. 72 FEP 887.

80. *Cf.* Haring v. Blumenthal, 471 F. Supp. 1172 (D.D.C. 1979), *cert. denied,* 452 U.S. 939 (1981). The court in *Haring* held that the Internal Revenue Service must accommodate a non-law enforcement employee who refused, for religious reasons, to work on certain tax-exempt organization applications. The court found no undue hardship in requiring the agency to assign the employee to work that did not offend his religious beliefs.

employers are more likely to prevail in their arguments that an employee's request for accommodation will create an undue hardship.

Summary

- Public-sector employees are protected by both Title VII and the Free Exercise clause of the First Amendment.
- If a public-sector employer adopts a rule with the objective of regulating religion and if the rule places a substantial burden on an employee's practice of a central religious belief, the First Amendment requires the employer to prove that it used the least restrictive means of achieving a compelling interest.
- The compelling interest/least restrictive alternative test does *not* apply when a state or local government employer adopts a neutral rule that incidentally interferes in an employee's religious practice. In such cases, however, the employee is still protected by Title VII.
- Public employers may directly regulate or ban employees' religious practices if those practices reasonably create the appearance that the government is endorsing or supporting religion. In such cases, the government has a compelling interest in avoiding a violation of the Establishment clause of the First Amendment.
- The courts have generally upheld the actions of public employers that limit or prohibit employee proselytizing to which the public is exposed; proselytizing in these circumstances creates the risk of a breach of the First Amendment's Establishment clause. The courts have shown greater leeway towards employees who direct their proselytizing solely towards their coworkers, as long as the proselytizing is neither disruptive nor harassing.
- Public employers that carry out law enforcement functions have generally had greater success in persuading the courts that accommodating religious practices will create an undue hardship. The courts have tended to be reluctant to interfere in the internal administration of an agency's law enforcement duties.

❈ CHAPTER 12

Religion in the
Federal Workplace

The previous chapter addressed the decisional law that applies to all public employers and employees—with one exception. Employees in the executive branch of the federal government are protected by the First Amendment and Title VII *and* by separate statutes and regulations relating to religious leave. In addition, almost all executive branch employees are covered by the recently promulgated White House "Guidelines on Religious Exercise and Religious Expression in the Federal Workplace."[1] This chapter addresses the issues that are unique to the federal government.

Federal Statutes and Regulations

Title VII bars all agencies of the executive branch of the federal government from discriminating based on religion.[2] Several provisions of the merit personnel system incorporate Title VII's requirements, while other statutes extend them to the legislative branch.[3] These statutes all apply

---

1. Reprinted at Appendix H. Hereinafter cited as the "Guidelines."

2. 42 U.S.C. § 2000e-16.

3. 5 U.S.C. § 7201(b) ("It is the policy of the United States to insure equal employment opportunities for employees without discrimination because of race, color, religion, sex, or national origin. The President shall use his existing authority to carry out this policy."); 5 U.S.C. § 2302 (prohibited personnel practice for federal executive agency to engage in discriminatory practices); 2 U.S.C. § 1301 *et seq.* (Congressional employees); 31 U.S.C. § 732 (General Accounting Office).

Title VII's principles of accommodation and disparate treatment to the federal workplace. To the extent that the courts have decided Title VII issues in claims by federal employees, those decisions are discussed elsewhere in this book. We will not repeat those discussions here, since the same principles apply in both the public and private sectors. Similarly, we refer the reader to the preceding chapter for an extended discussion of First Amendment jurisprudence. This chapter is limited to mandates that have been promulgated solely for the federal workplace and that, to some extent, deviate from the practices in the private sector.

Apart from the foregoing statutes, the statutory regulation of religion in the federal workplace is limited to providing compensatory leave for religious absences. Section 5550a of Title 5, United States Code, provides:

> (a) Not later than 30 days after the date of the enactment of this section, the Office of Personnel Management shall prescribe regulations providing for work schedules under which an employee whose personal religious beliefs require the abstention from work during certain periods of time, may elect to engage in overtime work for time lost for meeting those religious requirements. Any employee who so elects such overtime work shall be granted equal compensatory time off from his scheduled tour of duty (in lieu of overtime pay) for such religious reasons, notwithstanding any other provision of law. . . .

> (c) Regulations under this section may provide for such exceptions as may be necessary to efficiently carry out the mission of the agency or agencies involved.

Neither the statute nor the regulations provides examples of situations in which leave might interfere in an agency's mission. Instead, the regulations merely state that compensatory leave and absences for religious purposes shall be granted:

> To the extent that such modifications in work schedules do not interfere with the efficient accomplishment of an agency's mission, the agency shall in each instance afford the employee the opportunity to work compensatory overtime. . . . [4]

---

4. 5 C.F.R. § 550.1002(b).

While the EEOC's Guidelines on Discrimination Because of Religion interpret the term "undue hardship," as it is used in Section 701e(j) of Title VII, they do not indicate whether the agency views "undue hardship" and "interfer[ence] with the efficient accomplishment of any agency's mission" to be synonymous.

Employees who are absent for religious purposes may work the compensatory overtime either before or after the absence; if the work is performed after, it must be "within a reasonable amount of time."[5] The time absent may be calculated in days, hours, or increments of hours, leaving the employee with maximum flexibility in scheduling religious observances.[6] This *compensatory* overtime is paid at an employee's normal pay rate, regardless of when it is worked; the employee is *not* entitled to be paid one-and-one-half times the regular rate.[7]

White House Guidelines for Federal Employees

The foregoing approach to the religious practices of federal employees changed radically on August 14, 1997, when the White House issued "Guidelines on Religious Exercise and Religious Expression in the Federal Workplace." Although the Guidelines devote considerable attention to employees' accommodation rights, they also address other provocative issues such as proselytizing in the workplace and religious harassment. In all of these areas, the Guidelines make an important contribution to the debate over religious freedom in the workplace, and their standards may provide arguments to litigants in the private sector as to the reasonableness of accommodations, the limits of undue hardship, and the extent of permissible proselytizing.[8]

---

5. *Id.* at § 550.1002(c).

6. *Id.*

7. *Id.* The regulations explicitly exempt this form of compensatory overtime from the requirement of the Fair Labor Standards Act that overtime be paid at one-and-one-half times the regular hourly rate for work in excess of 40 hours in a work week. *See* 29 U.S.C. § 207.

8. For this reason, employers, unions, and employees in the private sector would also benefit from a review of the Guidelines and, especially, the many hypothetical examples that are provided.

The Guidelines exclude only military personnel and chaplains employed by the government; all other executive-branch employees are covered. The objectives of the Guidelines are clearly stated at the outset:

> Executive departments and agencies . . . shall permit personal religious expression by Federal employees to the greatest extent possible, consistent with requirements of law and interests in workplace efficiency as described in this set of Guidelines. Agencies shall not discriminate against employees on the basis of religion, require religious participation or non-participation as a condition of employment, or permit religious harassment. And agencies shall accommodate employees' exercise of their religion in the circumstances specified in these Guidelines.[9]

The Guidelines are broken down into several sections. One section sets forth the general principles underlying each of the subject areas addressed in the Guidelines (freedom of religious expression, hostile work environment, proselytizing, and so forth). A second section provides practical suggestions, including detailed hypothetical fact patterns that are intended to guide management and employees in resolving common conflicts.

A brief final section raises the question whether the Guidelines have any significant legal import:

> These Guidelines shall govern the internal management of the civilian executive branch. They are not intended to create any new right, benefit, or trust responsibility, substantive or procedural, enforceable at law or equity by a party against the United States, its agencies, its officers, or any person. Questions regarding interpretations of these Guidelines should be brought to the Office of the General Counsel or Legal Counsel in each department and agency.[10]

As explained below, several provisions of the Guidelines deviate from current decisional law; those provisions tend to provide much greater leeway to employee activities and, concomitantly, reduce flexibility to management. Yet, this section asserts that the Guidelines are not intended to

---

9. Guidelines, § 1.
10. *Id.* at § 3.

create any new legal rights. The intent seems to be that an employee may not bring suit under Title VII or the First Amendment and assert a breach of the Guidelines as a basis for a claim. Ultimately, the courts will have to decide this issue.

Accommodation of Religious Practices

The Guidelines' standards for accommodation are drawn from Section 701e(j) of Title VII, Section 5550a of Title 5, and from the Supreme Court's decision in *Ansonia Board of Education v. Philbrook.*[11] The Guidelines recognize an employee's right to take leave for religious purposes and the right to work overtime to compensate for the leave.[12] They also require that, if an employing agency extends accommodations to employees for nonreligious needs, the agency may not deny similar accommodations to employees who wish to attend to religious needs.[13]

The Guidelines borrow from *Trans World Airlines, Inc. v. Hardison*[14] the principle that an agency need not incur more than a de minimis cost in accommodating an employee's religious needs; however, the assertion of an undue hardship must be "real rather than speculative or hypothetical."[15] In this respect, a "real" hardship is one that causes "an actual cost to the agency or to other employees or an actual disruption of work."[16] An agency also is not compelled to undertake an action that is "barred by law."[17]

The Guidelines provide hypothetical fact patterns that are intended as guidance for managers and employees. For example, when an employee seeks time off for religious observance, the Guidelines state that the agency must grant the request when an adequate substitute employee is available or when there is no realistic imposition of an undue burden on the agency.[18] An employee who has religious objections to a particular

---

11. 479 U.S. 60 (1986).

12. Guidelines, § 2(E).

13. *Id.*

14. 432 U.S. 63 (1977).

15. Guidelines, § 2(E).

16. *Id.* at § 1(C).

17. *Id.* This presumably also means that an agency is not required to accommodate an employee whose actions would violate the First Amendment's Establishment clause.

18. *Id.*

work assignment should be reassigned, if doing so does not create an undue hardship.[19] However, as discussed in the preceding chapter, several circuit courts have held that law-enforcement agencies need not accede to an employee's request for reassignment or rescheduling in order to avoid religious conflicts.[20] Under these decisions, the employer appears not to have as great a burden of proving undue hardship as the White House Guidelines suggest. The Guidelines make no effort to reconcile the potential inconsistency with this precedent.

An additional conflict between precedent and the Guidelines arises out of the Guidelines' requirement that requests for accommodation be honored even when the religious conflict arises out of neutral work rules. As an example, the Guidelines state that a Jehovah's Witness who applies for a job should not be compelled to take a loyalty oath if it is in a form that is religiously objectionable. Also, dress codes that are neutral towards religion may be waived for employees who wear religious clothing or symbols (for example, crucifixes, yarmulkes, head scarf, or hijab); employees must be permitted to wear these articles during work, so long as they do not "unduly interfere with the functioning of the workplace."[21] Similarly, requirements that correctional officers wear short hair should not be enforced against employees whose religion compels long hair.[22] The intent here clearly is to prevent agencies from using the neutrality of a work rule as an excuse to avoid accommodating employees' religious needs:

> In those cases where an agency's work rule imposes a substantial burden on a particular employee's exercise of religion, the agency must go further: an agency should grant the employee an exemption from

---

19. To this extent, the Guidelines are consistent with the decision in Haring v. Blumenthal, 471 F. Supp. 1172 (D.D.C. 1979), *cert. denied,* 452 U.S. 939 (1981) (Catholic IRS employee who refused to work on applications for tax-exempt status from organizations that support abortion rights is entitled to have his beliefs accommodated under Title VII; because this work is only a small percentage of the employee's total duties, it is not an undue hardship for the agency to avoid assigning this work to him).

20. Beadle v. City of Tampa, 42 F.3d 633 (11th Cir.), *cert. denied,* 515 U.S. 1152 (1995); Ryan v. U.S. Dept. of Justice, 950 F.2d 458 (7th Cir. 1991), *cert. denied,* 504 U.S. 958 (1992).

21. Guidelines, § 1(C). Federal law has no analog to the Pennsylvania and Oregon "garb" laws.

22. *Id.*

that rule, unless the agency has a *compelling interest* in denying the exemption and there is no *less restrictive means* of furthering that interest.[23]

By embracing the "compelling interest" and "least restrictive alternative" tests, the Guidelines explicitly adopt the requirements of the Religious Freedom Restoration Act (RFRA),[24] notwithstanding the fact that the Supreme Court declared RFRA to be unconstitutional.[25] In so doing, the Guidelines require federal employers to meet a higher standard than would be imposed if the dispute were to arise in a state or local government. For example, in *TWA v. Hardison*,[26] the Supreme Court held that an employer is not required to accommodate an employee if it can prove that the accommodation would result in more than a de minimis cost. Under the Guidelines, in contrast, a federal employer can only avoid making an accommodation if it can point to a "compelling interest" justifying its action. If a federal agency must prove a compelling need for a neutral work rule that conflicts with an employee's religion, it might not find it so easy to avoid liability. The compelling-interest standard in the Guidelines appears to raise the bar of proof for the federal agency above and beyond the de minimis test of *Hardison.* Because private-sector employers and state and local governments do not need to prove a compelling interest, federal agencies stand alone in having to meet this standard for justifying neutral work rules.

A second example of the Guidelines establishing higher standards than required by the courts arises out of the Supreme Court's decision in *Ansonia Board of Education v. Philbrook*.[27] The Court held that an employer need offer only one reasonable accommodation to an employee and is not required to grant or even consider other reasonable alternatives proposed by the employee. However, the "least restrictive alternative" component of the Guidelines seems to require federal agencies to explore more than one reasonable accommodation. For example, if a shift swap is a reasonable accommodation that does not entail an undue hardship for a particular agency, such action would satisfy *Ansonia*. But, is it the least restric-

---

23. *Id.*
24. 42 U.S.C. § 2000bb.
25. City of Boerne v. Flores, 117 S.Ct. 2157 (1997).
26. 432 U.S. 63.
27. 479 U.S. 60.

tive accommodation? Do the Guidelines require a federal agency to offer several accommodations to an employee for selection of the least restrictive one? Private-sector employers and state and local governments have no similar obligation.

The foregoing discrepancies between the Guidelines and the prevailing case law under Title VII suggest that the accommodation of religious practices in the federal workplace will follow its own unique path.

Religious Expression by Employees and the Ban on the Establishment of Religion

The introduction to the discussion of "Religious Expression" in Section 1 sets the tone for the examples that follow:

> As a matter of law, agencies shall not restrict personal religious expression by employees in the Federal workplace except where the employee's interest in the expression is outweighed by the government's interest in the efficient provision of public services or where the expression intrudes upon the legitimate rights of other employees or creates the appearance, to a reasonable observer, of an official endorsement of religion. The examples cited in these Guidelines as permissible forms of religious expression will rarely, if ever, fall within these exceptions.[28]

Section 2 of the Guidelines extends this general rule to employee proselytizing:

> Many religions strongly encourage their adherents to spread the faith by persuasion and example at every opportunity, a duty that can extend to the adherents' workplace. As a general matter, proselytizing is entitled to the same constitutional protection as any other form of speech. Therefore, in the governmental workplace, proselytizing should not be singled out because of its content for harsher treatment than nonreligious expression.[29]

The Guidelines recognize that this broadly permissive approach to religious expression, including proselytizing in the workplace, faces a potential conflict with the Establishment clause of the First Amendment,

---

28. Guidelines, § 1(A).
29. *Id.* at § 2(A).

as well as the operating efficiency of an agency. The Guidelines therefore place several limits on the scope of employee expressions of religious faith. First, employees are warned that religious activities cannot supplant the business of the government:

> Agencies are not required, however, to permit employees to use work time to pursue religious or ideological agendas. Federal employees are paid to perform official work, not to engage in personal religious or ideological campaigns during work hours.[30]

As a general matter, employees' speech may be regulated if their interest "is outweighed by the interest of the Government, as an employer, in promoting the efficiency of the public services it performs. . . ."[31] This means more than the ability of management to impose content-neutral time, place, and means regulations. Employee speech

> can be regulated or discouraged if it impairs discipline by superiors, has a detrimental impact on close working relationships for which personal loyalty and confidence are necessary, impedes the performance of the speaker's duties or interferes with the regular operation of the enterprise, or demonstrates that the employee holds views that could lead his employer or the public reasonably to question whether he can perform his duties adequately.[32]

Second, the Guidelines warn that, because of First Amendment concerns, employees should not be permitted to engage in activities that "would lead a reasonable observer to conclude that the Government is sponsoring, endorsing or inhibiting religion generally or favoring or disfavoring a particular religion."[33] The need to prevent potential Establishment clause violations also leads to a prohibition on the use of "Government funds or resources (other than those facilities generally available to government employees) for private religious uses."[34]

There is an inherent tension between the rights of employees to engage in religious expression and the authority of managers to limit speech that impedes productivity or threatens government neutrality

---

30. *Id.* at § 1(A).
31. *Id.* at § 2(A).
32. *Id.* at § 2(A).
33. *Id.* at § 2(F).
34. *Id.*

vis à vis religion. For example, the Guidelines state that religious posters may be displayed only in "private work areas . . . and not on common walls." However, if employees are permitted to hang nonreligious posters in public areas seeking support for a nonprofit charitable activity, can employees hang similar posters for religious charities? If employees are permitted to use an agency's computer network to communicate "speech" to all other employees on the network, can religious speech be similarly communicated? Is the computer network akin to a "common wall" for posters and therefore a place from which all religious expression is banned? Only time will tell whether these sorts of questions will be relegated to the realm of the hypothetical or will ripen into actual workplace disputes.

The Guidelines repeatedly emphasize the presumption that religious speech is permissible and should be treated the same as other types of speech protected by the First Amendment. Work rules that permit certain forms of expression must be applied equally to the expression of religious views; to do otherwise would result in content-based discrimination against religion. Recognizing that these general principles are more easily stated than applied, the Guidelines provide detailed factual examples. These examples reinforce the premise that employees' discussions or displays of religion are presumptively lawful, except to the limited extent that they give the impression of governmental sponsorship or they become a disruptive force in the workplace. To avoid either of these two exceptions, employees are warned that they may not pursue religious activities during working time, may not "pursue religious or ideological agendas," and may not engage in expressive activities in areas open to the public.[35] On the other hand, supervisors may not limit or prohibit speech based solely on its content, religious or otherwise.[36] Supervisors also may not speculate as to potential disruptions in the workforce; restrictions based on "reasonable predictions of disruption" are permissible, but they may not be predicated "on merely hypothetical concerns having little basis in fact."[37]

Beyond these general principles, the Guidelines divide employee activities into four broad areas: (1) expression that is private or personal; (2) expression that may be heard or seen by other employees; (3) expres-

---

35. *Id.* at § 1(A).
36. *Id.*
37. *Id.*

sion intentionally directed towards other employees; and (4) expression in areas accessible to the public. The following are the rights and limitations in each of these four areas.

Private Work Areas

Employees have the greatest latitude in their own personal work spaces, since these areas are least likely to create conflicts with other employees or with the public.[38] Employees are therefore permitted to keep Bibles, Korans, religious symbols, and so on, in their *personal* work areas.[39] As a corollary, employees may wear religious medallions and messages (presumably buttons and the like) on their clothing, even though these items would be visible throughout the workplace.[40] They may also hang posters with religious messages on their office walls or otherwise display religious art and literature as long as they are not displayed in public areas; within offices, such items may be limited as to size and placement to the same extent that other, nonreligious posters are regulated.[41]

Expression Among Employees

The Guidelines recognize that some employees may wish to meet with and discuss religious issues with other employees. Assuming that the other employees are willing participants in these discussions, the only major proscription is that the employees not use work time for these activities.[42] Assuming that employees do not violate this rule, they may:

- Discuss religion in informal settings, such as cafeterias and hallways.[43]

---

38. Obviously, the impact on other employees or the public will vary, depending upon the layout of a particular office design. For example, offices with walls will be more private than modular work stations. Nevertheless, an employee's personal work space is the most private, and therefore the most protected, area in an office.

39. *Id.* at § 1(A)(1).

40. *Id.* at § 1(A)(2). This rule appears to apply to religious paraphernalia that are worn voluntarily and not because they are required by the employee's religion. To the extent that religious garb or symbols are theologically mandated, the rules governing accommodation would apply. For example, an orthodox Jewish employee could not be denied the right to wear a yarmulke unless doing so unduly interferes in the functioning of the office or violates some other compelling governmental interest.

41. *Id.* at § 1(A)(1).

42. *Id.* at 1(A)(2).

43. *Id.*

- Use office space (for example, a conference room) for meetings, Bible discussions, and so on, if such spaces are usually made available to employee groups for nonreligious gatherings.[44]

Supervisors are instructed that they should presume the propriety of these religious activities, *unless* they result in a disruption of workplace efficiency or if they occur in a context that could be reasonably interpreted as governmental sponsorship of the religious expressions.[45]

Expression Directed at Fellow Employees

As previously explained, the Guidelines accord the same protection to proselytizing as they do to other types of religious expression.[46] The Guidelines state that employees may try to "persuade" coworkers of their religious views. Employees are therefore presumptively protected when they "urge" fellow employees to engage in certain religious activities.

However, the treatment of the balance between the rights of the religious proselytizer and the rights of coworkers is somewhat confused. While employees may proselytize other employees in the office, supervisors are cautioned not to interfere in such activities merely because the proselytizing may be contentious: "In a country where freedom of speech and religion are guaranteed, citizens should expect to be exposed to ideas with which they disagree."[47] On the other hand, the Guidelines state that "employees must refrain from such expression [that is, proselytizing] when a fellow employee asks that it stop or otherwise demonstrates that it is unwelcome."[48] These two statements, if not contradictory, may be difficult to reconcile. Supervisors may not cut off religious proselytizing merely because it is contentious; on the other hand, supervisors *must* cut off such speech if another employee complains.

---

44. *Id.*

45. *Id.* It appears that the White House does not consider the mere usage of federal office space for religious meetings to cross the line of the First Amendment's Establishment clause. *See* Widmar v. Vincent, 454 U.S. 263 (1981) (a public university that makes its facilities available to student groups for meetings may not deny such usage to student religious groups). *See also* 20 U.S.C. § 4071, *et seq.* (Equal Access Act extends same principle to public secondary schools receiving federal funds).

46. Guidelines, at § 1(A)(3).

47. *Id.* at § 1(B)(3).

48. *Id.* at § 1(A)(3).

The concept of a hostile work environment based on religious speech is an evolving and relatively new area of the law.[49] The line between religious expression and religious harassment is not a bright one. The Guidelines attempt to illuminate this murky area of the law, but they founder on the subject of proselytizing.

In other areas of First Amendment jurisprudence, the sensitivity of the hearer is not the measure of a speaker's constitutional rights; speech that invites dispute cannot be restrained for that reason alone.[50] Under the Guidelines, however, one employee may be able to limit another employee's innocuous references to religious beliefs on the grounds that it is offensive to the hearer. Conversely, the presumptive rights of proselytizing employees may make supervisors reluctant to cut off expressive activities that actually create a hostile work environment. Supervisors who are asked to balance the interests of the speaker and listener in a proselytizing context will not have an easy time of it.

A further difficulty with the proselytizing guidelines involves supervisors. The White House posits that supervisors have the same First Amendment right to express their personal religious views as any other employee, as long as such actions are noncoercive.[51] If a supervisor engages in coercive activities, even under the guise of religious speech, then he or she may be guilty of religious discrimination. For example, it would be illegal for a supervisor to condition benefits of employment (for example, promotion or salary increases) on an employee either engaging in or refraining from religious activities.[52] The Guidelines therefore caution supervisors that their free exercise of religious expression must be presented in such a way as to make clear to employees that the views expressed are personal to the supervisor, are not government policy and are not tied to employees' terms and conditions of employment. A number of factual examples are then offered:[53]

- A supervisor may invite coworkers to a religious ceremony (for example, a bat mitzvah), but may not make statements such as "I

---

49. See Chapter 5.
50. Terminiello v. Chicago, 337 U.S. 1 (1949).
51. Guidelines, § 1(B)(2).
52. Id.
53. These examples are taken from Section 1(B)(2).

didn't see you in church this week. I expect to see you there this Sunday."

- A supervisor may post a notice of a religious event on a bulletin board devoted to personal announcements, but may not tell employees that they must attend a lunch-hour religious class in order to have access to a subsequent discussion on career advancement.
- A supervisor's statement to a colleague during lunch that religion is "important in one's life" is protected.
- A supervisor who is an atheist acts improperly if, over a period of years, he awards merit increases to employees who do not attend church and withholds such awards from churchgoing employees.
- A supervisor may express opinions at lunch that are either pro- or anti-abortion and may state a religious basis for those opinions. "Without more, neither of these comments coerces employees' religious conformity or conduct" and therefore are proper.

To some extent, these examples are so obvious as to hardly be instructive. More troubling is the fact that the balancing act suggested by the Guidelines pays scant attention to the inherently coercive position occupied by supervisors; subordinates *must* obey the lawful commands of supervisors. In many situations, a proselytizing supervisor who encourages religious activities by subordinates will not have to explicitly link the religious activities to the job; employees may well find the coercion to be implicit in the supervisor's comments. In other situations, those employees who feel most vulnerable about their jobs may undertake religious activities suggested by supervisors merely to curry favor or to improve their job prospects. Finally, if an employee feels that he or she has been subjected to a hostile work environment by a proselytizing coworker, that employee is not likely to complain to a supervisor if that supervisor is also engaged in proselytizing activities.

The Guidelines state that supervisors must be aware that their powers to hire, fire, and so forth, could be perceived by employees as coercive, even if not intended to be so. However, the suggested cure for that danger is for supervisors to be "careful" that they not erroneously convey a coercive intent. In the real world, that nostrum is not likely to provide comfort to employees concerned about a supervisor's religious activities on the job. Many supervisors hold residually coercive authority that employees will be disinclined to challenge. In short, permitting supervisors to prose-lytize subordinates is fraught with dangers that the Guidelines minimize or avoid altogether.[54]

Apart from the above difficulties, the Guidelines do provide some useful examples of the expressions that nonsupervisors can direct toward coworkers:

- "During a coffee break, one employee engages another in a polite discussion of why his faith should be embraced." If the coworker disagrees, but does not insist that the proselytizer stop, then supervisors should not take any action to stop the proselytizer's activity.[55]

- If one employee invites another employee to a religious service and the invitee states that such invitations are not welcome and should not be repeated, then the first employee should refrain from further invitations. However, the original invitation is still protected activity and is not subject to discipline.[56]

- An employee hands a coworker a "religious tract urging that she convert to another religion lest she be condemned to eternal dam-nation." If the proselytizing employee does not make any further comments, "[t]his speech typically should not be restricted."[57]

Expression in Public Areas

The greatest limitations on employee-speech rights are imposed in office areas to which the public has access.[58] Employees are warned that they must be

> sensitive to the Establishment Clause's requirement that expression not create the reasonable impression that the government is sponsor-

---

54. The Guidelines are not alone in avoiding this problem. The same concerns expressed here also apply to the Eighth Circuit's decision in Brown v. Polk County, Iowa, 61 F.3d 650 (8th Cir. 1995) (en banc), *cert. denied,* 516 U.S. 1158 (1996), in which the court held that it was improper for a public employer to terminate a supervisor who opened business meetings with prayers. See discussion in Chapter 11. Although the authors have reservations about the Guidelines' treatment of proselytizing by supervisors, it cannot be said that the Guidelines are unique in tilting the balance toward the First Amendment rights of the supervisor.

55. Guidelines, § 1(A)(3).

56. *Id.*

57. *Id.*

58. *Id.* at § 1(A)(4).

ing, endorsing, or inhibiting religion generally, or favoring or disfavoring a particular religion. This is particularly important in agencies with adjudicatory functions.[59]

The Guidelines do not provide any examples of improper conduct in public areas. They do, however, preserve certain employee rights, notwithstanding public access to their activities. Employees may wear religious medallions (assuming no safety concerns), display religious art or literature in personal work areas, and discuss religion among themselves, even if these displays or communications are accessible to the public, as long as the public would reasonably understand that the activities are personal to the employees and are not sponsored by the government.[60] To the extent that clashes arise between an employee's right to free expression and the government's obligation not to "establish" religion, resolution will necessarily turn on the individual facts of each case.[61]

Ban on Religious Discrimination

The rules governing religious discrimination are, for the most part, obvious and unexceptionable.[62] Drawing upon Title VII, agencies may not discriminate for or against employees based on religion with respect to hiring, promotion, pay, and discipline.[63] In addition, as previously discussed, supervisors may not use their free-speech rights in a coercive fashion. They may not make an employment benefit a quid pro quo for engaging in or refraining from religious activities.

The Guidelines reiterate that federal agencies will be bound by RFRA. Therefore, any agency rule that substantially burdens the exercise of religion may be deemed discriminatory unless it can be justified by a "compelling interest and is narrowly tailored to advance that interest."

---

59. *Id.*

60. *Id.*

61. There currently is insufficient jurisprudence upon which to safely predict the outcome of all such clashes. For example, suppose a government employee meets with welfare recipients in her cubicle, which is plastered with religious posters. Would the client understand that the posters are merely *personal* expressions of belief? The danger of an Establishment violation is considerable, but the Guidelines are unclear as to how they would treat this particular employee.

62. *Id.* at § 1(B).

63. *Id.* The Guidelines also cite Article VI, clause 3 of the Constitution, which provides that "no religious Test shall ever be required as a Qualification to any Office or public Trust under the United States."

One last aspect of this section is worth noting: "A supervisor may not impose more onerous work requirements on an employee who is an atheist because that employee does not share the supervisor's religious beliefs."[64] The notion that federal agencies must treat religion and the lack of religion with equal respect is echoed by the EEOC's very broad definition of religion. While the Supreme Court recognizes that the Constitution protects nonbelievers under the First Amendment,[65] their rights are less clearly defined in Title VII jurisprudence. By explicitly stating that atheists have the same rights as religious believers in the workplace, the Guidelines move into waters that are not entirely settled.

Hostile Work Environment and Harassment

The Guidelines adopt a definition of religious harassment that is consistent with the holdings of the several courts that have ruled on this matter:

> Employers violate Title VII's ban on discrimination by creating or tolerating a "hostile environment" in which an employee is subject to discriminatory intimidation, ridicule, or insult sufficiently severe or pervasive to alter the conditions of the victim's employment.[66]

This hostile environment may be created by management *or* by coworkers. The Guidelines state that a violation of Title VII can arise out of management's tolerance of religious harassment by nonsupervisory employees.[67]

In most cases the harassing speech will be explicitly anti-religious; however, abusive comments that are not explicitly religious in nature may still create a violation if they are inflicted upon an employee *because* of that employee's religious beliefs (or lack of beliefs).[68]

Recognizing the fine line between employees' free speech rights and the creation of a hostile environment, the Guidelines follow the lead of the courts in defining religious harassment. For speech to be violative of these Guidelines, it must be "sufficiently severe or pervasive to alter the conditions of employment."[69] Normally, the harassing conduct must be

---

64. *Id.* at § 1(B)(1)(c).

65. *See, e.g.,* Everson v. Board of Education, 330 U.S. 1, 16 (1947); Torcaso v. Watkins, 367 U.S. 488, 495 (1961).

66. Guidelines, § 2(D).

67. *Id.*

68. *Id.*

69. *Id. See also* § 1(B)(3).

repeated. Isolated comments that are disagreeable or even offensive may not rise to the level of creating a hostile environment. However, the Guidelines recognize that even a "single incident, if sufficiently abusive, might also constitute statutory harassment."[70]

To guard against the overly sensitive employee, the Guidelines caution that employees, like citizens in general, should expect to be exposed to ideas they find disagreeable: "a hostile environment is not created by the bare expression of speech with which some employees might disagree."[71] Supervisors are left with the delicate task of deciding whether a particular employee is being overly sensitive to workplace banter or is truly being victimized by hostile speech having a religious animus.[72] The following are examples of harassing conduct that the Guidelines identify as being worthy of censorship or punishment:[73]

- An employee who "repeatedly makes derogatory remarks to other employees with whom she is assigned to work about their faith or lack of faith."
- A group of employees subjects a fellow employee to a "barrage of comments" about his sex life, knowing that such questions would be offensive and discomforting to the victim because of his religious beliefs.[74]
- A group of employees sharing a common faith engage in a pattern of verbal attacks on coworkers of different faiths, calling them "heathens" and "sinners."

These examples do not present difficult fact patterns; no supervisor is likely to mistake the need to take action when confronted with these situations. The only example in which the Guidelines present an interesting "gray" area is the following:

- Two employees have an angry exchange in which one employee uses a derogatory comment about the other employee's religion.

---

70. *Id.* at § 1(B)(3).

71. *Id.*

72. *See* Oncale v. Sundowner Offshore Services, Inc., 118 S.Ct. 998 (1998), cautioning that offhand comments should not be mistaken for discrimination.

73. These examples are taken from Section 1(B)(3).

74. This example is undoubtedly offered to show that comments need not be explicitly religious to be violative of Title VII.

The comments are not repeated. "Unless the words are sufficiently severe or pervasive to alter the conditions of the insulted employee's employment or create an abusive working environment, this is not statutory religious harassment."[75]

This last example emphasizes the Guidelines' general approach to such conflicts: the presumption must be in favor of the expressive conduct.

The Guidelines also make it clear that employees do not engage in harassment merely because they exercise their free speech rights to wear religious jewelry, display religious art in their offices or engage in group prayer during nonworking time. While these activities may ruffle some feathers among coworkers, they are protected under the First Amendment and, without more, cannot rise to the level of religious harassment. Similarly, proselytizing will not be deemed harassing unless it persists after the targeted employee requests that it stop or otherwise makes clear that it is unwelcome.

Summary

- Federal employees are entitled to absent themselves from work for religious observances and may work "compensatory" overtime to make up for the absence. This overtime is paid at the employee's straight-time rate. The overtime may be worked before or after the religious observance.

- The White House "Guidelines on Religious Exercise and Religious Expression in the Federal Workplace" apply to virtually all civilian employees of the federal government. However, they do not carry the force of regulation and are not intended to give employees a cause of action for religious discrimination.

- The Guidelines adopt the accommodation principles set forth in the Supreme Court's decisions in *TWA v. Hardison* and *Ansonia v. Philbrook*.

- The Guidelines depart from prevailing law by counseling an agency to grant an employee an exemption from a work rule for religious reasons unless the agency has a compelling interest in

---

75. *Id.*

denying the exemption and there is no less restrictive means of furthering that interest. Neither private sector employers nor other public sector employers are required to meet this compelling-interest/least-restrictive alternative test.

- The Guidelines adopt Title VII's proscription against religious discrimination in the federal workplace, including conduct that creates a "hostile environment" in which employees are subjected to discriminatory intimidation, ridicule, or insult that is so severe or pervasive as to alter the conditions of employment.

- Religious proselytizing by federal employees is presumptively permissible under the Guidelines, although employees may not use government time or facilities to further proselytizing activities, may not disrupt official work, and may not create the appearance that the government is sponsoring, endorsing, or inhibiting religion. Employers may also prohibit religious proselytizing if it creates an abusive work environment or constitutes religious harassment.

- The Guidelines caution that the regulation of religious proselytizing should be tailored to the particular circumstances in which it occurs. While it may be appropriate to limit or prohibit religious speech directed to the public, the same speech is not necessarily objectionable when expressed within the confines of the workplace.

- Under the Guidelines, employees may wear religious medallions at work. Employees may also maintain posters, religious messages, Bibles, and so forth, within their individual work areas, but such materials may not be posted in public areas. Employers may limit the size and placement of religious posters, notices, and the like, within offices pursuant to rules that apply to nonreligious materials.

Appendixes

✦ APPENDIX A

Title VII, Civil Rights Act of 1964, as amended (42 U.S.C. § 2000e *et seq.*, selected provisions)

§ 2000e. Definitions

For the purposes of this subchapter—

(a) The term "person" includes one or more individuals, governments, governmental agencies, political subdivisions, labor unions, partnerships, associations, corporations, legal representatives, mutual companies, joint-stock companies, trusts, unincorporated organizations, trustees, trustees in cases under Title 11, or receivers.

(b) The term "employer" means a person engaged in an industry affecting commerce who has fifteen or more employees for each working day in each of twenty or more calendar weeks in the current or preceding calendar year, and any agent of such a person, but such term does not include (1) the United States, a corporation wholly owned by the Government of the United States, an Indian tribe, or any department or agency of the District of Columbia subject by statute to procedures of the competitive service (as defined in section 2102 of Title 5), or (2) a bona fide private membership club (other than a labor organization) which is exempt from taxation under section of 501(c) of Title 26, except that during the first year after March 24, 1972, persons having fewer than twenty-five employees (and their agents) shall not be considered employers.

(c) The term "employment agency" means any person regularly undertaking with or without compensation to procure employees for an employer or to procure for employees opportunities to work for an employer and includes an agent of such a person.

(d) The term "labor organization" means a labor organization engaged in an industry affecting commerce, and any agent of such an organization, and includes any organization of any kind, any agency, or employee representation committee, group, association, or plan so engaged in which employees participate and which exists for the purpose, in whole or in part, of dealing with employers concerning grievances, labor disputes, wages, rates of pay, hours, or other terms or conditions of employment, and any conference, general committee, joint or system board, or joint council so engaged which is subordinate to a national or international labor organization.

(e) A labor organization shall be deemed to be engaged in an industry affecting commerce if (1) it maintains or operates a hiring hall or hiring office which procures employees for an employer or procures for employees opportunities to work for an employer, or (2) the number of its members (or, where it is a labor organization composed of other labor organizations or their representatives, if the aggregate number of the members of such other labor organization) is (A) twenty-five or more during the first year after March 24, 1972, or (B) fifteen or more thereafter, and such labor organization—

(1) is the certified representative of employees under the provisions of the National Labor Relations Act, as amended [29 U.S.C.A. § 151 et seq.], or the Railway Labor Act, as amended [45 U.S.C.A. § 151 et seq.];

(2) although not certified, is a national or international labor organization or a local labor organization recognized or acting as the representative of employees of an employer or employers engaged in an industry affecting commerce; or

(3) has been chartered a local labor organization or subsidiary body which is representing or actively seeking to represent employees of employers within the meaning of paragraph (1) or (2); or

(4) has been chartered by a labor organization representing or actively seeking to represent employees within the meaning of paragraph (1) or (2) as the local or subordinate body through which such

employees may enjoy membership or become affiliated with such labor organization; or

(5) is a conference, general committee, joint or system board, or joint council subordinate to a national or international labor organization, which includes a labor organization engaged in an industry affecting commerce within the meaning of any of the preceding paragraphs of this subsection.

(f) The term "employee" means an individual employed by an employer, except that the term "employee" shall not include any person elected to public office in any State or political subdivision of any State by the qualified voters thereof, or any person chosen by such officer to be on such officer's personal staff, or an appointee on the policy making level or an immediate adviser with respect to the exercise of the constitutional or legal powers of the office. The exemption set forth in the preceding sentence shall not include employees subject to the civil service laws of a State government, governmental agency or political subdivision. With respect to employment in a foreign country, such term includes an individual who is a citizen of the United States.

(g) The term "commerce" means trade, traffic, commerce, transportation, transmission, or communication among the several States; or between a State and any place outside thereof; or within the District of Columbia, or a possession of the United States; or between points in the same State but through a point outside thereof.

(h) The term "industry affecting commerce" means any activity, business, or industry in commerce or in which a labor dispute would hinder or obstruct commerce or the free flow of commerce and includes any activity or industry "affecting commerce" within the meaning of the Labor-Management Reporting and Disclosure Act of 1959 [29 U.S.C.A. § 401 et seq.], and further includes any governmental industry, business, or activity.

(i) The term "State" includes a State of the United States, the District of Columbia, Puerto Rico, the Virgin Islands, American Samoa, Guam, Wake Island, the Canal Zone, and Outer Continental Shelf lands defined in the Outer Continental Shelf Lands Act [43 U.S.C.A. § 1331 et seq.].

(j) The term "religion" includes all aspects of religious observance and practice, as well as belief, unless an employer demonstrates that he is unable to reasonably accommodate to an employee's or prospective employee's religious observance or practice without undue hardship on the conduct of the employer's business.

*   *   *   *

§ 2000e–1. Applicability to foreign and religious employment

(a) Inapplicability of subchapter to certain aliens and employees of religious entities

This subchapter shall not apply to an employer with respect to the employment of aliens outside any State, or to a religious corporation, association, educational institution, or society with respect to the employment of individuals of a particular religion to perform work connected with the carrying on by such corporation, association, educational institution, or society of its activities.

(b) Compliance with statute as violative of foreign law

It shall not be unlawful under section 2000e–2 or 2000e–3 of this title for an employer (or a corporation controlled by an employer), labor organization, employment agency, or joint labor-management committee controlling apprenticeship or other training or retraining (including on-the-job training programs) to take any action otherwise prohibited by such section, with respect to an employee in a workplace in a foreign country if compliance with such section would cause such employer (or such corporation), such organization, such agency, or such committee to violate the law of the foreign country in which such workplace is located.

(c) Control of corporation incorporated in foreign country

(1) If an employer controls a corporation whose place of incorporation is a foreign country, any practice prohibited by section 2000e–2 and 2000e–3 of this title engaged in by such corporation shall be presumed to be engaged in by such employer.

(2) Sections 2000e–2 and 2000e–3 of this title shall not apply with respect to the foreign operations of an employer that is a foreign person not controlled by an American employer.

(3) For purposes of this subsection, the determination of whether an employer controls a corporation shall be based on—

(A) the interrelation of operations;

(B) the common management;

(C) the centralized control of labor relations; and

(D) the common ownership or financial control, of the employer and the corporation.

§ 2000e–2. Unlawful employment practices

(a) Employer practices

It shall be an unlawful employment practice for an employer—

(1) to fail or refuse to hire or to discharge any individual, or otherwise discriminate against any individual with respect to his compensation, terms, conditions, or privileges of employment, because of such individual's race, color, religion, sex, or national origin; or

(2) to limit, segregate, or classify his employees or applicants for employment in any way which would deprive or tend to deprive any individual of employment opportunities or otherwise adversely affect his status as an employee, because of such individual's race, color, religion, sex, or national origin.

(b) Employment agency practices

It shall be an unlawful employment practice for an employment agency to fail or refuse to refer for employment, or otherwise to discriminate against, any individual because of his race, color, religion, sex, or national origin or to classify or refer for employment any individual on the basis of his race, color, religion, sex, or national origin.

(c) Labor organization practices

It shall be an unlawful employment practice for a labor organization—

(1) to exclude or to expel from its membership, or otherwise to discriminate against, any individual because of his race, color, religion, sex, or national origin;

(2) to limit, segregate, or classify its membership or applicants for membership, or to classify or fail or refuse to refer for employment any individual, in any way which would deprive or tend to deprive any individual of employment opportunities, or would limit such employment opportunities or otherwise adversely affect his status as an employee or as an applicant for employment, because of such individual's race, color, religion, sex, or national origin; or

(3) to cause or attempt to cause an employer to discriminate against an individual in violation of this section.

(d) Training programs

It shall be an unlawful employment practice for any employer, labor organization, or joint labor-management committee controlling apprenticeship or other training or retraining, including on-the-job training programs to discriminate against any individual because of his race, color, religion, sex, or national origin in admission to, or employment in, any program established to provide apprenticeship or other training.

(e) Businesses or enterprises with personnel qualified on basis of religion, sex, or national origin; educational institutions with personnel of particular religion

Notwithstanding any other provision of this subchapter, (1) it shall not be an unlawful employment practice for an employer to hire and employ employees, for an employment agency to classify, or refer for employment any individual, for a labor organization to classify its membership or to classify or refer for employment any individual, or for an employer, labor organization, or joint labor-management committee controlling apprenticeship or other training or retraining programs to admit or employ any individual in any such program, on the basis of his religion, sex, or national origin in those certain instances where religion, sex, or national origin is a bona fide occupational qualification reasonably necessary to the normal operation of that particular business or enterprise, and (2) it shall not be unlawful employment practice for a school, college, university, or other educational institution or institution of learning to hire and employ employees of a particular religion if such school, college, university, or educational institution or institution of learning is, in whole or in substantial part, owned, supported, controlled, or managed by a particular religion or by a particular religious corporation, association, or society, or if the curriculum of such school, college, university, or other educational institution or institution of learning is directed toward the propagation of a particular religion.

*   *   *   *

(g) National security

Notwithstanding any other provision of this subchapter, it shall not be an unlawful employment practice for an employer to fail or refuse to hire and employ any individual for any position, for an employer to discharge any individual from any position, or for an employment agency to fail or refuse to refer any individual for employment in any position, or for a labor organization to fail or refuse to refer any individual for employment in any position, if—

(1) the occupancy of such position, or access to the premises in or upon which any part of the duties of such position is performed or is to be performed, is subject to any requirement imposed in the interest of the national security of the United States under any security program in effect pursuant to or administered under any statute of the United States or any Executive order of the President; and

(2) such individual has not fulfilled or has ceased to fulfill that requirement.

(h) Seniority or merit system; quantity or quality of production; ability tests; compensation based on sex and authorized by minimum wage provisions

Notwithstanding any other provision of this subchapter, it shall not be an unlawful employment practice for an employer to apply different standards of compensation, or different terms, conditions, or privileges of employment pursuant to a bona fide seniority or merit system, or a system which measures earnings by quantity or quality of production or to employees who work in different locations, provided that such differences are not the result of an intention to discriminate because of race, color, religion, sex, or national origin, nor shall it be an unlawful employment practice for an employer to give and to act upon the results of any professionally developed ability test provided that such test, its administration or action upon the results is not designed, intended or used to discriminate because of race, color, religion, sex or national origin. It shall not be an unlawful employment practice under this subchapter for any employer to differentiate upon the basis of sex in determining the amount of the wages or compensation paid or to be paid to employees of such employer if such differentiation is authorized by the provisions of section 206(d) of Title 29.

*   *   *   *

(j) Preferential treatment not to be granted on account of existing number or percentage imbalance

Nothing contained in this subchapter shall be interpreted to require any employer, employment agency, labor organization, or joint labor-management committee subject to this subchapter to grant preferential treatment to any individual or to any group because of race, color, religion, sex, or national origin of such individual or group on account of an imbalance which may exist with respect to the total number or percentage of persons of any race, color, religion, sex, or national origin employed by any employer, referred or classified for employment by any employment agency or labor organization, admitted to membership or classified by any labor organization, or admitted to, or employed in, any apprenticeship or other training program, in comparison with the total number or percentage of persons of such race, color, religion, sex, or national origin in any community, State, section, or other area, or in the available work force in any community, State, section, or other area.

(k) Burden of proof in disparate impact cases

(1)(A) An unlawful employment practice based on disparate impact is established under this subchapter only if—

(i) a complaining party demonstrates that a respondent uses a particular employment practice that causes a disparate impact on the basis of race, color, religion, sex, or national origin and the respondent fails to demonstrate that the challenged practice is job related for the position in question and consistent with business necessity; or

(ii) the complaining party makes the demonstration described in subparagraph (C) with respect to an alternative employment practice and the respondent refuses to adopt such alternative employment practice.

(B)(i) With respect to demonstrating that a particular employment practice causes a disparate impact as described in subparagraph (A)(i), the complaining party shall demonstrate that each particular challenged employment practice causes a disparate impact, except that if the complaining party can demonstrate to the court that the elements of a respondent's decisionmaking process are not capable of separation for analysis, the decisionmaking process may be analyzed as one employment practice.

(ii) If the respondent demonstrates that a specific employment practice does not cause the disparate impact, the respondent shall not be required to demonstrate that such practice is required by business necessity.

(C) The demonstration referred to by subparagraph (A)(ii) shall be in accordance with the law as it existed on June 4, 1989, with respect to the concept of "alternative employment practice".

(2) A demonstration that an employment practice is required by business necessity may not be used as a defense against a claim of intentional discrimination under this subchapter.

(3) Notwithstanding any other provision of this subchapter, a rule barring the employment of an individual who currently and knowingly uses or possesses a controlled substance, as defined in schedules I and II of section 102(6) of the Controlled Substances Act (21 U.S.C. 802(6)), other than the use or possession of a drug taken under the supervision of a licensed health care professional, or any other use or possession authorized by the Controlled Substances Act [21 U.S.C.A. § 801 et seq.] or any other provision of Federal law, shall be considered an unlawful employment practice under this subchapter only if such rule is adopted or applied with an intent to discriminate because of race, color, religion, or national origin.

(*l*) Prohibition of discriminatory use of test scores

It shall be an unlawful employment practice for a respondent, in connection with the selection or referral of applicants or candidates for employment or promotion, to adjust the scores of, use different cutoff scores for, or otherwise alter the results of, employment related tests on the basis of race, color, religion, sex, or national origin.

(m) Impermissible consideration of race, color, religion, sex, or national origin in employment practices

Except as otherwise provided in this subchapter, an unlawful employment practice is established when the complaining party demonstrates that race, color, religion, sex, or national origin was a motivating factor for any employment practice, even though other factors also motivated the practice.

(n) Resolution of challenges to employment practices implementing litigated or consent judgments or orders

(1)(A) Notwithstanding any other provision of law, and except as provided in paragraph (2), an employment practice that implements and is within the scope of a litigated or consent judgment or order that resolves a claim of employment discrimination under the Constitution or Federal civil rights laws may not be challenged under the circumstances described in subparagraph (B).

(B) A practice described in subparagraph (A) may not be challenged in a claim under the Constitution or Federal civil rights laws—

(i) by a person who, prior to the entry of the judgment or order described in subparagraph (A), had—

(I) actual notice of the proposed judgment or order sufficient to apprise such person that such judgment or order might adversely affect the interests and legal rights of such person and that an opportunity was available to present objections to such judgment or order by a future date certain; and

(II) a reasonable opportunity to present objections to such judgment or order; or

(ii) by a person whose interests were adequately represented by another person who had previously challenged the judgment or order on the same legal grounds and with a similar factual situation, unless there has been an intervening change in law or fact.

(2) Nothing in this subsection shall be construed to—

(A) alter the standards for intervention under rule 24 of the Federal Rules of Civil Procedure or apply to the rights of parties who have successfully intervened pursuant to such rule in the proceeding in which the parties intervened;

(B) apply to the rights of parties to the action in which a litigated or consent judgment or order was entered, or of members of a class represented or sought to be represented in such action, or of members of a group on whose behalf relief was sought in such action by the Federal Government;

(C) prevent challenges to a litigated or consent judgment or order on the ground that such judgment or order was obtained through collusion or fraud, or is transparently invalid or was entered by a court lacking subject matter jurisdiction; or

(D) authorize or permit the denial to any person of the due process of law required by the Constitution.

(3) Any action not precluded under this subsection that challenges an employment consent judgment or order described in paragraph (1) shall be brought in the court, and if possible before the judge, that entered such judgment or order. Nothing in the subsection shall preclude a transfer of such action pursuant to section 1404 of Title 28.

*   *   *   *

§ 2000e–5. Enforcement provisions

(a) Power of Commission to prevent unlawful employment practices

The Commission is empowered, as hereinafter provided, to prevent any person from engaging in any unlawful employment practice as set forth in section 2000e–2 or 2000e–3 of this title.

(b) Charges by persons aggrieved or member of Commission of unlawful employment practices by employers, etc.; filing; allegations; notice to respondent; contents of notice; investigation by Commission; contents of charges; prohibition on disclosure of charges; determination of reasonable cause; conference, conciliation, and persuasion for elimination of unlawful practices; prohibition on disclosure of informal endeavors to end unlawful practices; use of evidence in subsequent proceedings; penalties for disclosure of information; time for determination of reasonable cause

Whenever a charge is filed by or on behalf of a person claiming to be aggrieved, or by a member of the Commission, alleging that an employer, employment agency, labor organization, or joint labor-management committee controlling apprenticeship or other training or retraining, including on-the-job training programs, has engaged in an unlawful employment practice, the Commission shall serve a notice of the charge (including the date, place and circumstances of the alleged unlawful employment practice) on such employer, employment agency, labor organization, or joint labor-management committee (hereinafter referred to as the "respondent") within ten days, and shall make an investigation thereof. Charges shall be in writing under oath or affirmation and shall contain such information and be in such form as the Commission requires. Charges shall not be made public by the Commission. If the Commission determines after such investigation that there is not reasonable cause to believe that the charge is true, it shall dismiss the charge and promptly notify the person claiming to be aggrieved and the respondent of its action. In determining whether reasonable cause exists, the Commission shall accord substantial weight to final findings and orders made by State or local authorities in proceedings commenced under State or local law pursuant to the requirements of subsections (c) and (d) of this section. If the Commission determines after such investigation that there is reasonable cause to believe that the charge is true, the Commission shall endeavor to eliminate any such alleged unlawful employment practice by informal methods of conference, conciliation, and persuasion. Nothing said or done during and as a part of such informal endeavors may be made public by the Commission, its officers or employees, or used as evidence in a subsequent proceeding without the written consent of the persons concerned. Any person who makes public information in violation of this subsection shall be fined not more than $1,000 or imprisoned for not more than one year, or both. The Commission shall make its determination on reasonable cause as promptly as possible and, so far as practicable, not later than one hundred and twenty days from the filing of the charge or, where applicable under subsection (c) or (d) of this section, from the date upon which the Commission is authorized to take action with respect to the charge.

(c) **State or local enforcement proceedings; notification of State or local authority; time for filing charges with Commission; commencement of proceedings**

In the case of an alleged unlawful employment practice occurring in a State, or political subdivision of a State, which has a State or local law prohibiting the unlawful employment practice alleged and establishing or authorizing a State or local authority to grant or seek relief from such practice or to institute criminal proceedings with respect thereto upon receiving notice thereof, no charge may be filed under subsection (a) of this section by the person aggrieved before the expiration of sixty days after proceedings have been commenced under the State or local law, unless such proceedings have been earlier terminated, provided that such sixty-day period shall be extended to one hundred and twenty days during the first year after the effective date of such State or local law. If any requirement for the commencement of such proceedings is imposed by a State or local authority other than a requirement of the filing of a written and signed statement of the facts upon which the proceeding is based, the proceeding shall be deemed to have been commenced for the purposes of this subsection at the time such statement is sent by registered mail to the appropriate State or local authority.

(d) State or local enforcement proceedings; notification of State or local authority; time for action on charges by Commission

In the case of any charge filed by a member of the Commission alleging an unlawful employment practice occurring in a State or political subdivision of a State which has a State or local law prohibiting the practice alleged and establishing or authorizing a State or local authority to grant or seek relief from such practice or to institute criminal proceedings with respect thereto upon receiving notice thereof, the Commission shall, before taking any action with respect to such charge, notify the appropriate State or local officials and, upon request, afford them a reasonable time, but not less than sixty days (provided that such sixty-day period shall be extended to one hundred and twenty days during the first year after the effective day of such State or local law), unless a shorter period is requested, to act under such State or local law to remedy the practice alleged.

(e) Time for filing charges; time for service of notice of charge on respondent; filing of charge by Commission with State or local agency; seniority system

(1) A charge under this section shall be filed within one hundred and eighty days after the alleged unlawful employment practice occurred and notice of the charge (including the date, place and circumstances of the alleged unlawful employment practice) shall be served upon the person against whom such charge is made within ten days thereafter, except that in a case of an unlawful employment practice with respect to which the person aggrieved has initially instituted proceedings with a State or local agency with authority to grant or seek relief from such practice or to institute criminal proceedings with respect thereto upon receiving notice thereof, such charge shall be filed by or on behalf of the person aggrieved within three hundred days after the alleged unlawful employment practice occurred, or within thirty days after receiving notice that the State or local agency has terminated the proceedings under the State or local law, whichever is earlier, and a copy of such charge shall be filed by the Commission with the State or local agency.

(2) For purposes of this section, an unlawful employment practice occurs, with respect to a seniority system that has been adopted for an

intentionally discriminatory purpose in violation of this subchapter (whether or not that discriminatory purpose is apparent on the face of the seniority provision), when the seniority system is adopted, when an individual becomes subject to the seniority system, or when a person aggrieved is injured by the application of the seniority system or provision of the system.

(f) **Civil action by Commission, Attorney General, or person aggrieved; preconditions; procedure; appointment of attorney; payment of fees, costs, or security; intervention; stay of Federal proceedings; action for appropriate temporary or preliminary relief pending final disposition of charge; jurisdiction and venue of United States courts; designation of judge to hear and determine case; assignment of case for hearing; expedition of case; appointment of master**

(1) If within thirty days after a charge is filed with the Commission or within thirty days after expiration of any period of reference under subsection (c) or (d) of this section, the Commission has been unable to secure from the respondent a conciliation agreement acceptable to the Commission, the Commission may bring a civil action against any respondent not a government, governmental agency, or political subdivision named in the charge. In the case of a respondent which is a government, governmental agency, or political subdivision, if the Commission has been unable to secure from the respondent a conciliation agreement acceptable to the Commission, the Commission shall take no further action and shall refer the case to the Attorney General who may bring a civil action against such respondent in the appropriate United States district court. The person or persons aggrieved shall have the right to intervene in a civil action brought by the Commission or the Attorney General in a case involving a government, governmental agency, or political subdivision. If a charge filed with the Commission pursuant to subsection (b) of this section is dismissed by the Commission, or if within one hundred and eighty days from the filing of such charge or the expiration of any period of reference under subsection (c) or (d) of this section, whichever is later, the Commission has not filed a civil action under this section or the Attorney General has not filed a civil action in a case involving a government, gov-

ernmental agency, or political subdivision, or the Commission has not entered into a conciliation agreement to which the person aggrieved is a party, the Commission, or the Attorney General in a case involving a government, governmental agency, or political subdivision, shall so notify the person aggrieved and within ninety days after the giving of such notice a civil action may be brought against the respondent named in the charge (A) by the person claiming to be aggrieved or (B) if such charge was filed by a member of the Commission, by any person whom the charge alleges was aggrieved by the alleged unlawful employment practice. Upon application by the complainant and in such circumstances as the court may deem just, the court may appoint an attorney for such complainant and may authorize the commencement of the action without the payment of fees, costs, or security. Upon timely application, the court may, in its discretion, permit the Commission, or the Attorney General in a case involving a government, governmental agency, or political subdivision, to intervene in such civil action upon certification that the case is of general public importance. Upon request, the court may, in its discretion, stay further proceedings for not more than sixty days pending the termination of State or local proceedings described in subsections (c) or (d) of this section or further efforts of the Commission to obtain voluntary compliance.

(2) Whenever a charge is filed with the Commission and the Commission concludes on the basis of a preliminary investigation that prompt judicial action is necessary to carry out the purposes of this Act, the Commission, or the Attorney General in a case involving a government, governmental agency, or political subdivision, may bring an action for appropriate temporary or preliminary relief pending final disposition of such charge. Any temporary restraining order or other order granting preliminary or temporary relief shall be issued in accordance with rule 65 of the Federal Rules of Civil Procedure. It shall be the duty of a court having jurisdiction over proceedings under this section to assign cases for hearing at the earliest practicable date and to cause such cases to be in every way expedited.

(3) Each United States district court and each United States court of a place subject to the jurisdictions of the United States shall have jurisdiction of actions brought under this subchapter. Such an action may be

brought in any judicial district in the State in which the unlawful employment practice is alleged to have been committed, in the judicial district in which the employment records relevant to such practice are maintained and administered, or in the judicial district in which the aggrieved person would have worked but for the alleged unlawful employment practice, but if the respondent is not found within any such district, such an action may be brought within the judicial district in which the respondent has his principal office. For purposes of sections 1404 and 1406 of Title 28, the judicial district in which the respondent has his principal office shall in all cases be considered a district in which the action might have been brought.

(4) It shall be the duty of the chief judge of the district (or in his absence, the acting chief judge) in which the case is pending immediately to designate a judge in such district to hear and determine the case. In the event that no judge in the district is available to hear and determine the case, the chief judge of the district, or the acting chief judge, as the case may be, shall certify this fact to the chief judge of the circuit (or in his absence, the acting chief judge) who shall then designate a district or circuit judge of the circuit to hear and determine the case.

(5) It shall be the duty of the judge designated pursuant to this subsection to assign the case for hearing at the earliest practicable date and to cause the case to be in every way expedited. If such judge has not scheduled the case for trial within one hundred and twenty days after issue has been joined, that judge may appoint a master pursuant to rule 53 of the Federal Rules of Civil Procedure.

(g) Injunctions; appropriate affirmative action; equitable relief; accrual of back pay; reduction of back pay; limitations on judicial orders

(1) If the court finds that the respondent has intentionally engaged in or is intentionally engaging in an unlawful employment practice charged in the complaint, the court may enjoin the respondent from engaging in such unlawful employment practice, and order such affirmative action as may be appropriate, which may include, but is not limited to, reinstatement or hiring of employees, with or without back pay (payable by the employer, employment agency, or labor organization, as the case may be,

responsible for the unlawful employment practice), or any other equitable relief as the court deems appropriate. Back pay liability shall not accrue from a date more than two years prior to the filing of a charge with the Commission. Interim earnings or amounts earnable with reasonable diligence by the person or persons discriminated against shall operate to reduce the back pay otherwise allowable.

(2)(A) No order of the court shall require the admission or reinstatement of an individual as a member of a union, or the hiring, reinstatement, or promotion of an individual as an employee, or the payment to him of any back pay, if such individual was refused admission, suspended, or expelled, or was refused employment or advancement or was suspended or discharged for any reason other than discrimination on account of race, color, religion, sex, or national origin or in violation of section 2000e–3(a) of this title.

(B) On a claim in which an individual proves a violation under section 2000e–2(m) of this title and a respondent demonstrates that the respondent would have taken the same action in the absence of the impermissible motivating factor, the court—

(i) may grant declaratory relief, injunctive relief (except as provided in clause (ii)), and attorney's fees and costs demonstrated to be directly attributable only to the pursuit of a claim under section 2000e–2(m) of this title; and

(ii) shall not award damages or issue an order requiring any admission, reinstatement, hiring, promotion, or payment, described in subparagraph (A).

(h) Provisions of chapter 6 of Title 29 not applicable to civil actions for prevention of unlawful practices

The provisions of chapter 6 of Title 29 shall not apply with respect to civil actions brought under this section.

(i) Proceedings by Commission to compel compliance with judicial orders

In any case in which an employer, employment agency, or labor organization fails to comply with an order of a court issued in a civil action brought under this section, the Commission may commence proceedings to compel compliance with such order.

(j) Appeals

Any civil action brought under this section and any proceedings brought under subsection (i) of this section shall be subject to appeal as provided in sections 1291 and 1292, Title 28.

(k) Attorney's fee; liability of Commission and United States for costs

In any action or proceeding under this subchapter the court, in its discretion, may allow the prevailing party, other than the Commission or the United States, a reasonable attorney's fee (including expert fees) as part of the costs, and the Commission and the United States shall be liable for costs the same as a private person.

*   *   *   *

§ 2000e-16. Employment by Federal Government

(a) Discriminatory practices prohibited; employees or applicants for employment subject to coverage

All personnel actions affecting employees or applicants for employment (except with regard to aliens employed outside the limits of the United States) in military departments as defined in section 102 of title 5, in executive agencies as defined in section 105 of title 5 (including employees and applicants for employment who are paid from nonappropriated funds), in the United States Postal Service and the Postal Rate Commission, in those units of the Government of the District of Columbia having positions in the competitive service, and in those units of the judicial branch of the Federal Government having positions in the competitive service, and in the Government Printing Office, the General Accounting Office, and the Library of Congress shall be made free from any discrimination based on race, color, religion, sex, or national origin.

Equal Employment Opportunity Commission Guidelines

Guidelines on Discrimination Because of Religion (29 CFR Part 1605)

§ 1605.1 "Religious" nature of a practice or belief.

In most cases whether or not a practice or belief is religious is not at issue. However, in those cases in which the issue does exist, the Commission will define religious practices to include moral or ethical beliefs as to what is right and wrong which are sincerely held with the strength of traditional religious views. This standard was developed in *United States v. Seeger,* 380 U.S. 163 (1965) and *Welsh v. United States,* 398 U.S. 333 (1970). The Commission has consistently applied this standard in its decisions.[1] The fact that no religious group espouses such beliefs or the fact that the religious group to which the individual professes to belong may not accept such belief will not determine whether the belief is a religious belief of the employee or prospective employee. The phrase "religious practice" as used in these Guidelines includes both religious observances and practices, as stated in Section 701(j), 42 USC 2000e(j).

§ 1605.2 Reasonable accommodation without undue hardship as required by Section 701(j) of Title VII of the Civil Rights Act of 1964.

(a) **Purpose of this section.**

This section clarifies the obligation imposed by Title VII of the Civil Rights Act of 1964, as amended, (sections 701(j), 703 and 717) to accom-

---

1. *See* CD 76-104 (1976), CCH ¶ 6500; CD 71-2620 (1971), CCH ¶ 6283; CD 71-779 (1970), CCH ¶ 6180.

modate the religious practices of employees and prospective employees. This section does not address other obligations under Title VII not to discriminate on grounds of religion, nor other provisions of Title VII. This section is not intended to limit any additional obligations to accommodate religious practices which may exist pursuant to constitutional, or other statutory provisions; neither is it intended to provide guidance for statutes which require accommodation on bases other than religion such as § 503 of the Rehabilitation Act of 1973. The legal principles which have been developed with respect to discrimination prohibited by Title VII on the bases of race, color, sex, and national origin also apply to religious discrimination in all circumstances other than where an accommodation is required.

(b) Duty to accommodate.

(1) Section 701(j) makes it an unlawful employment practice under § 703(a)(1) for an employer to fail to reasonably accommodate the religious practices of an employee or prospective employee, unless the employer demonstrates that accommodation would result in undue hardship on the conduct of its business.[2]

(2) Section 701(j) in conjunction with § 703(c), imposes an obligation on a labor organization to reasonably accommodate the religious practices of an employee or prospective employee, unless the labor organization demonstrates that accommodation would result in undue hardship.

(3) Section 1605.2 is primarily directed to obligations of employers or labor organizations, which are the entities covered by Title VII that will most often be required to make an accommodation. However, the principles of Section 1605.2 also apply when an accommodation can be required of other entities covered by Title VII, such as employment agencies (§ 703(b)) or joint labor-management committees controlling apprenticeship or other training or retraining (§ 703(d)). (See, for example, § 1605.3(a) "Scheduling of Tests or Other Selection Procedures.")

(c) Reasonable Accommodation.

(1) After an employee or prospective employee notifies the employer or labor organization of his or her need for a religious accommodation, the

---

2. *See* Trans World Airlines, Inc. v. Hardison, [14 EPD ¶ 76201] 432 U.S. 63.74 (1977).

employer or labor organization has an obligation to reasonably accommodate the individual's religious practices. A refusal to accommodate is justified only when an employer or labor organization can demonstrate that an undue hardship would in fact result from each available alternative method of accommodation. A mere assumption that many more people, with the same religious practices as the person bring accommodated, may also need accommodation is not evidence of undue hardship.

(2) When there is more than one method of accommodation available which would not cause undue hardship, the Commission will determine whether the accommodation offered is reasonable by examining:

(i) The alternatives for accommodation considered by the employer or labor organization; and

(ii) The alternatives for accommodation, if any, actually offered to the individual requiring accommodation. Some alternatives for accommodating religious practices might disadvantage the individual with respect to his or her employment opportunities, such as compensation, terms, conditions, or privileges of employment. Therefore, when there is more than one means of accommodation which would not cause undue hardship, the employer or labor organization must offer the alternative which least disadvantages the individual with respect to his or her employment opportunities.

(d) Alternatives for Accommodating Religious Practices.

(1) Employees and prospective employees most frequently request an accommodation because their religious practices conflict with their work schedules. The following subsections are some means of accommodating the conflict between work schedules and religious practices which the Commission believes that employers and labor organizations should consider as part of the obligation to accommodate and which the Commission will consider in investigating a charge. These are not intended to be all-inclusive. There are often other alternatives which would reasonably accommodate an individual's religious practices when they conflict with a work schedule. There are also employment practices besides work scheduling which may conflict with religious practices and cause an individual to request an accommodation. See, for example, the Commission's finding number (3) from its Hearings on Religious Discrimination, in Appendix A to §§ 1605.2 and 1605.3. The principles expressed in these Guidelines apply as well to such requests for accommodation.

(i) Voluntary Substitutes and "Swaps."

Reasonable accommodation without undue hardship is generally possible where a voluntary substitute with substantially similar qualifications is available. One means of substitution is the voluntary swap. In a number of cases, the securing of a substitute has been left entirely up to the individual seeking the accommodation. The Commission believes that the obligation to accommodate requires that employers and labor organizations facilitate the securing of a voluntary substitute with substantially similar qualifications. Some means of doing this which employers and labor organizations should consider are: to publicize policies regarding accommodation and voluntary substitution; to promote an atmosphere in which such substitutions are favorably regarded; to provide a central file, bulletin board, or other means for matching voluntary substitutes with positions for which substitutes are needed.

(ii) Flexible Scheduling.

One means of providing reasonable accommodation for the religious practices of employees or prospective employees which employers and labor organizations should consider is the creation of a flexible work schedule for individuals requesting accommodation.

The following list is an example of areas in which flexibility might be introduced: flexible arrival and departure times; floating or optional holidays; flexible work breaks; use of lunch time in exchange for early departure; staggered work hours; and permitting an employee to make up time lost due to the observance of religious practices.[3]

(iii) Lateral Transfer and Change of Job Assignments.

When an employee cannot be accommodated either as to his or her entire job or an assignment within the job, employers and labor organizations should consider whether or not it is possible to change the job assignment or give the employee a lateral transfer.

(2) Payment of Dues to a Labor Organization.

Some collective bargaining agreements include a provision that each employee must join the labor organization or pay the labor organization a

---

3. On September 29, 1978, Congress enacted such a provision for the accommodation of Federal employees' religious practices. *See* Pub. L. 95-390, 5 U.S.C. 5550A [¶ 3475] "Compensatory Time Off for Religious Observances."

sum equivalent to dues. When an employee's religious practices do not permit compliance with such a provision, the labor organization should accommodate the employee by not requiring the employee to join the organization and by permitting him or her to donate a sum equivalent to dues to a charitable organization.

(e) Undue Hardship.

(1) Cost

An employer may assert undue hardship to justify a refusal to accommodate an employee's need to be absent from his or her scheduled duty hours if the employer can demonstrate that the accommodation would require "more than a *de minimis* cost."[4] The Commission will determine what constitutes "more than a *de minimis* cost" with due regard given to the identifiable cost in relation to the size and operating cost of the employer, and the number of individuals who will in fact need a particular accommodation. In general, the Commission interprets this phrase as it was used in the *Hardison* decision to mean that costs similar to the regular payment of premium wages of substitutes, which was at issue in *Hardison,* would constitute undue hardship. However, the Commission will presume that the infrequent payment of premium wages for a substitute or the payment of previum wages while a more permanent accommodation is being sought are costs which an employer can be required to bear as a means of providing a reasonable accommodation. Further, the Commission will presume that generally, the payment of administrative costs necessary for providing the accommodation will not constitute more than a *de minimis* cost. Administrative costs, for example, include those costs involved in rearranging schedules and recording substitutions for payroll purposes.

(2) Seniority Rights. Undue hardship would also be shown where a variance from a bona fide seniority system is necessary in order to accommodate an employee's religious practices when doing so would deny another employee his or her job or shift preference guaranteed by that system. *Hardison, supra,* 432 U.S. at 80. Arrangements for voluntary substitutes and swaps (see paragraph (d)(1)(i) of this section) do not constitute an undue hardship to the extent the arrangements do not violate a bona

---

4. *Hardison, supra,* 432 U.S. at 84.

fide seniority system. Nothing in the Statute or these Guidelines precludes an employer and a union from including arrangements for voluntary substitutes and swaps as part of a collective bargaining agreement.

§ 1605.3 Selection practices.

(a) Scheduling of Tests or Other Selection Procedures. When a test or other selection procedure is scheduled at a time when an employee or prospective employee cannot attend because of his or her religious practices, the user of the test should be aware that the principles enunciated in these guidelines apply and that it has an obligation to accommodate such employee or prospective employee unless undue hardship would result.

(b) Inquiries Which Determine An Applicant's Availability to Work During An Employer's Scheduled Working Hours.

(1) The duty to accommodate pertains to prospective employees as well as current employees. Consequently, an employer may not permit an applicant's need for a religious accommodation to affect in any way its decision whether to hire the applicant unless it can demonstrate that it cannot reasonably accommodate the applicant's religious practices without undue hardship.

(2) As a result of the oral and written testimony submitted at the Commission's Hearing on Religious Discrimination, discussions with representatives or organizations interested in the issue of religious discrimination, and the comments received from the public on these Guidelines as proposed, the Commission has concluded the use of preselection inquiries which determine an applicant's availability has an exclusionary effect on the employment opportunities of persons with certain religious practices. The use of such inquiries will, therefore, be considered to violate Title VII unless the employer can show that it:

(i) Did not have an exclusionary effect on its employees or prospective employees needing an accommodation for the same religious practices; or

(ii) Was otherwise justified by business necessity.

Employers who believe they have a legitimate interest in knowing the availability of their applicants prior to selection must consider procedures which would serve this interest and which would have a lesser exclusionary effect on persons whose religious practices need accommodation. An example of such a procedure is for the employer to state the normal work hours for the job and, after making it clear to the applicant that he or she is not required to indicate the need for any absences for religious practices during the scheduled work hours, ask the applicant whether he or she is otherwise available to work those hours. Then, after a position is offered, but before the applicant is hired, the employer can inquire into the need for a religious accommodation and determine, according to the principles of these Guidelines, whether an accommodation is possible. This type of inquiry would provide an employer with information concerning the availability of most of its applicants, while deferring until after a position is offered the identification of the usually small number of applicants who require an accommodation.

(3) The Commission will infer that the need for an accommodation discriminatorily influenced a decision to reject an applicant when : (i) prior to an offer of employment the employer makes an inquiry into an applicant's availability without having a business necessity justification; and (ii) after the employer has determined the applicant's need for an accommodation, the employer rejects a qualified applicant. The burden is then on the employer to demonstrate that factors other than the need for an accommodation were the reason for rejecting the qualified applicant, or that a reasonable accommodation without undue hardship was not possible.

Appendix A to §§ 1605.2 and 1605.3—Background Information

In 1966, the Commission adopted guidelines on religious discrimination which stated that an employer had an obligation to accommodate the religious practices of its employees or prospective employees unless to do so would create a "serious inconvenience to the conduct of the business." 29 CFR 1 605.1(a)(2), 31 FR 3870 (1966).

In 1967, the Commission revised these guidelines to state that an employer had an obligation to reasonably accommodate the religious practices of its employees or prospective employees, unless the employer could prove that to do so would create an "undue hardship". 29 CFR 1605.1(b)(c), 32 FR 10298.

In 1972, Congress amended Title VII to incorporate the obligation to accommodate expressed in the Commission's 1967 Guidelines by adding section 701(j).

In 1977, the United States Supreme Court issued its decision in the case of *Trans World Airlines, Inc. v. Hardison,* 432 U.S. 63 (1977). *Hardison* was brought under section 703(a)(1) because it involved facts occurring before the enactment of Section 701(j). The Court applied the Commission's 1967 Guidelines, but indicated that the result would be the same under Section 701(j). It stated that Trans World Airlines had made reasonable efforts to accommodate the religious needs of its employee, Hardison. The Court held that to require Trans World Airlines to make further attempts at accommodations—by unilaterally violating a seniority provision of the collective bargaining agreement, paying premium wages on a regular basis to another employee to replace Hardison, or creating a serious shortage of necessary employees in another department in order to replace Hardison—would create an undue hardship on the conduct of Trans World Airlines' business, and would therefore exceed the duty to accommodate Hardison.

In 1978, the Commission conducted public hearings on religious discrimination in New York City, Milwaukee, and Los Angeles in order to respond to the concerns raised by *Hardison.* Approximately 150 witnesses testified or submitted written statements.[5] The witnesses included employers, employees, representatives of religious and labor organizations and representatives of Federal, State and local governments.

The Commission found from the hearings that:

(1) There is widespread confusion concerning the extent of accommodation under the *Hardison* decision.

(2) The religious practices of some individuals and some groups of individuals are not being accommodated.

(3) Some of those practices which are not being accommodated are:

—Observance of a Sabbath or religious holidays;

—Need for prayer break during working hours;

—Practice of following certain dietary requirements;

—Practice of not working during a mourning period for a deceased relative;

—Prohibitions against medical examinations;

—Prohibitions against membership in labor and other organizations; and

—Practices concerning dress and other personal grooming habits.

---

5. The transcript of the Commission's Hearings on Religious Discrimination can be examined by the public at: The Equal Employment Opportunity Commission, 2401 E Street N.W., Washington, D.C. 20506.

(4) Many of the employers who testified had developed alternative employment practices which accommodate the religious practices of employees and prospective employees and which meet the employer's business needs.

(5) Little evidence was submitted by employers which showed actual attempts to accommodate religious practices with resultant unfavorable consequences to the employer's business. Employers appeared to have substantial anticipatory concerns but no, or very little, actual experience with the problems they theorized would emerge by providing reasonable accommodation for religious practices.

Based on these findings, the Commission is revising its Guidelines to clarify the obligation imposed by Section 701(j) to accommodate the religious practices of employees and prospective employees.

Policy Statement on Religious Accommodation Under Title VII

The Supreme Court, in *Ansonia Board of Education v. Philbrook,* 479 U.S. 60, 41 EDP ¶ 36,565 (1986), examined an employer's duty under § 701(j)[6] of Title VII of the Civil Rights Act of 1964, as amended (Title VII), to accommodate an employee's religious beliefs or practices. The issue before the Court was whether an employer who has already provided a means of reasonably accommodating an employee's religious needs must provide an employee's preferred means of accommodation where it would not cause undue hardship on the conduct of the employer's business. *Ansonia,* 479 U.S. at 66. The Supreme Court held "that an employer has met its obligation under § 701(j) when it demonstrates that it has offered a reasonable accommodation to the employee." *Id.* at 69.

In *Ansonia* a school teacher's religious beliefs required that he refrain from secular employment on six occasions during the school year in order to observe holy days. *Ansonia,* 479 U.S. at 62–63. The Ansonia Board of Education's collective bargaining agreement with the Ansonia Federation of Teachers provided three days of leave for mandatory religious observance; these were not charged against an employee's annual leave or accu-

---

6. Section 701(j) provides that "[t]he term religion includes all aspects of religious observance and practice, as well as belief, unless an employer demonstrates that he is unable to reasonably accommodate to an employee's or prospective employee's religious observance or practice without undue hardship on the conduct of the employer's business."

mulated sick leave. *Id.* at 63–64. The collective bargaining agreement also provided for the use of up to three days of accumulated sick leave for "necessary personal business" but limited the personal business reasons to those not otherwise specified in the contract. *Id.* at 64. Use of the personal business leave for religious observance was specifically excluded. *Id.*

Philbrook sought to be allowed to use the three days of personal business leave for religious observance rather than having to take unpaid leave for the three additional days of religious observance. *Id.* Alternatively, Philbrook requested that he be allowed to pay the cost of hiring a substitute which was significantly less than the amount deducted from his salary for each unauthorized absence. *Id.* at 65. Because the school board consistently rejected Philbrook's proposals he filed a complaint with the Connecticut Commission on Human Rights and Opportunities, with the EEOC, and eventually in federal district court alleging that the prohibition on the use of the necessary personal business leave for religious observance violated § 703(a)(1) & (2). *Id.*

After the district court concluded that Philbrook had failed to prove a case of religious discrimination, the Court of Appeals reversed the lower court and held that "[w]here the employer and employee each propose a reasonable accommodation, Title VII requires the employer to accept the proposal the employee prefers unless that accommodation causes undue hardship on the employer's conduct of his business." *Id.* at 66, *citing* 757 F.2d 476, 484 (2nd Cir. 1985). The Supreme Court rejected the Court of Appeal's conclusion, finding no basis in the language or the legislative history of Title VII for requiring an employer to choose any particular means of accommodation as long as the accommodation offered is reasonable. *Id.* at 68. The Court concluded that where an employer has reasonably accommodated an employee's religious needs the employer need not show that each of the employee's alternative accommodations would result in undue hardship. *Id.* "[T]he extent of undue hardship on the employer's business is at issue only where the employer claims that it is unable to offer any reasonable accommodation without such hardship." *Id.* at 68–69.

The Court of Appeals had found support for its position in the Commission's guidelines on religious discrimination. The Commission's guidelines provide that "when there is more than one means of accommodation which would not cause undue hardship, the employer or labor organization must offer the alternative which least disadvantages the individual with respect to his or her employment opportunities."[7] The Supreme Court noted that the guideline, "[t]hough superficially consistent with the burden imposed by the Court of Appeals, . . . by requiring the employer to choose the option that least disadvantages an individual's *employment opportunities,* contains a significant limitation not found in the court's standard." *Id.* at 70 n.6 (emphasis in original). The Court added that it would find the guideline inconsistent with Title VII "[t]o the extent that [it], like the Court of Appeals, requires [an] employer to accept any alternative favored by the employee short of undue hardship . . . ." *Id.* It is the Commission's position that the guideline does not require an employer to provide any alternative favored by the employee and is, therefore, consistent with the Supreme Court's holding in *Ansonia.*

The Commission, in its amicus brief filed in *Ansonia,* took the position that the Court of Appeals had overstated the extent of an employer's accommodation obligations under Title VII. Brief for the United States and the Equal Employment Opportunity Commission as Amici Curiae at 15, *Ansonia,* 479 U.S. 60 (1986). "[The court's] conclusion that an employer must, absent a showing of undue hardship, accept the particular accommodation preferred by the employee is inconsistent with the clear import of the statutory language." *Id.* "The sole judicial inquiry is whether the employer's proposed accommodation is reasonable." *Id.* at 16.

The Commission explained in its brief what reasonable accommodation involves. "An employer's duty of reasonable accommodation includes beliefs and employment requirements and to preserve the employee's employment status. *Id.* (citation omitted). "Neither the employee's subjective assessment of the accommodation nor his secular, *non*-employment related needs are relevant" to the determination of reasonableness. *Id.* at 17 (emphasis in original). The Commission noted in its brief that this position was not inconsistent with the EEOC guidelines since they "confirm that only impacts on the employee's employment status are relevant." *Id.* at 17 n.16. The Commission further reasoned that where the burden on an employee's employment status is more than de minimis or inconsequential, the employer's attempt to accommodate is unreasonable. *Id.*

Although the Supreme Court did not make a determination that the school board's accommodation was in fact reasonable, it found that requiring an employee to take unpaid leave for religious observance that

---

7. 29 C.F.R. § 1605.2(c)(2).

exceeded the amount allowed by a collective bargaining agreement would generally be reasonable. *Id.* Unpaid leave would not constitute a reasonable accommodation, however, if paid leave were provided for all purposes except religious ones. *Id.* The case was remanded to determine whether the three days of leave designated for "necessary personal business" was limited to personal business not already provided for in the collective bargaining agreement or whether it was generally used for increasing the amount of leave for secular purposes while leave used for religious purposes was restricted.

In conclusion, the holding in *Ansonia* does not invalidate the Commission's guidelines on religious accommodation. The guidelines should be consulted when determining the reasonableness of an accommodation offered by an employer. Whether a particular religious accommodation is reasonable must be determined on a case by case basis. Where leave of absence for secular purposes is granted more liberally than for religious purposes the accommodation is not reasonable. Where the burden on an employee's employment status is more than de minimis or inconsequential an accommodation is unreasonable.

The Compliance Manual will be revised in light of the Supreme Court's decision in *Ansonia.* The following should be regarded as in conflict with *Ansonia:*

§ 628.5(a)—"The employer satisfies its duty to an employee or prospective employee once it offers all reasonable means of accommodation without undue hardship."[8] (p. 628-15); "[O]nce a union offers all reasonable means of accommodation to a member or prospective member which would not result in undue hardship, it will have satisfied its obligations under Title VII." (p. 628-17).

---

8. See § 628.5(a), p. 625-15. The manual supports this statement with a reference to C.D. No. 81-28, CCH EEOC Decisions (1983) ¶ 6818, which states that "[w]hen an employer offers all available means of reasonable accommodation which would not result in undue hardship, it has met its burden [of reasonable accommodation]." It is true that an employer who has already offered all available means of accommodation, as the respondent in the Commission Decision had, has met its Title VII obligation. However, it is not necessary after *Ansonia* for an employer to offer all available means of reasonable accommodation which would not result in undue hardship in order to meet its obligation under Title VII.

§ 628.10(c) Procedures

(12) If respondent attempted to accommodate the religious needs of the charging party, it must be determined that all reasonable means of accommodating charging party were actually offered and that undue hardship would in fact have resulted from each available alternative that was offered.

Policy Statement on Religious Objections to Unionism

I. Analysis

Title VII case law establishes that a reasonable accommodation is made when religious objectors to unionism are allowed to make payments to a nonreligious charitable organization as a substitute for the payment of union dues.[9] Once a reasonable accommodation is reached, the statutory inquiry is at an end. Thus, an employee who refuses to pay dues to a labor organization and also refuses to donate to a charitable organization a sum equivalent to the amount required for union dues may be lawfully discharged, unless the employee has good faith religious objections to donating to the charities listed in the collective bargaining agreement, in which case other acceptable charities must be identified.

Title VII of the Civil Rights Act of 1964, 42 U.S.C. §§ 2000e-2(a) and 2000e-2(c), provides that it is an unlawful employment practice for either an employer or a union to discriminate against an individual because of the individual's religion. Section 701(j) of the Act, 42 U.S.C. 2000e(j), defines religion to include all aspects of religious observance and practice. An employee whose religious beliefs include conscientious objections to joining or financially supporting labor organizations may not be required to join or financially support a labor union. In *International Association of Machinists and Aerospace Workers, District Lodge 751 v. Boeing Co.,* 833 F.2d 165, 45 EPD ¶ 37,593 (9th Cir. 1987), *cert. denied,* 56 U.S.L.W. 3715 (U.S. Apr. 18, 1988) (No. 87-1484), the court held that an employee with sincerely held religious objections to unionism need not be a member of an organized religious group which opposes unions to be entitled to

---

9. The related issue of accommodation of an individual's religious objections to association with a particular union because of that union's specific activities will be addressed by the Commission in a subsequent policy guidance.

the protection of the religious accommodation provision of Title VII.[10]
See also *EEOC v. Davy Tree Surgery Co.*, 43 EPD ¶ 37059 (N.D. Cal.
1987). *See generally Tooley v. Martin Marietta Corp.*, 648 F.2d 1239, 26
EPD ¶ 31, 907 (9th Cir. 1981), *cert. denied, sub. nom. United Steelworkers,
Local 8141 v. Tooley*, 454 U.S. 1098, 27 EPD ¶ 32,269 (1981); *Nottleson v.
Smith Steel Workers, Local 19806*, 643 F.2d 445, 25 EPD ¶ 31,599 (7th
Cir. 1981), *cert. denied*, 454 U.S. 1046, 27 EPD ¶ 32,193 (1981); *Anderson
v. General Dynamics, Convair Aerospace Division*, 589 F.2d 397, 18 EPD
¶ 8652 (9th Cir. 1978), *cert. denied*, 442 U.S. 921, 19 EPD ¶ 9246
(1979).

To establish a prima facie case of religious discrimination under Sections 701(j) and 703(a)(1) of Title VII, 42 U.S.C. §§ 2000e(j) and 2000e-
2(a)(1), the employee must show that (1) (s)he holds conscientious objections to joining or financially supporting labor organizations; (2) (s)he
informed his/her employer and the union about his/her religious views
that were in conflict with the union security agreement; and (3) (s)he was
discharged for his/her refusal to join the union and to pay union dues. The
burden is then on the employer and union to show reasonable accommodation efforts or undue hardship justifying nonaccommodation. *Anderson
v. General Dynamics, Convair Aerospace Division*, 589 F.2d at 401. *See also
Smith v. Pyro Mining Co.*, 827 F.2d 1081 (6th Cir. 1987); *McDaniel v.
Essex International, Inc.*, 571 F.2d 338, 16 EPD ¶ 8137 (6th Cir. 1978).

A reasonable accommodation is made when religious objectors to unionism are allowed to make payments to a nonreligious charitable organization as a substitute for the payment of union dues. EEOC, Guidelines on
Discrimination Because of Religion (Guidelines), 29 C.F.R. 1605.2(d)(2)
(1987).[11]

---

10. By contrast to Title VII, Section 19 of the National Labor Relations Act
(NLRA), 29 U.S.C. § 169, requires that a religious objector be a member of a bona fide
religion which has historically held conscientious objections to joining or financially supporting labor organizations.

11. The NLRA is consistent with the Commission's Guidelines. Section 19 of the
NLRA is more specific than Title VII and allows those employees who object to union
membership or the payment of dues to pay an equivalent amount to a non-religious and
non-labor oriented charity designated by agreement, or, if not designated, chosen by the
employee.

This charitable substitution is the only accommodation the employer/ union need offer. Title VII requires reasonable accommodation. It does not require employers to accommodate the religious practices of an employee in exactly the way the employee would like to be accommodated. See *Ansonia Board of Education v. Philbrook,* 479 U.S. 60, 41 EPD ¶ 36,565 (1986); *Pinsker v. Joint District No. 28J,* 735 F.2d 388, 34 EPD ¶ 34,410 (10th Cir. 1984); *Brener v. Diagnostic Center Hospital,* 671 F.2d 141, 28 EPD ¶ 32,550 (5th Cir. 1982).

In *Stern v. Teamsters General Local Union No. 200,* 626 F. Supp. 1043, 40 EDP ¶ 36,355 (E.D. Wis. 1986), the plaintiff, a former employee, brought an action against his former employer and recognized union at his former work place alleging that he had been fired because, pursuant to his religious beliefs, he had refused to join the union. Stern also refused to pay the equivalent of union dues to any of the nonreligious charities named as alternatives in the collective bargaining agreement. The court found that the offer to allow payment to a nonreligious charity listed in the collective bargaining agreement was a reasonable accommodation and the only accommodation the union need offer. Thus, Stern was lawfully discharged.

The court relied upon Section 19 of the NLRA and found that the union offered the alternative approved by Congress. The court quoted the legislative history of Section 19; "[T]he bill would . . . reconcile the National Labor Relations Act with section 701(j) of the Equal Employment Opportunity Act. . . . The option of allowing a qualifying individual the ability to pay the equivalent of dues to a nonreligious charity clearly constitutes a 'reasonable accommodation' to the individual's religious beliefs." H.R. Rep. No. 496, 96th Cong., 2d Sess. reprinted in 1980 U.S. Cong. & Ad. News 7158, 7159. Relying on the legislative history, the court concluded that since Section 19 is more recent than Title VII and the Commission's Guidelines, the offer to allow payment to a non-religious charity listed in the collective bargaining agreement is the only accommodation the union need offer.

In *Ansonia,* the Supreme Court held that, where the employer or union and the employee each propose a reasonable accommodation that would not cause undue hardship, the employer/union does not have to accept the employee's alternative. Rather, the employer/union will meet its obligation simply by offering a reasonable accommodation, regardless of possible alternatives. The court stated: "[W]here the employer has already reasonably accommodated the employee's religious needs, the statutory inquiry is at an end. The employer need not further show that each of the employee's alternative accommodations would result in undue hardship." *Ansonia,* 479 U.S. at 68. Since it is well established that a reasonable accommodation is reached when a religious objector is allowed to pay the equivalent of union dues to a charity listed in the collective bargaining agreement, the statutory inquiry is at an end unless the employee's good faith religious beliefs forbid him/her from contributing to any of the charities listed in the collective bargaining agreement.

In that case, a contribution to those charities would not constitute a reasonable accommodation of his/her religious beliefs because it would not resolve the conflict between the employee's work and religious requirements. One alternative which might resolve the conflict is allowing the employee to contribute to a charity which is not on the list but which is acceptable to the employee, the union, and the employer. Whether any alternative is reasonable and will not present an undue hardship must be decided on a case-by-case basis, in light of the union's size, operational costs, and the number of individuals who will need accommodation. How to make this determination is discussed in more detail in the Compliance Manual, Volume II, § 628, Religious Accommodation.

II. Charge Resolution

If a charge raises the issue of religious discrimination based on the failure of the union to reasonably accommodate an employee's religious objections to unionism and financial support of unions, a *prima facie* case of religious discrimination must be established. It must be shown: (1) that (s)he had a good faith belief that union membership and dues payments were contrary to his/her religious beliefs; (2) that (s)he informed his/her employer and union that his/her religious views conflicted with the union security agreement; and (3) that (s)he was discharged for his/her refusal to join the union and/or pay dues. The burden is then on the employer and union to show reasonable accommodation efforts or undue hardship justifying nonaccommodation.

Policy Guidance: Religious Organizations that Pay Women Less than Men in Accordance with Religious Beliefs

Subject Matter

A religious organization or institution may not pay women less than men even if such a policy is pursuant with its religious beliefs. Religious institutions are covered by the Equal Pay Act (EPA) and Title VII of the Civil Rights Act of 1964, as amended (Title VII), in regard to sex discrimination in wages. They may not justify their refusal to comply with the Equal Pay Act or Title VII on constitutional grounds since the statutes neither infringe upon the organizations' free exercise of their religious beliefs nor violate the establishment clause of the first amendment.

The Free Exercise Clause

The free exercise clause prohibits legislation of religious beliefs. To determine whether a generally valid governmental regulation, such as the EPA and/or Title VII, violates the free exercise clause of the Constitution, courts weigh three factors: (1) the magnitude of the statute's impact on the exercise of a religious belief; (2) the existence of a compelling state interest justifying the burden imposed upon the exercise of the religious belief; and (3) the extent to which recognition of an exemption from the statute would impede objectives sought to be advanced by the statute. *Wisconsin v. Yoder,* 406 U.S. 205 (1972); *Sherbert v. Verner,* 374 U.S. 398 (1963). Application of Title VII and/or the EPA to religious discrimination has been found not to violate the free exercise clause in numerous cases, including some which presented a direct conflict between sincerely held religious beliefs and the state interest in eliminating sex discrimination.

In *EEOC v. Pacific Press Publishing Ass'n,* 676 F.2d 1272, 29 EPD ¶ 32,817 (9th Cir. 1982), the plaintiff, an employee of a religiously affiliated publishing house, alleged that she was denied monetary allowances paid to similarly situated male employees in violation of Title VII. The court held that the institution's free exercise of its religious beliefs was not violated by requiring that the institution pay similarly situated men and women equal wages. However, the clash between the state interest and religious beliefs was not present as to this aspect of the case, since "the Church proclaims that it does not believe in discriminating against women or minority groups and that its policy is to pay wages without discrimination. . . ." *Id.* at 1279, 29 EPD at 25,808. *EEOC v. Fremont Christian School,* 781 F.2d 1362, 39 EPD ¶ 35,872 (9th Cir. 1986), involved an employer policy of according health insurance only to married men and not to married women because of its religious belief that only men could be the head of the household. There, too, the court held that the Free Exercise Clause did not preclude imposing Title VII and Equal Pay Act requirements on the school. It reasoned that there was not significant impact on the school's religious beliefs because the church did not believe in discriminating against women, and that the state has a compelling interest in eliminating discrimination. *See also Tony and Susan Alamo Foundation v. Secretary of Labor,* 471 U.S. 290, 36 EPD ¶ 35,147 (1985) (requiring adherence to the Fair Labor Standard Act's minimum wage law does not interfere with a free exercise of religion even where employees protested the act's application; but facts show no direct conflict between the religious beliefs and the FLSA).

Nevertheless, the court in *Pacific Press* did discuss balancing the defendant's free exercise rights against the state's interest in Title VII, where the two do directly clash. Besides the claim of unequal wages, the employee there also brought a claim of retaliatory discharge. The employer asserted that the charge of discrimination brought by the complainant "violat[ed] . . . church doctrines which prohibit lawsuits by members against the church." *Id.* at 1280. As the court said, "Unlike the wage discrimination claim, there is a substantial impact on the exercise of religious beliefs because EEOC's jurisdiction to prosecute . . . will impose liability on Press for disciplinary actions based on religious doctrine." *Id.*

The court concluded, however, that "the government's compelling interest in assuring equal employment opportunities justifies this burden." *Id. See also Tony and Susan Alamo,* 471 U.S. at 309 (compelling government interest in enforcing minimum wage laws; failure to do so would have anti-competitive effect). The Commission believes that this result properly balances the interests at stake, and thus disagrees with the contrary result implied by the court of appeals for the Sixth Circuit in *Dayton Christian Schools v. Ohio Civil Rights Commission,* 766 F.2d 932, 37 EPD ¶ 35,336 (6th Cir. 1985), *rev'd on other grounds and vacated,* 106 S.Ct. 2718, 40 EPD ¶ 36,195 (1986).

In *Dayton Christian Schools,* the court of appeals held, *inter alia,* that Ohio could not constitutionally apply its state law against gender discrimination to a parochial school when the school discriminates pursuant to religious beliefs. Since the Ohio statute and Title VII are identical in providing no exemption for theologically based sex discrimination, it is likely that the Sixth Circuit would have reached the same result, had the suit been brought under Title VII.[12]

The Commission concludes that there is no valid free exercise claim that permits employers to pay unequal wages based on sex in violation of Title VII and the Equal Pay Act. Both the Ninth and Sixth Circuits have applied the test we have discussed, differing only in their assessment of the impact that an exception in favor of religious groups would have on enforcement of sex discrimination laws.

As the Ninth Circuit said in *Pacific Press,* Congress has manifested an intent "to protect employees of religious employers. The effect of a broad religious-organization exemption would be to withdraw Title VII's protection from employees" of religious organizations. 676 F.2d at 1280. Thus, the impact of such an exemption for religious employers would be profound and widespread, contrary to the conclusion of the Sixth Circuit in *Dayton Christian Schools* that "[a]ccommodation of the religious beliefs in this case would not significantly interfere with the state's fulfillment of its goal of eradicating discrimination in employment." 766 F.2d at 955. As Judge Clark wrote for the Fifth Circuit in *EEOC v. Mississippi College,* 626 F.2d 477, 489 [23 FEP Cases 1501] (5th Cir. 1980), *cert. denied,* 453 U.S. 912 [26 FEP Cases 64] (1981), "creating an exemption . . . greater than that provided by § 702 would seriously undermine the means chosen by Congress to combat discrimination . . . . Although the number of religious educational institutions is minute in comparison to the num-

---

12. In reversing, the Supreme Court did not reach the merits of the claim that the Constitution would be violated by applying the antidiscrimination law where the discrimination was based on religious beliefs. Thus, the Sixth Circuit decision still represents that court's thinking on the issue. Nevertheless, the Supreme Court's decision lends strong support to the Commission's position. It held that the state interest in eliminating sex discrimination was sufficiently important to bring the case within the principle that federal courts should abstain from enjoining state proceedings unless necessary to prevent irreparable injury and that the state agency's investigation violated no constitutional provision.

ber of employers subject to Title VII, their effect upon society at large is great. . . ."

The Commission also notes that Congress has manifested a strong desire not to allow religious organizations to be exempt from statutory prohibitions of sex discrimination.[13] In enacting § 702 of Title VII which allows religious organizations to discriminate on the basis of religion, Congress expressly rejected numerous proposed amendments that would exempt religious organizations from liability for theologically-based sex and other discrimination. *See Pacific Press,* 676 F.2d at 1276-77 (reviewing history of rejected proposals to broaden the religious exemption). It is, therefore, evident that Congress has determined that to broaden the exemption already provided, in fact, would seriously undermine one of the purposes of the statute: to end sex discrimination in employment.

A religious exemption to the EPA is not justified by the EPA's provision excepting from its coverage an employment practice based on "any other factor other than sex" (in this case religious beliefs). 29 U.S.C. § 206(d)(1)(iv). *See EEOC v. Fremont Christian School,* 781 F.2d 1362 (holding that the religiously based "head of household" policy, denying fringe benefits to married women, is not a factor other than sex).

Further, several district courts have held that the application of the EPA to religious institutions does not violate the free exercise clause, although those cases were not ones in which the employer asserted a sincerely held belief that conflicted with the enforcement of the EPA. *Marshall v. Pacific Union Conference of Seventh Day Adventists,* 14 EPD ¶ 7806 (C.D. Cal. 1977), held that the application of the Equal Pay Act to lay persons employed at schools owned and operated by a religious institution is not an unconstitutional impingement on religious beliefs. *See also Russell v. Belmont College,* 31 EPD ¶ 33,520 (M.D. Tenn. 1982) (church-

---

13. The Section-by-Section analysis of H.R. 1746, the Equal Employment Opportunity Act of 1972, states that:

> The limited exemption . . . for religious . . . associations . . . has been broadened to allow such entities to employ individuals of a particular religion in all their activities. . . . Such organizations remain subject to the provisions of Title VII with regard to race, color, sex, or national origin.

Reprinted in LEGISLATIVE HISTORY OF THE EQUAL EMPLOYMENT OPPORTUNITY ACT OF 1972 at 1844, 1845.

controlled educational institution not exempt from EPA; the EPA provides only narrow exemptions from its remedial coverage, none of which fit the institution). It is therefore the policy of the Commission to enforce both the EPA and Title VII in appropriate cases of sex discrimination by religious organizations.

The Establishment Clause

Nor does the establishment clause of the First Amendment prohibit application of Title VII or the Equal Pay Act to religious institutions. To withstand scrutiny under the establishment clause, the statute: (1) must have a secular purpose; (2) must neither advance not inhibit religion as its primary effect; and (3) must not foster excessive governmental entanglement with religion. *Lemon v. Kurtzman,* 403 U.S. 602 612-14 (1971). *See also Committee for Public Education and Religious Liberty v. Regan,* 444 U.S. 646, 653 (1980); *Roemer v. Maryland Public Works Board,* 426 U.S. 736 (1976). There is no question that Title VII and the Equal Pay Act meet the first two parts of this test. First, they have a secular purpose, i.e., they require equal pay for equal work and end to sex discrimination. Second, as discussed in *Pacific Press,* 676 F.2d at 1281-82, and *Fremont Christian School,* 781 F.2d at 1369-70, the Acts do not have the primary effect of advancing or inhibiting religion. The third part of the *Lemon* test is crucial: whether application of Title VII and the EPA create excessive governmental entanglement between the EEOC and the religious institution. To determine whether governmental entanglement is excessive we must examine the character and purposes of the institutions that are benefitted, the nature of the aid that the state provides, and the resulting relationship between the federal government and the religious institution. *Lemon,* 403 U.S. at 615.

The nature of the regulation's intrusion and the resulting relationship between the government and the religious institution are closely related. The potential for continuous supervision is the critical entanglement issue and Title VII's enforcement mechanisms will not result in ongoing scrutiny of the religious institution's operations. The court in *Mississippi College* stated that the relationship between the federal government and the religious institution that results from the application of Title VII is limited both in scope and effect. No relationship is created between the institution and government until and unless the organization violates or is alleged to have violated the act. Then the organization is subject only to limited investigation and *de novo* judicial determination. EEOC's relationship to religious employers threatens no more entanglement than other statutes which apply to religious institutions. *Pacific Press,* 676 F.2d at 1282, 29 EPD at 25,810; *EEOC v. Mississippi College,* 626 F.2d at 487-88, 24 EPD at 17,706; *Russell v. Belmont College,* 31 EPD at 29,423; *Marshall,* 14 EPD at 5958-59.

Ministerial Exception

Courts have developed an exception to the above analysis where the employment relationship is between a church and its ministers. In the few cases addressing the issue, courts have concluded that because ministers are the "lifeblood" of the church, any state interference in the relationship would violate the religious clauses of the First Amendment. That proposition was first articulated by the Fifth Circuit in *McClure v. Salvation Army,* 460 F.2d 553, 558, 4 EPD ¶ 7719, (5th Cir. 1972), *cert. denied,* 409 U.S. 896 (1972). It involved a female minister who alleged, among other things, that she was underpaid because of her sex. The court reasoned that:

> [t]he minister is the chief instrument by which the church seeks to fulfill its purpose. Matters touching on this relationship must necessarily be recognized as of prime ecclesiastical concern. Just as the initial function of selecting a minister is a matter of church administration and government, so are the functions which accompany such a selection. It is unavoidably true that these include the determination of a minister's salary, his place of assignment, and the duty he is to perform in the furtherance of the religious mission of the church.

460 F.2d at 559.

The Fifth Circuit reaffirmed the distinction between ministers and lay persons in *EEOC v. Southwestern Baptist Theological Seminary,* 651 F.2d 277, 26 EPD ¶ 32,107 (5th Cir. 1981), *cert. denied,* 456 U.S. 905, 28 EPD ¶ 32548 (1982). The court there held that the seminary-defendant had to comply with the EEOC filing requirements—except for employees found to be ministers of the church. See also *Marshall v. Pacific Union Conference,* 14 EPD ¶ 7806 at 5958 (C.D. Cal. 1977) (noting that government was not seeking to apply EPA to clergy, but only to lay employees of church). *Cf. Kedroff v. St. Nicholas Cathedral of the Russian Orthodox Church in America,* 344 U.S. 94,116 (1952) ("freedom to select the clergy . . . must now be said to have federal constitutional protection as a part of the free exercise of religion against state interference").

The Fourth Circuit has held that this "ministerial exception" includes "clergy" who are not technically ministers but who function in that capacity. In *Rayburn v. General Conference of Seventh-Day Adventists,* 772 F.2d 1164, 1165, 38 EPD ¶ 35,555 (4th Cir. 1985), *cert. denied,* 106 S.Ct. 3333, 40 EPD ¶ 36,207 (1986), a white female alleged race and sex discrimination after she was denied a position on the pastoral staff as an "associate in pastoral care (a female who has received seminary training but has a different title from her male counterpart because in the Seventh-day Adventist Church women may not stand for ordination)." The pastoral staff duties entailed teaching baptismal and Bible classes, pastoring the singles group, occasional preaching, and other evangelical, liturgical, and counseling responsibilities. An associate in pastoral care may also receive a "commissioned minister credential" or a "commissioned minister license," although she may never be ordained. The court found that because of her role in the church the charging party fell within the ministerial exception though she may never become an ordained minister in the church. It observed that:

> The fact that an associate in pastoral care can never be an ordained minister in her church is likewise immaterial. The "ministerial exception" to Title VII first articulated in *McClure v. Salvation Army,* [citation omitted] does not depend on the ordination but upon the function of the position, *EEOC v. Southwestern Baptist Seminary.* (citation omitted) "As a general rule, if the employee's primary duties consist of teaching, spreading the faith, church governance, supervision of a religious order, or supervision or participation in religious ritual and worship, he or she should be considered 'clergy.'" This approach necessarily requires a court to determine whether a position is important to the spiritual and pastoral mission of the church.

Id. at 1168-69 (citations omitted).[14] See also *Assemany v. Archdiocese of Detroit,* 49 FEP Cases 169 (Mich.Ct.App. 1989) (holding, under a state age discrimination statute, that a church musical director could be "clergy" for purposes of the exception).

The Commission will carefully examine the nature of the relationship between the individual and the church and on a case by case basis to determine whether to apply the ministerial exception or whether the individual should be considered "clergy." For example, it questions the court's conclusion in *Assemany.*

When a charge alleging sex discrimination in wages is filed against a religious institution, the charge can be analyzed under the EPA and/or Title VII. It should also be noted that Title VII covers types of wage discrimination not actionable under the EPA. Therefore, if an action cannot be brought under the EPA, it may nevertheless be a violation if Title VII. See EEOC Compliance Manual, Volume II, § 633, Wages.

---

14. The *Rayburn* court also noted that Title VII is an "interest of the highest order" which will often "overbalance legitimate claims to the free exercise of religion." *Id.* at 1169. Thus, Title VII will apply to decisions "such as those relating to a secular teacher in a church approved school" *citing EEOC v. Mississippi College* and *EEOC v. Pacific Press Publishing Co.*

▓ A P P E N D I X   C

Executive Order No. 11246
(selected provisions)

Under and by virtue of the authority vested in me as President of the United States by the Constitution and statutes of the United States, it is ordered as follows:

*   *   *   *

PART II—NONDISCRIMINATION IN EMPLOYMENT BY GOVERNMENT CONTRACTORS AND SUBCONTRACTORS

SUBPART A—DUTIES OF THE SECRETARY OF LABOR

Sec. 201. The Secretary of Labor shall be responsible for the administration and enforcement of Parts II and III of this Order. The Secretary shall adopt such rules and regulations and issue such orders as are deemed necessary and appropriate to achieve the purposes of Parts II and III of this Order.

SUBPART B—CONTRACTORS' AGREEMENTS

Sec. 202. Except in contracts exempted in accordance with Section 204 of this Order, all Government contracting agencies shall include in every Government contract hereafter entered into the following provisions:

"During the performance of this contract, the contractor agrees as follows:

"(1) The contractor will not discriminate against any employee or applicant for employment because of race, color, religion, sex, or national origin. The contractor will take affirmative action to ensure that applicants are employed, and that employees are treated during employment, without regard to their race, color, religion, sex or national origin. Such action shall include, but not be limited to the following: employment, upgrading, demotion, or transfer; recruitment or recruitment advertising; layoff or termination; rates of pay or other forms of compensation; and selection for training, including apprenticeship. The contractor agrees to post in conspicuous places, available to employees and applicants for employment, notices to be provided by the contracting officer setting forth the provisions of this nondiscrimination clause.

"(2) The contractor will, in all solicitations or advertisements for employees placed by or on behalf of the contractor, state that all qualified applicants will receive consideration for employment without regard to race, color, religion, sex or national origin.

"(3) The contractor will send to each labor union or representative of workers with which he has a collective bargaining agreement or other contract or understanding, a notice, to be provided by the agency contracting officer, advising the labor union or workers' representative of the contractor's commitments under Section 202 of Executive Order No. 11246 of September 24, 1965, and shall post copies of the notice in conspicuous places available to employees and applicants for employment.

"(4) The contractor will comply with all provisions of Executive Order No. 11246 of Sept. 24, 1965, and of the rules, regulations, and relevant orders of the Secretary of Labor.

"(5) The contractor will furnish all information and reports required by Executive Order No. 11246 of September 24, 1965, and by the rules, regulations, and orders of the Secretary of Labor, or pursuant thereto, and will permit access to its books, records, and accounts by the contracting agency and the Secretary of Labor for purposes of investigation to ascertain compliance with such rules, regulations, and orders.

"(6) In the event of the contractor's noncompliance with the nondiscrimination clauses of this contract or with any of such rules, regulations, or orders, this contract may be canceled, terminated or suspended in whole or in part and the contractor may be declared ineligible for further Government contracts in accordance with procedures authorized in Executive Order No. 11246 of Sept. 24, 1965, and such other sanctions may be imposed and remedies invoked as provided in Executive Order No. 11246 of September 24, 1965, or by rule, regulations, or order of the Secretary of Labor, or as otherwise provided by law.

"(7) The contractor will include the provisions of paragraphs (1) through (7) in every subcontract or purchase order unless exempted by rules, regulations, or orders of the Secretary of Labor issued pursuant to Section 204 of Executive Order No. 11246 of September 24, 1965 [Section 204 of this Order], so that such provisions will be binding upon each subcontractor or vendor. The contractor will take such action with respect to any subcontract or purchase order as may be directed by the Secretary of Labor as a means of enforcing such provisions including sanctions for noncompliance: *Provided, however,* That in the event the contractor becomes involved in, or is threatened with, litigation with a subcontractor or vendor as a result of such direction, the contractor may request the United States to enter into such litigation to protect the interests of the United States."

Sec. 203. (a) Each contractor having a contract containing the provisions prescribed in Section 202 shall file, and shall cause each of his subcontractors to file, Compliance Reports with the contracting agency or the Secretary of Labor as may be directed. Compliance Reports shall be filed within such times and shall contain such information as to the practices, policies, programs, and employment policies, programs, and employment statistics of the contractor and each subcontractor, and shall be in such form, as the Secretary of Labor may prescribe.

(b) Bidders or prospective contractors or subcontractors may be required to state whether they have participated in any previous contract subject to the provisions of this Order, or any preceding similar Executive order, and in that event to submit, on behalf of themselves and their proposed subcontractors, Compliance Reports prior to or as an initial part of their bid or negotiation of a contract.

(c) Whenever the contractor or subcontractor has a collective bargaining agreement or other contract or understanding with a labor union or an agency referring workers or providing or supervising apprenticeship or training for such workers, the Compliance Report shall include such information as to such labor union's or agency's practices and policies affecting compliance as the Secretary of Labor may prescribe: *Provided,* That to the extent such information is within the exclusive possession of a labor union or an agency referring workers or providing or supervising apprenticeship or training and such labor union or agency shall refuse to furnish such information to the contractor, the contractor shall so certify to the Secretary of Labor as part of its Compliance Report and shall set forth what efforts he has made to obtain such information.

(d) The Secretary of Labor may direct that any bidder or perspective contractor or subcontractor shall submit, as part of his Compliance Report, a statement in writing, signed by an authorized officer or agent on behalf of any labor union or any agency referring workers or providing or supervising apprenticeship or other training, with which the bidder or prospective contractor deals, with supporting information, to the effect that the signer's practices and policies do not discriminate on the grounds of race, color, religion, sex or national origin, and that the signer either will affirmatively cooperate in the implementation of the policy and provisions of this order or that it consents and agrees that recruitment, employment, and the terms and conditions of employment under the proposed contract shall be in accordance with the purposes and provisions of the order. In the event that the union, or the agency shall refuse to execute such a statement, the Compliance Report shall so certify and set forth what efforts have been made to secure such a statement and such additional factual material as the Secretary of Labor may require.

Sec. 204. The Secretary of Labor may, when he deems that special circumstances in the national interest so require, exempt a contracting agency from the requirement of including any or all of the provisions of Section 202 of this Order in any specific contract, subcontract, or purchase order. The Secretary of Labor may, by rule or regulations, also exempt certain classes of contracts, subcontracts, or purchase orders (1) whenever work is to be or has been performed outside the United States and no recruitment of workers within the limits of the United States is involved; (2) for standard commercial supplies or raw materials; (3) involving less than specified amounts of money or specified numbers of workers; or (4) to the extent that they involve subcontracts below a specified tier. The Secretary of Labor may also provide, by rule, regulation, or order, for the exemption of facilities of a contractor which are in all respects separate and distinct from activities of the contractor related to the performance of the contract: *Provided,* That such an exemption will not interfere with or impede the effectuation of the purposes of this Order: *And provided further,* That in the absence of such an exemption all facilities shall be covered by the provisions of this Order.

SUBPART C—POWER AND DUTIES OF THE SECRETARY OF LABOR AND THE CONTRACTING AGENCIES

Sec. 205. The Secretary of Labor shall be responsible for securing compliance by all Government contractors and subcontractors with this Order and any implementing rules or regulations. All contracting agencies shall comply with the terms of this Order and any implementing rules, regulations, or orders of the Secretary of Labor. Contracting agencies shall cooperate with the Secretary of Labor and shall furnish such information and assistance as the Secretary may require.

Sec. 206. (a) The Secretary of Labor may investigate the employment practices of any Government contractor or subcontractor to determine whether or not the contractual provisions specified in § 202 of this Order have been violated. Such investigation shall be conducted in accordance with the procedures established by the Secretary of Labor.

(b) The Secretary of Labor may receive and investigate complaints by employees or prospective employees of a Government contractor or subcontractor which allege discrimination contrary to the contractual provisions specified in Section 202 of this Order.

Sec. 207. The Secretary of Labor shall use his best efforts, directly and through interested Federal, State, and local agencies, contractors, and all other available instrumentalities to cause any labor union engaged in work under Government contracts or any agency referring workers or providing or supervising apprenticeship or training for or in the course of such work to cooperate in the implementation of the purposes of this Order. The Secretary of Labor shall, in appropriate cases, notify the Equal Employment Opportunity Commission, the Department of Justice, or other appropriate Federal agencies whenever it has reason to believe that the practices of any such labor organization or agency violate Title VI or Title VII of the Civil Rights Act of 1964 [sections 2000d to 2000d-4 of this title and this subchapter] or other provision of Federal law.

Sec. 208. (a) The Secretary of Labor, or any agency, officer, or employee in the executive branch of the Government designated by rule, regulation, or order of the Secretary, may hold such hearings, public or private, as the Secretary may deem advisable for compliance, enforcement, or educational purposes.

(b) The Secretary of Labor may hold, or cause to be held, hearings in accordance with Subsection (a) of this Section prior to imposing, ordering, or recommending the imposition of penalties and sanctions under this Order. No order for debarment of any contractor from further Government contracts under Section 209(a)(6) shall be made without affording the contractor an opportunity for a hearing.

SUBPART D—SANCTIONS AND PENALTIES

Sec. 209. (a) In accordance with such rules, regulations, or orders as the Secretary of Labor may issue or adopt, the Secretary may:

(1) Publish, or cause to be published, the names of contractors or unions which it has concluded have complied or have failed to comply with the provisions of this Order or of the rules, regulations, and orders of the Secretary of Labor.

(2) Recommend to the Department of Justice that, in cases in which there is substantial or material violation or the threat of substantial or material violation of the contractual provisions set forth in Section 202 of this Order, appropriate proceedings be brought to enforce those provisions, including the enjoining, within the limitations of applicable law, of organizations, individuals, or groups who prevent directly or indirectly, or seek to prevent directly or indirectly, compliance with the provisions of this Order.

(3) Recommend to the Equal Employment Opportunity Commission or the Department of Justice that appropriate proceedings be instituted under Title VII of the Civil Rights Act of 1964 [this sub-chapter].

(4) Recommend to the Department of Justice that criminal proceedings be brought for the furnishing of false information to any contracting agency or to the Secretary of Labor as the case may be.

(5) After consulting with the contracting agency, direct the contracting agency to cancel, terminate, suspend, or cause to be canceled, terminated, or suspended, any contract, or any portion or portions thereof, for failure of the contractor or subcontractor to comply with equal employment opportunity provisions of the contract. Contracts may be canceled, terminated, or suspended absolutely or continuance of contracts may be conditioned upon a program for future compliance approved by the Secretary of Labor.

(6) Provide that any contracting agency shall refrain from entering into further contracts, or extensions or other modifications of existing contracts, with any noncomplying contractor, until such contractor has satisfied the Secretary of Labor that such contractor has established and

will carry out personnel and employment policies in compliance with the provisions of this Order.

(b) Pursuant to rules and regulations prescribed by the Secretary of Labor, the Secretary shall make reasonable efforts, within a reasonable time limitation, to secure compliance with the contract provisions of this Order by methods of conference, conciliation, mediation, and persuasion before proceedings shall be instituted under subsection (a)(2) of this Section, or before a contract shall be canceled or terminated in whole or in part under subsection (a)(5) of this Section.

Sec. 210. Whenever the Secretary of Labor makes a determination under Section 209, the Secretary shall promptly notify the appropriate agency. The agency shall take the action directed by the Secretary and shall report the results of the action it has taken to the Secretary of Labor within such time as the Secretary shall specify. If the contracting agency fails to take the action directed within thirty days, the Secretary may take the action directly.

Sec. 211. If the Secretary of Labor shall so direct, contracting agencies shall not enter into contracts with any bidder or prospective contractor unless the bidder or prospective contractor has satisfactorily complied with the provisions of this Order or submits a program for compliance acceptable to the Secretary of Labor.

Sec. 212. When a contract has been canceled or terminated under Section 209(a)(5) or a contractor has been debarred from further Government contracts under Section 209(a)(6) of this Order, because of noncompliance with the contract provisions specified in Section 202 of this Order, the Secretary of Labor shall promptly notify the Comptroller General of the United States.

SUBPART E—CERTIFICATES OF MERIT

Sec. 213. The Secretary of Labor may provide for issuance of a United States Government Certificate of Merit to employers or labor unions, or other agencies which are or may hereafter be engaged in work under Government contracts, if the Secretary is satisfied that the personnel and employment practices of the employer, or that the personnel, training, apprenticeship, membership, grievance and representation, upgrading, and other practices and policies of the labor union or other agency conform to the purposes and provisions of this Order.

Sec. 214. Any Certificate of Merit may at any time be suspended or revoked by the Secretary of Labor if the holder thereof, in the judgment of the Secretary, has failed to comply with the provisions of this Order.

Sec. 215. The Secretary of Labor may provide for the exemption of any employer, labor union, or other agency from any reporting requirements imposed under or pursuant to this Order if such employer, labor union, or other agency has been awarded a Certificate of Merit which has not been suspended or revoked.

PART III—NONDISCRIMINATION PROVISIONS IN FEDERALLY ASSISTED CONSTRUCTION CONTRACTS

Sec. 301. Each executive department and agency which administers a program involving Federal financial assistance shall require as a condition for the approval of any grant, contract, loan, insurance, or guarantee thereunder, which may involve a construction contract, that the applicant for Federal assistance undertake and agree to incorporate, or cause to be incorporated, into all construction contracts paid for in whole or in part with funds obtained from the Federal Government or borrowed on the credit of the Federal Government pursuant to such grant, contract, loan, insurance, or guarantee, or undertaken pursuant to any Federal program involving such grant, contract, loan, insurance, or guarantee, the provisions prescribed for Government contracts by Section 202 of this Order or such modification thereof, preserving in substance the contractor's obligations thereunder, as may be approved by the Secretary of Labor, together with such additional provisions as the Secretary deems appropriate to establish and protect the interest of the United States in the enforcement of those obligations. Each such applicant shall also undertake and agree (1) to assist and cooperate actively with the Secretary of Labor in obtaining the compliance of contractors and subcontractors with those contract provisions and with the rules, regulations and relevant orders of the Secretary, (2) to obtain and to furnish to the Secretary of Labor such information as the Secretary may require for the supervision of such compliance, (3) to carry out sanctions and penalties for violation of such obligations imposed upon contractors and subcontractors by the Secretary of Labor pursuant to Part II, Subpart D, of this Order, and (4) to refrain from entering into any contract subject to this Order, or extension or other modification of such a contract with a contractor debarred from Government contracts under Part II, Subpart D, of this Order.

Sec. 302. (a) "Construction contract" as used in this Order means any contract for the construction, rehabilitation, alteration, conversion, extension, or repair of buildings, highways, or other improvements to real property.

(b) The provisions of Part II of this Order shall apply to such construction contracts, and for purposes of such application the administering department or agency shall be considered the contracting agency referred to therein.

(c) The term "applicant" as used in this Order means an applicant for Federal assistance or, as determined by agency regulation, other program participant, with respect to whom an application for any grant, contract, loan, insurance, or guarantee is not finally acted upon prior to the effective date of this Part, and it includes such an applicant after he becomes a recipient of such Federal assistance.

Sec. 303. (a). The Secretary of Labor shall be responsible for obtaining the compliance of such applicants with their undertakings under this Order. Each administering department and agency is directed to cooperate with the Secretary of Labor and to furnish the Secretary such information and assistance as the Secretary may require in the performance of the Secretary's functions under this Order.

(b) In the event an applicant fails and refuses to comply with the applicant's undertakings pursuant to this Order, the Secretary of Labor may, after consulting with the administering department or agency, take any or all of the following actions: (1) direct any administering department or agency to cancel, terminate, or suspend in whole or in part the agreement, contract or other arrangement with such applicant with respect to which the failure or refusal occurred; (2) direct any administering department or agency to refrain from extending any further assistance to the applicant under the program with respect to which the failure or refusal occurred until satisfactory assurance of future compliance has been received by the Secretary of Labor from such applicant; and (3) refer the case to the Department of Justice or the Equal Employment Opportunity Commission for appropriate law enforcement or other proceedings.

(c) In no case shall action be taken with respect to an applicant pursuant to clause (1) or (2) of subsection (b) without notice and opportunity for hearing.

Sec. 304. Any executive department or agency which imposes by rule, regulation, or order requirements of nondiscrimination in employment, other than requirements imposed pursuant to this Order, may delegate to the Secretary of Labor by agreement such responsibilities with respect to compliance standards, reports, and procedures as would tend to bring the administration of such requirements into conformity with the administration of requirements imposed under this Order: *Provided,* That actions to effect compliance by recipients of Federal financial assistance with requirements imposed pursuant to Title VI of the Civil Rights Act of 1964 [sections 2000d to 2000d-4 of this title] shall be taken in conformity with the procedures and limitations prescribed in Section 602 thereof [Section 2000d-1 of this title] and the regulations of the administering department or agency issued thereunder.

▨ A P P E N D I X D

Department of Labor Guidelines Office of Federal Contract Compliance Programs (41 C.F.R. Ch. 60)

Part 60-50—Guidelines on Discrimination Because of Religion or National Origin

§ 60-50.1 Purpose and scope.

(a) The purpose of the provisions in this part is to set forth the interpretations and guidelines of the Office of Federal Contract Compliance Programs regarding the implementation of Executive Order 11246, as amended, for promoting and insuring equal employment opportunities for all persons employed or seeking employment with Government contractors and subcontractors or with contractors and subcontractors performing under federally assisted construction contracts, without regard to religion or national origin.

(b) Members of various religious and ethnic groups, primarily but not exclusively of Eastern, Middle, and Southern European ancestry, such as Jews, Catholics, Italians, Greeks, and Slavic groups, continue to be excluded from executive, middle-management, and other job levels because of discrimination based upon their religion and/or national origin. These guidelines are intended to remedy such unfair treatment.

(c) These guidelines are also intended to clarify the obligations of employers with respect to accommodating to the religious observances and practices of employees and prospective employees.

(d) The employment problems of black, Spanish-surnamed Americans, orientals, and American Indians are treated under Part 60-2 of this chapter and under other regulations and procedures implementing the requirements of Executive Order 11246, as amended. Accordingly, the remedial provisions of § 60-50.2(b) shall not be applicable to the employment problems of these groups.

(e) Nothing contained in this Part 60-50 is intended to supersede or otherwise limit the exemption set forth in § 60-1.5(a)(5) of this chapter for contracts with certain educational institutions.

§ 60-50.2 Equal employment policy.

(a) *General requirements.* Under the equal opportunity clause contained in section 202 of Executive Order 11246, as amended, employers are prohibited from discriminating against employees or applicants for employment because of religion or national origin, and must take affirmative action to insure that applicants are employed, and that employees are treated during employment, without regard to their religion or national origin. Such action includes, but is not limited to the following: Employment, upgrading, demotion, or transfer: Recruitment or recruitment advertising; layoff or termination; rates of pay or other forms of compensation; and selection for training, including apprenticeship.

(b) *Outreach and positive recruitment.* Employers shall review their employment practices to determine whether members of the various religious and/or ethnic groups are receiving fair consideration for job opportunities. Special attention shall be directed toward executive and middle-management levels, where employment problems relating to religion and national origin are most likely to occur. Based upon the findings of such reviews, employers shall undertake appropriate outreach and positive recruitment activities, such as those listed below, in order to remedy existing deficiencies. It is not contemplated that employers necessarily will undertake all of the listed activities. The scope of the employer's efforts shall depend upon all the circumstances, including the nature and extent of the employer's deficiencies and the employer's size and resources.

(1) Internal communication of the employer's obligation to provide equal employment opportunity without regard to religion or national origin in such a manner as to foster understanding, acceptance, and support among the employer's executive, management, supervisory, and all other employees and to encourage such persons to take the necessary action to aid the employer in meeting this obligation.

(2) Development of reasonable internal procedures to insure that the employer's obligation to provide equal employment opportunity without regard to religion or national origin is being fully implemented.

(3) Periodically informing all employees of the employer's commitment to equal employment opportunity for all persons, without regard to religion or national origin.

(4) Enlisting the assistance and support of all recruitment sources (including employment agencies, college placement directors, and business associates) for the employer's commitment to provide equal employment opportunity without regard to religion or national origin.

(5) Reviewing employment records to determine the availability of promotable and transferable members of various religious and ethnic groups.

(6) Establishment of meaningful contacts with religious and ethnic organizations and leaders for such purposes as advice, education, technical assistance, and referral of potential employees.

(7) Engaging in significant recruitment activities at educational institutions with substantial enrollments of students from various religious and ethnic groups.

(8) Use of the religious and ethnic media for institutional and employment advertising.

§ 60-50.3 Accommodations to religious observance and practice.

An employer must accommodate to the religious observances and practices of an employee or prospective employee unless the employer demonstrates that it is unable to reasonably accommodate to an employee's or prospective employee's religious observance or practice without undue hardship on the conduct of the employer's business. As part of this obligation, an employer must make reasonable accommodations to the religious observances and practices of an employee or prospective employee who regularly observes Friday evening and Saturday, or some other day of the week, as his Sabbath and/or who observes certain religious holidays during the year and who is conscientiously opposed to performing work or engaging in similar activity on such days, when such accommodations can be made without undue hardship on the conduct of the employer's business. In determining the extent of an employer's obligations under this section, at least the following factors shall be considered: (a) Business necessity, (b) financial costs and expenses, and (c) resulting personnel problems.

§ 60-50.4 Enforcement.

The provisions of this part are subject to the general enforcement, compliance review, and complaint procedures set forth in Subpart B of Part 60-1 of this chapter.

§ 60-50.5 Nondiscrimination.

The provisions of this part are not intended and shall not be used to discriminate against any qualified employee or applicant for employment because of race, color, religion, sex, or national origin.

▨ APPENDIX E

National Labor Relations Act (29 U.S.C. § 169)

§ 169. Employees with religious convictions; payment of dues and fees.

Any employee who is a member of and adheres to established and traditional tenets or teachings of a bona fide religion, body, or sect which has historically held conscientious objections to joining or financially supporting labor organizations shall not be required to join or financially support any labor organization as a condition of employment; except that such employee may be required in a contract between such employees' employer and a labor organization in lieu of periodic dues and initiation fees, to pay sums equal to such dues and initiation fees to a nonreligious, nonlabor organization charitable fund exempt from taxation under section 501(c)(3) of Title 26, chosen by such an employee from a list of at least three such funds, designated in such contract or if the contract fails to designate such funds, then to any such fund chosen by the employee. If such employee who holds conscientious objections pursuant to this section requests the labor organization to use the grievance-arbitration procedure on the employee's behalf, the labor organization is authorized to charge the employee for the reasonable cost of using such procedure.

APPENDIX F

Federal Personnel Laws and Regulations Relating to Religious Accommodation (5 U.S.C. § 5550a; 5 C.F.R. Ch. I, Part 550)

§ 5550a. Compensatory time off for religious observances.

(a) Not later than 30 days after the date of the enactment of this section, the Office of Personnel Management shall prescribe regulations providing for work schedules under which an employee whose personal religious beliefs require the abstention from work during certain periods of time, may elect to engage in overtime work for time lost for meeting those religious requirements. Any employee who so elects such overtime work shall be granted equal compensatory time off from his scheduled tour of duty (in lieu of overtime pay) for such religious reasons, notwithstanding any other provision of law.

(b) In the case of any agency described in subparagraphs (C) through (G) of section 5541(1) of this title, the head of such agency (in lieu of the Office) shall prescribe the regulations referred to in subsection (a) of this section.

(c) Regulations under this section may provide for such exceptions as may be necessary to efficiently carry out the mission of the agency or agencies involved.

5 C.F.R. Chapter I, Subpart J—Adjustment of Work Schedules for Religious Observances

§ 550.1001 Coverage.

This subpart applies to each employee in or under an executive agency as defined by section 105 of title 5, United States Code.

§ 550.1002 Compensatory time off for religious observances.

(a) These regulations are issued pursuant to title IV of Public Law 95-390, enacted September 29, 1978. Under the law and these regulations, an employee whose personal religious beliefs require the abstention from work during certain periods of time may elect to engage in overtime work for time lost for meeting those religious requirements.

(b) To the extent that such modifications in work schedules do not interfere with the efficient accomplishment of an agency's mission, the agency shall in each instance afford the employee the opportunity to work compensatory overtime and shall in each instance grant compensatory time off to an employee requesting such time off for religious observances when the employee's personal religious beliefs require that the employee abstain from work during certain periods of the workday or workweek.

(c) For the purpose stated in paragraph (b) of this section, the employee may work such compensatory overtime before or after the grant of compensatory time off. A grant of advanced compensatory time off should be repaid by the appropriate amount of compensatory overtime work within a reasonable amount of time. Compensatory overtime shall be credited to an employee on an hour for hour basis or authorized fractions thereof. Appropriate records will be kept of compensatory overtime earned and used.

(d) The premium pay provisions for overtime work in subpart A of part 550 of title 5, Code of Federal Regulations, and section 7 of the Fair Labor Standards Act of 1938, as amended, do not apply to compensatory overtime work performed by an employee for this purpose.

⬛ APPENDIX G

Religious Freedom Restoration Act (42 U.S.C. § 2000bb) [declared unconstitutional in *City of Boerne v. Flores,* 117 S.Ct. 2157 (1997)]

§ 2000bb. Congressional findings and declaration of purposes

(a) Findings

The Congress finds that—

(1) the framers of the Constitution, recognizing free exercise of religion as an unalienable right, secured its protection in the First Amendment to the Constitution;

(2) laws "neutral" toward religion may burden religious exercise as surely as laws intended to interfere with religious exercise;

(3) governments should not substantially burden religious exercise without compelling justification;

(4) in Employment Division v. Smith, 494 U.S. 872 (1990) the Supreme Court virtually eliminated the requirement that the government justify burdens on religious exercise imposed by laws neutral toward religion; and

(5) the compelling interest test as set forth in prior Federal court rulings is a workable test for striking sensible balances between religious liberty and competing prior governmental interests.

(b) Purposes

The purposes of this chapter are—

(1) to restore the compelling interest test as set forth in Sherbert v. Verner, 374 U.S. 398 (1963) and Wisconsin v. Yoder, 406 U.S. 205 (1972) and to guarantee its application in all cases where free exercise of religion is substantially burdened; and

(2) to provide a claim or defense to persons whose religious exercise is substantially burdened by government.

§ 2000bb-1. Free exercise of religion protected

(a) In general

Government shall not substantially burden a person's exercise of religion even if the burden results from a rule of general applicability, except as provided in subsection (b) of this section.

(b) Exception

Government may substantially burden a person's exercise of religion only if it demonstrates that application of the burden to the person—

(1) is in furtherance of a compelling governmental interest; and

(2) is the least restrictive means of furthering that compelling governmental interest.

(c) Judicial relief

A person whose religious exercise has been burdened in violation of this section may assert that violation as a claim or defense in a judicial proceeding and obtain appropriate relief against a government. Standing to assert a claim or defense under this section shall be governed by the general rules of standing under article III of the Constitution.

§ 2000bb-2. Definitions

As used in this chapter—

(1) the term "government" includes a branch, department, agency, instrumentality, and official (or other person acting under color of law) of the United States, a State, or a subdivision of a State;

(2) the term "State" includes the District of Columbia, the Commonwealth of Puerto Rico, and each territory and possession of the United States;

(3) the term "demonstrates" means meets the burdens of going forward with the evidence and of persuasion; and

(4) the term "exercise of religion" means the exercise of religion under the First Amendment to the Constitution.

§ 2000bb-3. Applicability

(a) In general

This chapter applies to all Federal and State law, and the implementation of that law, whether statutory or otherwise, and whether adopted before or after November 16, 1993.

(b) Rule of construction

Federal statutory law adopted after November 16, 1993 is subject to this chapter unless such law explicitly excludes such application by reference to this chapter.

(c) Religious belief unaffected

Nothing in this chapter shall be construed to authorize any government to burden any religious belief.

§ 2000bb-4. Establishment clause unaffected

Nothing in this chapter shall be construed to affect, interpret, or in any way address that portion of the First Amendment prohibiting laws respecting the establishment of religion (referred to in this section as the "Establishment Clause"). Granting government funding, benefits, or exemptions, to the extent permissible under the Establishment Clause, shall not constitute a violation of this chapter. As used in this section, the term "granting", used with respect to government funding, benefits, or exemptions, does not include the denial of government funding, benefits, or exemptions.

▓ A P P E N D I X   H

White House Guidelines on Religious Exercise and Religious Expression in the Federal Workplace (August 14, 1997)

The following Guidelines, addressing religious exercise and religious expression, shall apply to all civilian executive branch agencies, officials, and employees in the Federal workplace.

These Guidelines principally address employees' religious exercise and religious expression when the employees are acting in their personal capacity within the Federal workplace and the public does not have regular exposure to the workplace. The Guidelines do not comprehensively address whether and when the government and its employees may engage in religious speech directed at the public. They also do not address religious exercise and religious expression by uniformed military personnel, or the conduct of business by chaplains employed by the Federal Government. Nor do the Guidelines define the rights and responsibilities of nongovernmental employers—including religious employers—and their employees. Although these Guidelines, including the examples cited in them, should answer the most frequently encountered questions in the Federal workplace, actual cases sometimes will be complicated by additional facts and circumstances that may require a different result from the one the Guidelines indicate.

Section 1. Guidelines for Religious Exercise and Religious Expression in the Federal Workplace. Executive departments and agencies ("agencies") shall permit personal religious expression by Federal employees to the greatest extent possible, consistent with requirements of law and interest in workplace efficiency as described in this set of Guidelines. Agencies shall not discriminate against employees on the basis of religion, require religious participation or non-participation as a condition of employment, or permit religious harassment. And agencies shall accommodate employees' exercise of their religion in the circumstances specified in these Guidelines. These requirements are but applications of the general principle that agencies shall treat all employees with the same respect and consideration, regardless of their religion (or lack thereof).

A. Religious Expression. As a matter of law, agencies shall not restrict personal religious expression by employees in the Federal Workplace except where the employee's interest in the expression is outweighed by the government's interest in the efficient provision of public services or where the expression intrudes upon the legitimate rights of other employees or creates the appearance, to a reasonable observer, of an official endorsement of religion. The examples cited in these Guidelines as permissible forms of religious expression will rarely, if ever, fall within these exceptions.

As a general rule, agencies may not regulate employees' personal religious expression on the basis of its content or viewpoint. In other words, agencies generally may not suppress employees' private religious speech in the workplace while leaving unregulated other private employee speech that has a comparable effect on the efficiency of the workplace—including ideological speech on politics and other topics—because to do so would be to engage in presumptively unlawful content or viewpoint discrimination. Agencies, however, may, in their discretion, reasonably regulate the time, place and manner of all employee speech, provided such regulations do not discriminate on the basis of content or viewpoint.

The Federal Government generally has the authority to regulate an employee's private speech, including religious speech, where the employee's interest in that speech is outweighed by the government's interest in promoting the efficiency of the public services it performs. Agencies should exercise this authority evenhandedly and with restraint, and with regard for the fact that Americans are used to expressions of disagreement on controversial subjects, including religious ones. Agencies are not required, however, to permit employees to use work time to pursue religious or ideological agendas. Federal employees are paid to perform official work, not to engage in personal religious or ideological campaigns during work hours.

(1) **Expression in Private Work Areas.** Employees should be permitted to engage in private religious expression in personal work areas not regularly open to the public to the same extent that they may engage in nonreligious private expression, subject to reasonable content- and viewpoint-neutral standards and restrictions: such religious expression must be permitted so long as it does not interfere with the agency's carrying out of its official responsibilities.

Examples

(a) An employee may keep a Bible or Koran on her private desk and read it during breaks.

(b) An agency may restrict all posters, or posters of a certain size, in private work areas, or require that such posters be displayed facing the employee, and not on common walls; but the employer typically cannot single out religious or anti-religious posters for harsher or preferential treatment.

(2) **Expression Among Fellow Employees.**

Employees should be permitted to engage in religious expression with fellow employees, to the same extent that they may engage in comparable nonreligious private expression, subject to reasonable and content-neutral standards and restrictions: such expression should not be restricted so long as it does not interfere with workplace efficiency. Though agencies are entitled to regulate such employee speech based on reasonable predictions of disruption, they should not restrict speech based on merely hypothetical concerns, having little basis in fact, that the speech will have a deleterious effect on workplace efficiency.

Examples

(a) In informal settings, such as cafeterias and hallways, employees are entitled to discuss their religious views with one another, subject only to the same rules of order as apply to other employee expression. If an agency permits unrestricted nonreligious expression of a controversial nature, it must likewise permit equally controversial religious expression.

(b) Employees are entitled to display religious messages on items of clothing to the same extent that they are permitted to display other comparable messages. So long as they do not convey any governmental endorsement of religion, religious messages may not typically be singled out for suppression.

(c) Employees generally may wear religious medallions over their clothes or so that they are otherwise visible. Typically, this alone will not affect workplace efficiency, and therefore is protected.

(3) Expression Directed at Fellow Employees.

Employees are permitted to engage in religious expression directed at fellow employees, and may even attempt to persuade fellow employees of the correctness of their religious views, to the same extent as those employees may engage in comparable speech not involving religion. Some religions encourage adherents to spread the faith at every opportunity, a duty that can encompass the adherent's workplace. As a general matter, proselytizing is as entitled to constitutional protection as any other form of speech—as long as a reasonable observer would not interpret the expression as government endorsement of religion. Employees may urge a colleague to participate or not to participate in religious activities to the same extent that, consistent with concerns of workplace efficiency, they may urge their colleagues to engage in or refrain from other personal endeavors. But employees must refrain from such expression when a fellow employee asks that it stop or otherwise demonstrates that it is unwelcome. (Such expression by supervisors is subject to special consideration as discussed in Section B(2) of these guidelines.)

Examples

(a) During a coffee break, one employee engages another in a polite discussion of why his faith should be embraced. The other employee disagrees with the first employee's religious exhortations, but does not ask that the conversation stop. Under these circumstances, agencies should not restrict or interfere with such speech.

(b) One employee invites another employee to attend worship services at her church, though she knows that the invitee is a devout adherent of another faith. The invitee is shocked, and asks that the invitation not be repeated. The original invitation is protected, but the employee should honor the request that no further invitations be issued.

(c) In a parking lot, a non-supervisory employee hands another employee a religious tract urging that she convert to another religion lest she be condemned to eternal damnation. The proselytizing employee says nothing further and does not inquire of his colleague whether she followed the pamphlet's urging. This speech typically should not be restricted.

Though personal religious expression such as that described in these examples, standing alone, is protected in the same way, and to the same extent, as other constitutionally valued speech in the Federal workplace, such expression should not be permitted if it is part of a larger pattern of verbal attacks on fellow employees (or a specific employee) not sharing the faith of the speaker. Such speech, by virtue of its excessive or harassing nature, may constitute religious harassment or create a hostile work environment, as described in Part B(3) of these Guidelines, and an agency should not tolerate it.

(4) **Expression in Areas Accessible to the Public.** Where the public has access to the Federal workplace, all Federal employers must be sensitive to the Establishment Clause's requirement that expression not create the reasonable impression that the government is sponsoring, endorsing, or inhibiting religion generally, or favoring or disfavoring a particular religion. This is particularly important in agencies with adjudicatory functions.

However, even in workplaces open to the public, not all private employee religious expression is forbidden. For example, Federal employees may wear personal religious jewelry absent special circumstances (such as safety concerns) that might require a ban on all similar nonreligious jewelry. Employees may also display religious art and literature in their personal work areas to the same extent that they may display other art and literature, so long as the viewing public would reasonably understand the religious expression to be that of the employee acting in her personal capacity, and not that of the government itself. Similarly, in their private time employees may discuss religion with willing coworkers in public spaces to the same extent as they may discuss other subjects, so long as the public would reasonably understand the religious expression to be that of the employees acting in their personal capacities.

B. Religious Discrimination. Federal agencies may not discriminate against employees on the basis of their religion, religious beliefs, or views concerning religion.

(1) **Discrimination in Terms and Conditions.** No agency within the executive branch may promote, refuse to promote, hire, refuse to hire, or otherwise favor or disfavor, an employee or potential employee because of his or her religion, religious beliefs, or views concerning religion.

Examples

(a) A Federal agency may not refuse to hire Buddhists, or impose more onerous requirements on applicants for employment who are Buddhists.

(b) An agency may not impose, explicitly or implicitly, stricter promotion requirements for Christians, or impose stricter discipline on Jews than on other employees, based on their religion. Nor may Federal agencies give advantages to Christians in promotions, or impose lesser discipline on Jews than on other employees, based on their religion.

(c) A supervisor may not impose more onerous work requirements on an employee who is an atheist because that employee does not share the supervisor's religious beliefs.

(2) **Coercion of Employee's Participation or Nonparticipation in Religious Activities.** A person holding supervisory authority over an employee may not, explicitly or implicitly, insist that the employee participate in religious activities as a condition of continued employment, promotion, salary increases, preferred job assignments, or any other incidents of employment. Nor may a supervisor insist that an employee refrain from participating in religious activities outside the workplace except pursuant to otherwise legal, neutral restrictions that apply to employees' off-duty conduct and expression in general (e.g., restrictions on political activities prohibited by the Hatch Act).

This prohibition leaves supervisors free to engage in some kinds of speech about religion. Where a supervisor's religious expression is not coercive and is understood as his or her personal view, that expression is protected in the Federal workplace in the same way and to the same extent as other constitutionally valued speech. For example, if surrounding circumstances indicate that the expression is merely the personal view of the supervisor and that employees are free to reject or ignore the supervisor's point of view or invitation without any harm to their careers or professional lives, such expression is so protected.

Because supervisors have the power to hire, fire, or promote, employees may reasonably perceive their supervisors' religious expression as coercive, even if it was not intended as such. Therefore, supervisors should be careful to ensure that their statements and actions are such that employees do not perceive any coercion of religious or non-religious behavior (or respond as if such coercion is occurring), and should, where necessary, take appropriate steps to dispel such misperceptions.

Examples

(a) A supervisor may invite co-workers to a son's confirmation in a church, a daughter's bat mitzvah in a synagogue, or to his own wedding at a temple. But a supervisor should not say to an employee: "I didn't see you in church this week. I expect to see you there this Sunday."

(b) On a bulletin board on which personal notices unrelated to work regularly are permitted, a supervisor may post a flyer announcing an Easter musical service at her church, with a handwritten notice inviting co-workers to attend. But a supervisor should not circulate a memo announcing that he will be leading a lunch-hour Talmud class that employees should attend in order to participate in a discussion of career advancement that will convene at the conclusion of the class.

(c) During a wide-ranging discussion in the cafeteria about various non-work related matters, a supervisor states to an employee her belief that religion is important in one's life. Without more, this is not coercive, and the statement is protected in the Federal workplace in the same way, and to the same extent, as other constitutionally valued speech.

(d) A supervisor who is an atheist has made it known that he thinks that anyone who attends church regularly should not be trusted with the public weal. Over a period of years, the supervisor regularly awards merit increases to employees who do not attend church routinely, but not to employees of equal merit who do attend church. This course of conduct would reasonably be perceived as coercive and should be prohibited.

(e) At a lunch-table discussion about abortion, during which a wide range of views are vigorously expressed, a supervisor shares with those he supervises his belief that God demands full respect for unborn life, and that he believes it is appropriate for all persons to pray for the unborn. Another supervisor expresses the view that abortion should be kept legal because God teaches that women must have control over their own bodies. Without more, neither of these comments coerces employees' religious conformity or conduct. Therefore, unless the supervisors take further steps to coerce agreement with their view or act in ways that could reasonably be perceived as coercive, their expressions are protected in the Federal workplace in the same way and to the same extent as other constitutionally valued speech.

(3) **Hostile Work Environment and Harassment.** The law against workplace discrimination protects Federal employees from being subjected to a hostile environment, or religious harassment, in the form of religiously discriminatory intimidation, or pervasive or severe religious ridicule or insult, whether by supervisors or fellow workers. Whether particular conduct gives rise to a hostile environment, or constitutes impermissible religious harassment, will usually depend upon its frequency or repetitiveness, as well as its severity. The use of derogatory language in an assaultive manner can constitute statutory religious harassment if it is severe or invoked repeatedly. A single incident, if sufficiently abusive, might also constitute statutory harassment. However, although employees should always be guided by general principles of civility and workplace efficiency, a hostile environment is not created by the bare expression of speech with which some employees might disagree. In a country where freedom of speech and religion are guaranteed, citizens should expect to be exposed to ideas with which they disagree.

The examples below are intended to provide guidance on when conduct or words constitute religious harassment that should not be tolerated in the Federal workplace. In a particular case, the question of employer liability would require consideration of additional factors, including the extent to which the agency was aware of the harassment and the actions the agency took to address it.

Examples

(a) An employee repeatedly makes derogatory remarks to other employees with whom she is assigned to work about their faith or lack of faith. This typically will constitute religious harassment. An agency should not tolerate such conduct.

(b) A group of employees subjects a fellow employee to a barrage of comments about his sex life, knowing that the targeted employee would be discomforted and offended by such comments because of his religious beliefs. This typically will constitute harassment, and an agency should not tolerate it.

(c) A group of employees that share a common faith decides that they want to work exclusively with people who share their views. They engage in a pattern of verbal attacks on other employees who do not share their views, calling them heathens, sinners, and the like. This conduct should not be tolerated.

(d) Two employees have an angry exchange of words. In the heat of the moment, one makes a derogatory comment about the other's religion. When tempers cool, no more is said. Unless the words are sufficiently severe or pervasive to alter the conditions of the insulted employee's employment or create an abusive working environment, this is not statutory religious harassment.

(e) Employees wear religious jewelry and medallions over their clothes or so that they are otherwise visible. Others wear buttons with a generalized religious or anti-religious message. Typically, these expressions are personal and do not alone constitute religious harassment.

(f) In her private work area, a Federal worker keeps a Bible or Koran on her private desk and reads it during breaks. Another employee displays a picture of Jesus and the text of the Lord's Prayer in her private work area. This conduct, without more, is not religious harassment, and does not create an impermissible hostile environment with respect to employees who do not share those religious views, even if they are upset or offended by the conduct.

(g) During lunch, certain employees gather on their own time for prayer and Bible study in an empty conference room that employees are generally free to use on a first-come, first-served basis. Such a gathering does not constitute religious harassment even if other employees with different views on how to pray might feel excluded or ask that the group be disbanded.

C. Accommodation of Religious Exercise. Federal law requires an agency to accommodate employees' exercise of their religion unless such accommodation would impose an undue hardship on the conduct of the agency's operations. Though an agency need not make an accommodation that will result in more than a *de minimis* cost to the agency, that cost or hardship nevertheless must be real rather than speculative or hypothetical: the accommodation should be made unless it would cause an actual cost to the agency or to other employees or an actual disruption of work, or unless it is otherwise barred by law.

In addition, religious accommodation cannot be disfavored vis-a-vis other, nonreligious accommodations. Therefore, a religious accommodation cannot be denied if the agency regularly permits similar accommodations for nonreligious purposes.

Examples

(a) An agency must adjust work schedules to accommodate an employee's religious observance—for example, Sabbath or religious holiday observance—if an adequate substitute is available, or if the employee's absence would not otherwise impose an undue burden on the agency.

(b) An employee must be permitted to wear religious garb, such as a crucifix, a yarmulke, or a head scarf or hijab, if wearing such attire during the work day is part of the employee's religious practice or expression, so long as the wearing of such garb does not unduly interfere with the functioning of the workplace.

(c) An employee should be excused from a particular assignment if performance of that assignment would contravene the employee's religious beliefs and the agency would not suffer undue hardship in reassigning the employee to another detail.

(d) During lunch, certain employees gather on their own time for prayer and Bible study in an empty conference room that employees are generally free to use on a first-come, first-served basis. Such a gathering may not be subject to discriminatory restrictions because of its religious content.

In those cases where an agency's work rule imposes a substantial burden on a particular employee's exercise of religion, the agency must go further: an agency should grant the employee an exemption from that rule, unless the agency has a compelling interest in denying the exemption and there is no less restrictive means of furthering that interest.

Examples

(a) A corrections officer whose religion compels him or her to wear long hair should be granted an exemption from an otherwise generally applicable hair-length policy unless denial of an exemption is the least restrictive means of preserving safety, security, discipline or other compelling interests.

(b) An applicant for employment in a governmental agency who is a Jehovah's Witness should not be compelled, contrary to her religious beliefs, to take a loyalty oath whose form is religiously objectionable.

D. Establishment of Religion. Supervisors and employees must not engage in activities or expression that a reasonable observer would interpret as Government endorsement or denigration of religion or a particular religion. Activities of employees need not be officially sanctioned in order to violate this principle; if, in all the circumstances, the activities would leave a reasonable observer with the impression that Government was endorsing, sponsoring, or inhibiting religion generally or favoring or disfavoring a particular religion, they are not permissible. Diverse factors, such as the context of the expression or whether official channels of communication are used, are relevant to what a reasonable observer would conclude.

Examples

(a) At the conclusion of each weekly staff meeting and before anyone leaves the room, an employee leads a prayer in which nearly all employees participate. All employees are required to attend the weekly meeting. The supervisor neither explicitly recognizes the prayer as an official function nor explicitly states that no one need participate in the prayer. This course of conduct is not permitted unless under all the circumstances a reasonable observer would conclude that the prayer was not officially endorsed.

(b) At Christmas time, a supervisor places a wreath over the entrance to the office's main reception area. This course of conduct is permitted.

Section 2. Guiding Legal Principles. In applying the guidance set forth in section 1 of this order, executive branch departments and agencies should consider the following legal principles.

A. Religious Expression. It is well-established that the Free Speech Clause of the First Amendment protects Government employees in the workplace. This right encompasses a right to speak about religious subjects. The Free Speech Clause also prohibits the Government from singling out religious expression for disfavored treatment: "[P]rivate religious speech, far from being a First Amendment orphan, is as fully protected under the Free Speech Clause as Secular private expression," Capitol Sq. Review Bd. v. Pinette, 115 S.Ct. 2448 (1995). Accordingly, in the Government workplace, employee religious expression cannot be regulated because of its religious character, and such religious speech typically cannot be singled out for harsher treatment than other comparable expression.

Many religions strongly encourage their adherents to spread the faith by persuasion and example at every opportunity, a duty that can extend to the adherents' workplace. As a general matter, proselytizing is entitled to the same constitutional protection as any other form of speech. Therefore, in the governmental workplace, proselytizing should not be singled out because of its content for harsher treatment than nonreligious expression.

However, it is also well-established that the Government in its role as employer has broader discretion to regulate its employees' speech in the workplace than it does to regulate speech among the public at large. Employees' expression on matters of public concern can be regulated if the employees' interest in the speech is outweighed by the interest of the Government, as an employer, in promoting the efficiency of the public services it performs through its employees. Governmental employers also posses substantial discretion to impose content-neutral and viewpoint-neutral time, place, and manner rules regulating private employee expression in the workplace (though they may not structure or administer such rules to discriminate against particular viewpoints). Furthermore, employee speech can be regulated or discouraged if it impairs discipline by superiors, has a detrimental impact on close working relationships for which personal loyalty and confidence are necessary, impedes the performance of the speaker's duties or interferes with the regular operation of the enterprise, or demonstrates that the employee holds views that could lead his employer or the public reasonably to question whether he can perform his duties adequately.

Consistent with its fully protected character, employee religious speech should be treated, within the Federal workplace, like other expression on issues of public concern: in a particular case, an employer can discipline an employee for engaging in speech if the value of the speech is outweighed by the employer's interest in promoting the efficiency of the public services it performs through its employee. Typically, however, the religious speech cited as permissible in the various examples included in these Guidelines will not unduly impede these interests and should not be regulated. And rules regulating employee speech, like other rules regulating speech, must be carefully drawn to avoid any unnecessary limiting or chilling of protected speech.

B. Discrimination in Terms and Conditions. Title VII of the Civil Rights Act of 1964 makes it unlawful for employers, both private and public, to "fail or refuse to hire or to discharge any individual, or otherwise to discriminate against any individual with respect to compensation, terms, conditions, or privileges of employment, because of such individual's . . . religion." 42 U.S.C. § 2000e-2(a)(1). The Federal Government also is bound by the equal protection component of the Due Process Clause of the Fifth Amendment, which bars intentional discrimination on the basis of religion. Moreover, the prohibition on religious discrimination in employment applies with particular force to the Federal Government, for Article VI, clause 3 of the Constitution bars the Government from enforcing any religious test as a requirement for qualification to any Office. In addition, if a Government law, regulation or practice facially discriminates against employees' private exercise of religion or is intended to infringe upon or restrict private religious exercise, then that law, regulation, or practice implicates the Free Exercise Clause of the First Amendment. Last, under the Religious Freedom Restoration Act, 42 U.S.C. § 2000bb-1, Federal governmental action that substantially burdens a private party's exercise of religion can be enforced only if it is justified by a compelling interest and is narrowly tailored to advance that interest.

C. Coercion of Employees' Participation or Nonparticipation in Religious Activities. The ban on religious discrimination is broader than simply guaranteeing nondiscriminatory treatment in formal employment decisions such as hiring and promotion. It applies to all terms and conditions of employment. It follows that the Federal Government may not require or coerce its employees to engage in religious activities or to refrain from engaging in religious activity. For example, a supervisor may not demand attendance at (or a refusal to attend) religious services as a condition of continued employment or promotion, or as a criterion affecting assignment of job duties. Quid pro quo discrimination of this sort is illegal. Indeed, wholly apart from the legal prohibitions against coercion, supervisors may not insist upon employees' conformity to religious behavior in their private lives any more than they can insist on conformity to any other private conduct unrelated to employees' ability to carry out their duties.

D. Hostile Work Environment and Harassment. Employers violate Title VII's ban on discrimination by creating or tolerating a "hostile environment" in which an employee is subject to discriminatory intimidation, ridicule, or insult sufficiently severe or pervasive to alter the conditions of the victim's employment. This statutory standard can be triggered (at the very least) when an employee, because of her or his religion or lack thereof, is exposed to intimidation, ridicule, and insult. The hostile conduct—which may take the form of speech—need not come from supervisors or from the employer. Fellow employees can create a hostile environment through their own words and actions.

The existence of some offensive workplace conduct does not necessarily constitute harassment under Title VII. Occasional and isolated utterances of an epithet that engenders offensive feelings in an employee typically would not affect conditions of employment, and therefore would not in and of itself constitute harassment. A hostile environment, for Title VII purposes, is not created by the bare expression of speech with which one disagrees. For religious harassment to be illegal under Title VII, it must be sufficiently severe or pervasive to alter the conditions of employment and create an abusive working environment. Whether conduct can be the predicate for a finding of religious harassment under Title VII depends on the totality of the circumstances, such as the nature of the verbal or physical conduct at issue and the context in which the alleged incidents occurred. As the Supreme Court has said in an analogous context:

> [W]hether an environment is "hostile" or "abusive" can be determined only by looking at all the circumstances. These may include the frequency of the discriminatory conduct; its severity; whether it is physically threatening or humiliating, or a mere offensive utterance; and whether it unreasonably interferes with an employee's work performance. The effect on the employee's psychological well-being is, of course, relevant to determining whether the plaintiff actually found the environment abusive. *Harris v. Forklift Systems, Inc.,* 510 U.S. 17, 23 (1993).

The use of derogatory language directed at an employee can rise to the level of religious harassment if it is severe or invoked repeatedly. In particular, repeated religious slurs and negative religious stereotypes, or continued disparagement of an employee's religion or ritual practices, or lack thereof, can constitute harassment. It is not necessary that the harassment be explicitly religious in character or that the slurs reference religion: it is sufficient that the harassment is directed at an employee because of the employee's religion or lack thereof. That is to say, Title VII can be violated by employer tolerance of repeated slurs, insults and/or abuse not explicitly religious in nature if that conduct would not have occurred but for the targeted employee's religious belief or lack of religious belief. Finally, although proselytization directed at fellow employees is generally permissible (subject to the special considerations relating to supervisor expression discussed elsewhere in these Guidelines), such activity must stop if the listener asks that it stops or otherwise demonstrates that it is unwelcome.

E. Accommodation of Religious Exercise. Title VII requires employers "to reasonably accommodate . . . an employee's or prospective employee's religious observance or practice" unless such accommodation would impose an "undue hardship on the conduct of the employer's business." 42 U.S.C. § 2000e(j). For example, by statute, if an employee's religious beliefs require her to be absent from work, the

Federal Government must grant that employee compensation time for overtime work, to be applied against the time lost, unless to do so would harm the ability of the agency to carry out its mission efficiently. 5 U.S.C. § 5550a.

Though an employer need not incur more than *de minimis* costs in providing an accommodation, the employer hardship nevertheless must be real rather than speculative or hypothetical. Religious accommodation cannot be disfavored relative to other, nonreligious, accommodations. If an employer regularly permits accommodation for nonreligious purposes, it cannot deny comparable religious accommodation: "Such an arrangement would display a discrimination against religious practices that is the antithesis of reasonableness." *Ansonia Bd. of Educ. v. Philbrook,* 479 U.S. 60, 71 (1986).

In the Federal Government workplace, if neutral workplace rules—that is, rules that do not single out religious or religiously motivated conduct for disparate treatment—impose a substantial burden on a particular employee's exercise of religion, the Religious Freedom Restoration Act requires the employer to grant the employee an exemption from that neutral rule, unless the employer has a compelling interest in denying an exemption and there is no less restrictive means of furthering that interest. 42 U.S.C. § 2000bb-1.

F. Establishment of Religion. The Establishment Clause of the First Amendment prohibits the Government—including its employees—from acting in a manner that would lead a reasonable observer to conclude that the Government is sponsoring, endorsing or inhibiting religion generally or favoring or disfavoring a particular religion. For example, where the public has access to the Federal workplace, employee religious expression should be prohibited where the public reasonably would perceive that the employee is acting in an official, rather than a private, capacity, or under circumstances that would lead a reasonable observer to conclude that the Government is endorsing or disparaging religion. The Establishment Clause also forbids Federal employees from using Government funds or resources (other than those facilities generally available to government employees) for private religious uses.

Section 3. General. These Guidelines shall govern the internal management of the civilian executive branch. They are not intended to create any new right, benefit, or trust responsibility, substantive or procedural, enforceable at law or equity by a party against the United States, its agencies, its officers, or any person. Questions regarding interpretations of these Guidelines should be brought to the Office of the General Counsel or Legal Counsel in each department and agency.

Table of Cases

C

Index